The CONDUCT *of the* CORPORATION

THE
Conduct OF THE
CORPORATION

W I L B E R T E.
M O O R E

Random House · NEW YORK

FIRST PRINTING

THIS IS JEANNE'S BOOK

PREFACE

T H I S book is about the modern business corporation, both as a collectivity and as an assembly of persons. "The Conduct of the Corporation" thus refers to the way representatives of that singular organization act in a highly complex and occasionally hazardous environment, to the way various standardized parts of the system act and interact internally, and to the way types and categories of persons behave at work.

The six parts of this book bear titles that testify to playful alliteration. Part One, Challenge, comprises a single chapter that explores the current uncertainty about the place of the large corporations in American life and the resulting ambiguity about the powers and rewards of their executives and managers. Most of the rest of the book is designed to explore the internal organization and external relations of large business enterprises, emphasizing their comforting or deadly certainty as well as the sources of variation and lack of predictability.

Part Two, Conjugation, is concerned with the orderly bringing together of highly specialized human components into a single complex network of jobs, authorities, communications, and rules. In a more formal treatise these chapters would comprise the "principles" or even the "theory" of complex organization. Part Three, Counterpoint, attends to the side of human behavior in corporations that, if not seamy, at least has a pattern different from that appearing on the "face" side. Here I shall note a variety of departures from established "theory," but departures so regular and predictable that they must be incorporated into any realistic theory of corporate conduct.

Parts Two and Three, then, deal with organization, official and otherwise. They set the stage. Part Four, Characters, provides the cast for the drama, the players who act out their several parts well or ill, in hope or despair, in arrogance or humility. These are the "organization men," but we shall want to emphasize that they wear many faces, not a standard mask of vacuous charm.

Organizations change, partly through unintentional and even mindless vacillation and evolution, partly through deliberate action. Part Five, Change, explores the sources, types, and directions of movement in the dramatic plot. The action concludes in Part Six, Circumscription, for here we encounter the friendly and unfriendly interests that invest in the corporation, buy from it, sell to it, compete with it, or harass it in courts and legislative chambers. Although corporations, or rather their members, may play a prominent part in developing a rationale, a *raison d'être*, to help resolve the uncertainties explored in Chapter I, the external environment and particularly the public as a political force are likely to be finally decisive.

This book does not have a single thesis, argued and documented with exquisite detail. Rather it expounds many theses—perhaps as many as Martin Luther's 95 propositions tacked on the church door at Wittenberg. Having no church door handy, and in any event having in mind a somewhat more secular reading public, I have put my allegations about the conduct of corporations between the covers of a book. I cannot confidently expect that the contents will have an effect on history like that of the good friar of Wittenberg. I may, however, hope for a faintly increased measure of understanding, if not of morality and ultimate Truth.

My point of view is that of the friendly critic, and I have tried to keep traces of either shrillness or grimness out of the tonal quality of the writing. Like some 85 per cent of the labor force, I am employed by an "administrative organization," a university which has an occasionally charming and frequently alarming resemblance to all other examples of the species, including corporations. When I poke fun, the joke is frequently on all of us poor organized people.

Although I hold the brave belief that this book is factual, not fictional, illustrations are generally "typical" situations, and unless specifically noted do not refer to any particular company or its denizens. If the shoe fits, that is because so many feet are alike.

Wilbert E. Moore

ACKNOWLEDGMENTS

OBSERVATION of and thinking, talking, and writing about the contemporary American corporation have been among my major preoccupations for over two decades. To recount all of the sources of information and incitement over the years would be impossible as well as tedious. I do want, however, to record the special value of my experience as Director of the Organizational Behavior Project at Princeton University in 1950-1953, under a Ford Foundation "Behavioral Science" grant to the University. That Project provided the means for gaining insights as well as increased knowledge concerning complex organizations and human behavior within them. The opportunity to serve as a guest of or consultant to several corporations has also added its share to the perspectives I present in this book.

I have not attempted to leave "scholarly tracks" throughout the book. Only an occasional reference is made to other books. The "References" at the end of the book indicate some of the principal sources that I have found most useful and stimulating.

Parts of several chapters have been adapted from previous short publications of mine. Chapter 10 represents a revision and expansion of a paper on "The Corporation as a Welfare State," published in the *Proceedings of the American Philosophical Society* for December, 1960. Some of Chapter 15 is adapted from a paper on "Technological Change and Industrial Organization," to be published in a symposium sponsored by the International Social Science Council in Paris. In Chapter 20 several paragraphs are adapted from "Affluence, Softness and Growth," which appeared in *Challenge* magazine for December, 1959. The main outlines of Chapters 16, 19, 20, and 21 were originally developed in an article,

"The Corporation and the Significant Future," for the April, 1959, issue of *Marketing Times*, published by General Electric.

I am grateful to the respective publishers for permission to use these materials in the present volume.

Several people have given me the benefit of a critical reading of the manuscript in whole or part. I want to thank, and absolve, Gerald W. Breese, Peter M. Wilson, and Robert B. Yegge. For detailed editorial and technical comments I want especially to thank Charles H. Page. My wife, Jeanne Yates Moore, also read the manuscript, heard it read to her, and typed it. In these long-suffering roles she checked my interpretations against her own business experience and my mode of exposition against the standards of civilized discourse. The dedication of the book to her represents an acknowledgment of debt, not its repayment.

W. E. M.

CONTENTS

Part One
CHALLENGE

WHEREIN anxious executives are depicted as decisively worried
about the merit of their positions and the salaries they receive
but may not earn, and WHEREIN the low suspicion is entertained
that corporate managers are accountable to no one.

*Who's in Charge Here? . . . The Merits of Managers . . . Invasion of
Privacy*

Part Two
CONJUGATION

WHEREIN starts the quest for the essential features of corporations
as social structures and mortal men temporarily serve immortal
organizations.

*Mission . . . Livelihood . . . Order, Discipline, Hierarchy . . . Ration-
ality . . . Immortality*

Part Three

COUNTERPOINT

Part Four

CHARACTERS

WHEREIN the inconsistency between individual and corporate goals is related to questions of why people work, and evil persons and practices are regarded with mixed fear and hope.

Bribed Cooperation . . . Commitment and Identification . . . Conditioned Love . . . Endemic Pathologies (Favoritism. . Lethargy, Sabotage. . Corruption. . Technicism. . Saintliness. . Survivalism) . . . Useful Troublemakers (Memory and Conscience Keepers. . Conscientious Objectors. . Court Jesters. . Creators. . Sinners)

WHEREIN the notion that all good management men aim for the top, dooming most to frustration, is defeated, and the discussion of corporate careers distinguishes between those who run breathlessly and those who sit quietly, mostly knitting.

Ladders and Escalators . . . The Rat Race and the Treadmill . . . Tenure and Pasture Lots . . . The Old Love and the New

WHEREIN the men who represent the corporation to outside interests are shown to be the spokesmen for those interests in corporate councils, not always happily.

The Rise of "Relations" . . . The Interests of Clients

Part One

CHALLENGE

I

MANAGEMENT IN MORAL CRISIS

W HEREIN *anxious executives are depicted as decisively worried about the merit of their positions and the salaries they receive but may not earn, and* W HEREIN *the low suspicion is entertained that corporate managers are accountable to no one.*

·TIME was that a businessman in the United States needed no more justification for his position and for his rewards than his admirable eagerness to make an honest dollar. The businessman invested his money in production or distribution, and if his costs did not exceed his returns on sales, he made an honorable profit. If he were exceptionally shrewd in his transactions, or exceptionally fortunate in his lucky guesses and favorable circumstances, he might, still honorably, make a good deal of money. The size of the rewards, and the justice with which they were acquired by some and not by others, did not go unquestioned. The major criticism of the "capitalist system" arose in the Nineteenth Century, when the system was relatively "pure," but the critics did not then become convincing to majority opinion and have never succeeded since in the United States. The system, meanwhile, has changed radically.

Those may have been the good old days or the bad old days,

but they are in either case irretrievably lost for a substantial portion of the men who manage the factories and stores, the mines, and even some of the farms. These men are not, properly speaking, capitalists. Rather, they are managers. The difference is fundamental, although it does not entirely appear on the surface.

The crucial difference between the "typical" businessman in the second half of the Twentieth Century and his counterpart in the Nineteenth Century is that the modern manager operates with other people's money. He may also operate with some of his own, and in many small concerns and a few large ones his investment may outweigh all others. Still, if he uses other people's money also, he owes them some responsibility for his stewardship, some accountability for costs and returns.

The contemporary business corporation, which has so radically altered the economic shape of the American economy and the moral position of its managers, was not intended to do either. Corporations, as "legal persons," were not established primarily to broaden the base of investments, but only to reduce the hazards of failure. By the principle of "limited liability," investors in losing enterprises lost only their investment, not all other assets to the point that the debt was settled or assets exhausted. This feature proved to be very attractive, however, and men with ideas—promoters—were shortly found raising capital to implement their ideas by selling "shares" in the enterprise. If some of the promises were overly optimistic or downright dishonest, if fancy certificates turned out to be the company's only tangible assets, the investor's risk was still limited to the loss of the money he improvidently parted with. The problem here was only one of business ethics and the development of rules for fair dealing. Those rules have evolved, aided by occasional scandals, but they have not resolved the fundamental issues posed by the contemporary corporation. Those issues still involve the moral justification for the position and power, the responsibilities and rewards of corporate managers.

The wide pooling of investments, an essentially accidental by-product of the invention of the corporation, has made possible the establishment of truly giant business concerns, with assets running to billions of dollars. If we take the 200 largest manufacturing companies as representing big business, they account for about half of the assets invested in manufacturing and for a similar share of the industrial labor force.

What this means for the position of the businessman, or rather for the corporate manager, is partly clear, partly murky. A few hundred men, the chief executives of big business, control tremendous financial resources, and therefore the economic well-being of investors, employees, and indeed whole communities and even states. They also constitute the supreme political authorities in vast private governments fully equipped with laws and policemen, if not with legislatures and courts.

These men are not precisely actors in search of an author, but they or their hired spokesmen are in search of a rationale, a reason for the corporation, a moral basis for executive power, and a justification of their selection to represent the corporation and to exercise its power.

Who's in Charge Here?

For at least three decades there has been a growing realization that the modern corporation is a "peculiar institution," as Southerners used to call Negro slavery. For convenience, and possibly even for accuracy, this realization can be said to have originated with the publication in 1932 of *The Modern Corporation and Private Property* by Adolph A. Berle, Jr., and Gardiner C. Means. One central thesis of that book was that "management" has been separated from "ownership," that is, that the election of managers by stockholders is only nominal. In the large corporations, the authors noted, management tends to be self-perpetuating, and if attentive at all to the wishes of stockholders, then only to a few with substantial holdings that may still be a very small fraction of all shares. Thus a kind of dollar democracy, the investor having as many votes as he has shares, becomes in effect an oligarchy representing the powerful few or even an autocracy accountable to no constituents at all.

The separation of ownership and management may be called the Berle-Means doctrine. As such it has achieved wide acceptance, though not without modification and criticism. The notion of "ownership," for example, is drastically altered if it is shorn of traditional notions of powers of control. It is more correct to view corporate wealth as a new form of property, with different persons having different rights in the same aggregate of assets. Stockholders as investors have rights different from those of bond owners as creditors. Workers tend to have property rights in their jobs and managers have proprietary powers of use normally accorded only to owners under older notions of private property.

The "sterilization" of investment is not complete. It is true that the dissatisfied investor is more likely to sell his stock, to change a piece of paper, than, in conjunction with others, to change the management. Yet stockholders do have some reserve rights. Even in corporations that have the pleasant immunity deriving from minute subdivision of claims among very large numbers of equity owners, accumulated discontent may lead to solicitation of anti-management proxies with the aim of changing the administration. Even where the equity dispersion is extreme, with no stockholder owning more than a tiny fraction of the shares, managers will generally not dare to retain all earnings for reinvestment as a continuous practice. Stockholders seeking current returns are likely to be sufficiently numerous and vocal to be threatening.

Nevertheless, stockholders do accord to management very extensive latitude in the exercise of corporate power. Singly they have virtually no choice, and collective action is both difficult and expensive even if it were sought. The vote of "no confidence" by sale of the stock—of course, many such sales are for other reasons —may have a restraining influence on the managers if the reaction is sufficiently general to depress the market price of the stock. Rising market values are taken as a favorable sign by managers, even if they own no stock themselves. And rising values make the quest for new capital easier and often less expensive in terms of the returns that must be paid to investors, many of whom will be more interested in capital gains—appreciation in market value of assets—than in current dividends.

Whether the investor is aiming for dividends or profits from buying and selling shares, he remains remarkably permissive— perhaps, in the words of a former Yale football coach speaking about university alumni, "sullen but not rebellious." As a single individual he has, to repeat, very little choice in the matter.

Managers, then, have acquired a large degree of independence from stockholders in most of the large corporations. By now, nearly all interested parties know this, except, it would often seem, lawyers and judges, who, because they are bound by legal language and precedent, will be the last to get the word, or to hear it officially. The language of the courts still has the "owners" in control and managers as hirelings doing the owners' bidding. This leads occasionally to some judicial nonsense, equalled only by finding the corporation, as a "legal person," guilty of criminal offenses. Yet courts will occasionally entertain stockholder suits against management and, significantly, will occasionally uphold management's use of resources in behalf of the company's social responsibilities despite the depleted reserves available for dividend distribution. Out of such judicial decisions there may evolve, in the slow way of the law, a set of guides to the positive powers and duties of corporations.

Perhaps the most accurate way to depict the position of contemporary corporate management is one of relative autonomy but subject to restraints and "veto powers" beyond some limits. Stockholders exercise potential restraints, as noted, and creditors may do so at an earlier juncture. Suppliers of materials set limiting conditions, and customers do too. Competitors exercise restraining influence, and, in some markets, may have the ultimate sanction of forcing a company out of the market. Employees, individually or as organized groups, may bargain or withhold their services altogether. The public, particularly as presented by the agencies of government, provides rules and penalties, orders and restraints.

Management is accountable to none of these interests—and to all of them. In particular, the interests of stockholders are not automatically superior to all others; those interests are only some among many.

The first part of the moral crisis of management then is, "Whom do they represent?" It would be altogether too cynical to reply simply, "Themselves." Yet the interests of the organization itself and of its leaders in particular are strongly represented. Other interests are more distant, and somewhat intermittent. Within the limits of freedom permitted by external constraints, organizational and especially managerial interests tend to be supreme.

Berle and Means, thirty years ago, suggested that managers have become "trustees," and the notion has gained some ground since. Trustees, especially if one takes the example of non-profit organizations like universities, reach balanced judgments on policies that affect many different interests. They are also sensitive to the preservation of continuities with the past, maintaining at least some temporal consistency with the charter and accumulated traditions. They also take a responsible view of the future, moderating present advantage with concern for leaving the organization in a healthy state for their successors.

The notion of trusteeship is an attractive one, as it lends a kind of responsible dignity and sense of service to positions of power. Above all, it implies that the trustee is "disinterested," dedicated to the organization's welfare but not to his own aggrandizement.

That is the essential trouble. Measured by the yardstick of money, the chief beneficiaries of the contemporary corporation are precisely the ones who set the policies and control the conditions for carrying them out. If the relationship is one of trust—a fiduciary position in the archaic language of the law—how does it happen that the trustees have their hands in the till?

The difficulties multiply, however. Managers, no longer owners or precisely representative of owners, have become "professionals." As professionals, they claim "the authority necessary to do the job." But who determines the job? The test of the market, that is, the determination of utility to society or suitable segments of it, by profitable production of goods and services, will not suffice. Profits may accrue from fraud, from producing harmful or dangerous products. Profits may be enhanced by collusion among producers to fix prices, leaving suppliers of customers no liberty of action, no bargaining power. In these situations, the public has generally intervened and will certainly continue to do so. But that in itself reveals that self-regulation is an unsatisfactory rationale for freedom of action.

On the positive side, large corporations also must act "above" the level of mere market considerations. Their very size, and the dependence of the economy and the nation on their continuation, removes the privilege of business failure and gives rise to notions of "social responsibility." The notions are not novel among corporate managers. Indeed, they are stressed. But one has the sense that the stress is defensive and apprehensive, a little too loud, a little too virtuous. For it is offered as a justification not only for corporate size and success but also for the power and privileges of managers, as though justifying their rewards by the exceptional service they are rendering rather than for the risks they are taking, which are in fact hard to detect and in any event involve other people's money.

The idea of "responsible management," although spoken glibly by those who claim it, is remarkably slippery. Managers are not the elected representatives of any organizational constituency. Rather they are chosen from above, by their administrative superiors. And how are their superiors chosen? By *their* superiors. There is an end to this progression, however, in the Board of Directors. Although membership on the Board is ratified by those stockholders who take the trouble to sign their proxies, it is essentially determined by the current Board. In other words, the final accountability for a system of graded power rests with a rather disembodied collection of company officers and "representatives" of stockholders, financial institutions, law firms, and possibly the "public."

Managers are elected neither by constituents nor, in effect, by stockholders. They cannot claim for themselves the rights of property or the biologically inherited "divine right" of kings to rule. They lack the doctrine of "apostolic succession" that would preserve a spiritual linkage with the original founder. Their accession to power is more likely to be marked by a cocktail party than by the rich color of the inauguration of a national president (who has an electorate) or a university president (who has various constituencies including, notably, trustees) or of the head of a church (who has his authority from God alone).

And who is to judge the results of managerial efforts? The market test is partly operative, but only partly. When competition is not too severe, or at least not total and totally threatening, and when stockholders have little basis for judging the efficiency and care with which the company is operated, the relative autonomy of management permits simultaneous achievement of "acceptable" performance and substantial use of funds for unnecessary salaries and amenities. Care for the "stockholders' money" is given suitable verbal support, especially in pious platitudes for the public. In fact, however, the pleas and demands of the organization for higher salaries, for more people at senior advisory positions, and for thicker carpets and prettier secretaries, are more audible. And the money is in the control of the executives, not in the stockholders' pockets. As charitable contributions the expenses might be hard to justify. But as "costs" of production, their merits are rarely challenged.

The notion of trusteeship is virtually the only one in our institutional system that fits the corporate executive and the rest of management. But the fit is only approximate. The legal and moral status of management can no longer be justified in traditional, proprietary terms. Other terms are not yet firmly established. They may not be for some time to come, but both legislative and judicial actions are likely to move increasingly toward public circumscription of the powers and duties of the modern captains of industry.

The Merits of Managers

Even if there were no uncertainties about the moral position of managers, there would still be questions about the way managers are selected. Except where conditions of ownership or sentiment intrude, as with hiring a representative of the founding family for an important post, the first presumption about managers is that they are competent. That is, there is an expectation of competitive selection, with talents and duties approximately matched. It is, of course, possible to find incompetents in high places, but not as a general rule. The difficulty is less likely to be grossly bad or perverse judgment than it is to be great uncertainty about the talents sought for the job to be done.

If management is professional, what are its standards? By what reliable tests, founded on a body of knowledge and skills and recognized by fellow professionals, are talent and performance to be judged? To ask the question does not imply that the answers are embarrassingly missing. Partial accuracy, greater at the extremes than in the middle ranges of positions and performances, is certainly available. The concern of the managers themselves over the legitimacy of their positions leads to attempts to standardize judgments. If this encourages a considerable amount of distorted self-justification, there are enough people pressing different criteria of excellence to prevent pure self-delusion or pure and collective charlatanism.

It is, I believe, of some significance that most of the graduate schools of business administration have followed Harvard's lead in teaching mainly by the "case method." Now to a substantial degree cases *are* the law, but in other fields of professional practice cases at best provide a kind of vicarious experience that may or may not have substantial carry-over to, say, actual administrative problems. By avoiding administrative principles the courses invite the suspicion that there are none. I think this is not true, and this book is a testimony to that conviction. However, until there is established a body of abstract principles capable of application in a wide variety of situations, and until training in these principles readily distinguishes the true professional from the amateur or the man qualified only by a limited range of experience that he cannot generalize, the attempt to "professionalize" management must be regarded as rather incomplete.

To the presumption of competence must be added the presumption of responsibility. But that brings us right back to the question of accountability. If modern business management were truly professional, its practitioners would have developed a binding code of ethics, protective of both professional standards and of clients, and enforced chiefly by the professional body itself. Moves in this direction are not wanting, but they are pretty feeble and halting. I think this stems once more from the uncertainty as to whose interests management should represent. In particular, there is a confusion between service to the employer, as represented by the administrative superior, and to the "client," who may be the subordinate, the person who is "managed."

A few ethical problems will serve to illustrate the uncertain state of managerial morality. Several critics of corporate conduct have noted, and regretted, the practice of supervising the social life of employees and particularly of managerial employees. Such "irrelevant" criteria of competence as joining the right organizations, voting the right way, and marrying the right (socially graceful) wife may be powerful influences on a managerial career. What is lacking here is any clear-cut line between job-relevant and "private" conduct and thus any sharp limit on the exercise of the employer's influence over the employee.

The question of influence or power over the subordinate is also posed in the unlikely context of sweet charity. Officers of some national charities and of local "community chests" or "united funds" have hit upon an extremely efficient solicitation device, namely, through employers. For reasons of "public relations," if for no others, executives of business concerns are likely to find it difficult to reject such proposals. The consequence, however, is that fund solicitation is made through channels, that is, from bosses to subordinates, often with an explicit notation of the expected contribution for each salary level, which the boss knows to the last digit. In the circumstances the contribution is no longer voluntary, but another example of taxation without representation. If managers had a more highly developed sense of moral responsibility for their subordinates, or at least some sense of what constitutes an abuse of power, they would send the fund-raisers back to ringing doorbells or writing letters. Without any such clear moral standards, managers are fair game for legitimate-sounding pressures.

Management, its spokesmen claim, is a leadership of ability. One can assent or dissent only if the ability is specified in other than self-confirming ways ("He has the position, he must have ability."). I am not going to list and debate the various virtues that good managers are said to possess. But I do suggest that the case for merit can only be established when its foundations and testing procedures are more firmly founded than they presently are.

The question of selection can be rephrased as, are the right people rewarded? The uncertainty of the answer adds to the sense of moral unease shared by those who enjoy the rewards as well as by their unsuccessful competitors and by outsiders as well. The question gets honed to a sharp edge when the amount of the rewards is considered.

The *average* level of salaries of managers even in leading corporations is not exceptionally high. The average, moreover, is strongly affected by a relatively few top salaries, and those are the ones that excite attention. For leading corporate executives, salaries over a quarter of a million of dollars annually are fairly common, and higher ones are not exactly rare. These are exclusive of stock bonuses and stock options at reduced rates which may effectively double the executive's income. Such stock plans are portrayed to quiescent stockholders as executive incentive plans, 250,000 dollars presumably not being an adequate lure to turn in an exemplary performance. They are, of course, really tax-avoiding schemes for part of executive compensation, as the profit from sales of stocks is taxed as capital gains at a maximum of 25 per cent rather than at the steeply graded income tax rate.

Now these salaries compare very favorably with the 17,000 dollar salary of full generals or admirals, the 35,000 dollar income of Supreme Court justices, and even the 100,000 dollar honorarium to the President of the United States. The "justification" of executive salaries in corporations rests upon the presumed scarcity of talent and the highly competitive market for the limited supply. Yet the peculiar talents of the highest-paid executives as compared with those at much lower salaries, even within the business world, are rather difficult to specify, and invite the suspicion that they do not exist.

There is a notable correlation between the size of corporations and the salaries of their chief officers. This appears immediately sensible, on the assumption that managing a large concern requires more talent than managing a small one. Yet for this assumption there is scant evidence. It is possible that the 20,000 dollar-a-year president of a small concern doing two million dollars of annual business has a more difficult and demanding job than the president of the corporation so large and luxurious that specialized staffs take on many functions that the lesser executive must do for himself.

Part of the explanations of high executive salaries scarcely constitute justifications. The first explanation is organizational. In a large organization there are many steps from the bottom to the top, and the idea prevails that each step should entail a net increment in income over the one below it, often around 15 per cent. If there were no income taxes, or if they were assessed at a flat rate, this would still not result in very high salaries at the top. In a 15-layer organization with a 4,000-dollar base wage and a 15 per cent increment by rank, the top salary would be only slightly over 28,000 dollars or around a ratio of 7 to 1. Although some of the differentials are substantially steeper than 15 per cent, a principal factor in the high executive salaries is the graduated income tax, which makes the preservation of net differentials an increasingly costly affair. The result in terms of gross pay may be a differential of 100 to 1, although the net ratio is much narrower.

The other explanation of high executive salaries is less impersonal, less "circumstantial." Executive salaries are determined by the boards of directors, and executive officers are also members of the board. Good manners may prevent their voting on their own salaries, but the independence of boards and executives from external supervision or control does, I suggest, encourage all of the spurious rationalizations for what may amount to plunder or legal embezzlement.

The question is, if there were a truly open market and no arbitrary assumptions about minimum income differentials by rank, could able executive talent be secured for much less money? The inference from the income levels in other fields demanding unusual abilities is that it could. The cost of executive salaries to consumers and stockholders is not great, and within the organization high salaries may encourage managerial ambition. Whether the differentials also result in some sense of unfairness for those who clearly are no longer candidates for high salaries is simply not known. Executive salaries certainly excite adverse comments outside the organization, and I have suggested that this arises from a doubt that has some merit and not simply from ignorant envy.

Managers, I have argued, and particularly the top managers or executives of the large corporations, find themselves without a sure basis for their autonomous power, for their own selection to wield this power, or for their financial compensation for doing so. There is enough evidence of doubt and anxiety, of tension-produced disorders, of emotional instability among the successful as well as those merely straining for success, to suggest that something more troublesome than hard work presses upon the coordinators and decision-makers. And if this does not reveal itself to the manager through his own insight, there are enough outside pressures and criticism to keep turning up the dilemmas and ambiguities of corporate behavior.

Invasion of Privacy

This book represents an attempt to comprehend the corporation in its many manifestations: not only as the setting in which managers manage but also as the principal producer of goods and purveyor of services and as the way of working life of a large segment of the American population.

Contemporary corporations, and particularly the giant ones, represent the substantial strength of "private enterprise." Their products and services when entered in the economists' national balance sheets, appear in the "private sector." Privacy, however, is always limited by the official exercise of the public interest and by the unofficial but inveterate curiosity of neighbors when they think something mysterious is going on.

The concept of the corporation is steeped in semantic confusion. Though private in the sense that they are not owned and operated by agencies of government, many corporations are also public in the sense that their stock is widely dispersed among individuals and institutions, traded in national markets, and registered with public agencies. It is this public quality which sets the corporation apart from traditional notions of private enterprise, which permits such happy public relations inventions as "people's capitalism," and which incidentally provides some aid and comfort to the curious. It is the privacy of this major segment of private enterprise that we intend to invade.

Corporations come in various shapes, sizes, and types of business. I shall maintain that obvious differences do not remove underlying similarities, and indeed that one may generalize about all administrative organizations. However, our primary focus will be on the large, diversified, national, publicly held corporations.

This string of adjectives is less restrictive than it is redundant. Size encourages or requires diversification of products. Together these characteristics bespeak a national or even international market. And all this is quite unlikely to be based on a single personal fortune but rather to represent the pooled investments of many, both absolutely rich and relatively poor.

Size, in fact, implies these corporate characteristics and many others as well: the formality of procedures, which requires a substantial, sustained-yield forest to supply the paper for memos and records; the endless parleys among potentates of fractional business empires; the awesome internal differences in individual power and income; the threat to the individual from such massive collectivism, whether that threat is based on terroristic tactics or on a surfeit of goodies.

The size of the largest corporations does impress. By one conventional and arbitrary distinction, the "giant" corporation is one of the 200 largest. Membership in this select group is not constant from year to year and especially from decade to decade. And the rank-order is also subject to change as different economic activities prosper or decline. In *Fortune* magazine's annual survey, companies are ranked by sales, but also by assets, profits, and average number of employees. There is of course considerable correlation among these various measures of size.

Since I am not going to be concerned in any major way with "concentration" in the American economy, whether viewed benevolently or with alarm, the boundary line on what is "large" need not be very precise. Many of the 300 corporations that trail the giants share most of their characteristics of internal organization and external relations. And to the private citizen contemplating his assets, a company worth a mere 49 million dollars, as was the 500th in *Fortune's* 1961 survey, is large enough to qualify as big business.

Despite the moral dilemmas it presents and despite the frustration of human individuality that any organization entails, the large corporation offers a fairly satisfactory living and way of life to millions of breadwinners. The durability of the corporation must be viewed somewhat more benevolently than the simple, cynical acceptance of ineradicable sin. The moral crisis arising from the uncertainty as to what, in the final sense, the corporation and its managers are doing here is not sufficiently grave to inhibit action. The workman goes to his bench, the engineer to his drafting board, and the manager to his desk. For the organized life also provides a high level of order, sufficient, perhaps, to make uncertainty tolerable.

Part Two

CONJUGATION

I I

WORK AS THE WAY TO SALVATION

*W H E R E I N starts the quest for the essential
features of corporations as social structures and
mortal men temporarily serve
immortal organizations.*

A v a s t majority of the people who work for a living in the United
States work for employers. Wage and salary earners comprise
about 85 per cent of the total labor force. Now it is true that
many of these have few if any fellow employees, like the doctor's
receptionist or the mechanic in a small garage. It is also true,
however, that well over half of the laboring population work in
establishments that are big enough to have an "administrative
structure." A minimum definition of such an organization is that
it has at least two levels of managerial authority. One immediate
implication of such an organization is that for at least part of
the work force, the boss has a boss. The probability clearly increases with the size of the organization.

In the technical language of sociology, an administrative organization is known by the shorter term "bureaucracy," and the
growing proportion of workers employed in such organizations is
summarized by the phrase "bureaucratization of the labor force."

But because non-sociological people often insist on applying the term "bureaucracy" only to governmental agencies and on giving it a mostly negative connotation, calling up pictures of incompetence and pettifogging adherence to senseless procedures, bureaucracy can scarcely be used in polite conversations about business. The alternative is to use the more cumbersome but less prejudicial term "administrative organization."

Although the business community and other sensible people have rejected bureaucracy as a correct word for private organizations, it is difficult to conceal the fact that the form of the administrative organization was developed historically in such public areas as armies and civil government before it came to be adopted and adapted for more prosaic uses. The reasons for the crude similarities are not difficult to find. Armies require the coordination of considerable numbers of people doing a variety of tasks and maintaining disciplined performance of assignments that will achieve rather precise objectives for the organization as a whole. So does the production of refrigerators. Public administration requires the subordination of officials to the policies and directives determined by the chief authorities and the faithful execution of their delimited duties. So does management of a corporate branch plant.

I do not mean to belabor the public origin of private modes of organization or the contemporary comparisons between them. (There are differences too.) I do mean to underscore the fact that administrative organization represents a common solution to common problems of coordinating human effort for cooperative goals.

In this and the remaining chapters of Part Two we shall be engaged in an enterprise known in certain academic circles as "model construction." This will not be a working model, suitable for a patent application, but rather a standard against which actual performance can be compared. Our model of the complex administrative organization will thus not be an absolutely accurate description of real organizations. Rather it will be the ideal that people in real organizations try to achieve or evade and, in a sinful world, more nearly succeed in evading than achieving. To dismiss an ideal not fully achieved as inconsequential is the commonest error of simple cynics. The question is, how different would the situation be if there were no ideal standard? The answer must usually be, very different.

Mission

Strictly speaking, organizations do not have goals or ends or purposes. These are subjective concepts properly attributable only to individuals, including those who formulate and pursue objectives on behalf of organizations. For some purposes the distinction between individual and organization is tedious, but for others it is not, as for example the question of degree of correspondence between individual goals and the welfare of organizations that individuals represent. Administrative organizations may, however, properly be said to have a *mission*, meaning a set of specific, limited, and ordered objectives.

All of the qualifications just noted are important. An administrative organization is not established or continued for vague purposes of friendly interaction but rather for objectives that can be clearly stipulated and the degree of achievement constantly or periodically appraised. Such organizations are generally badly equipped to fulfill all of life's functions or their members' interests. But they are equipped to accomplish limited functions that require complex cooperation. If more than one objective is part of the mission, it is unlikely that all can be simultaneously "maximized" in all situations, so that a priority ordering is needed as the basis for choice in cramped quarters.

If the mission is clear, definite, and feasible, then its achievement is "simply" one of organizing and motivating human action for all the subsidiary and instrumental tasks. As a wise philosopher, the late Ralph Barton Perry, once noted with reference to the doctrine that the end justifies the means, what else could? The mission determines, or at least limits, and justifies the actual organization.

Now all this may seem logical but a bit abstract. The business corporation appears to be set up to produce and sell a limited range of goods and services at a profit to its investors. It thus seems to qualify on "mission," and one can routinely pass on to the next part of the model. But the situation is not so simple. Corporations, and particularly the giant ones, tend to violate every one of the limits on "mission." They adopt objectives such as personality development of employees, support of education, and various attributes of "good corporate citizenship," and hire staffs to implement these additional functions. And in prosperous times there is little evidence of the ordering of these objectives. That tends to come about, if at all, by the painful process of cost cutting when reduced income restrains even the most benevolent dispositions.

There is, in fact, a general tendency for successful and continuing organizations to accumulate functions. The special feature of the business corporation is that it has been able to do so for the most part because of its freedom from detailed accountability to investors. Thus the pursuit of objectives having little to do with the company's mission in the market shows up as "costs" of operations rather than as expenditures of disposable resources for various desirable purposes.

It is not even absolutely clear what primary objectives the corporation pursues. One can stir a lively dispute in both company corridors and the halls of learning by raising the question of the role of profits. Few will deny that the corporation is expected to survive by a favorable balance between income and outlay. The alternative courses require borrowing, which is likely to have early limits, or subsidies from public or private angels, which violates principles of competitive tests of capacity for survival. But does the corporation seek to "maximize" profits? Not if one takes into account costs unrelated to production and sales. Defenders of the "profit motive" then usually shift to the claim that corporations attempt to maximize long-run profits. That claim in turn raises sticky problems of definition and testing. If the run is long enough, the question doesn't matter any more. A fair case can be made for the view that large corporations set their competitive strategy in terms of position (rank) in the market, which may not coincide with optimal profit-producing strategies. But withal, the one sure thing that corporations, or their officers, seek to do is survive, and they seek to survive as affluently as convenient if not as profitably as possible.

Livelihood

Membership in a corporation may or may not be a way of life, but it is certainly a way of earning a living. The second characteristic of our model administrative organization is the clarity of organizational membership. In most instances the test is a very simple one—being on the payroll. This criterion will leave some fuzziness around the edges, as when we encounter the member of the Board of Directors who is not otherwise a company officer, draws his principal salary elsewhere, and in fact receives a rather modest fee for attending Board meetings. But such "external" Board members may be almost as harmless as the emasculated stockholder, save for decisions on major capital expenditures or picking the company's senior officers.

The jobs to be done, the positions to be filled, are determined in principle by the mission of the corporation, including considerations of magnitude (how big an operation? at what level of capacity?). An important qualification has to be entered here, however. Personnel demands will also be greatly affected by what we may loosely call "technology," that is, the mechanical and administrative means for achieving the mission. At any particular time, technology may be taken as a condition. Through time, it is of course a variable that both affects and is affected by the numbers and qualities of workers.

The corporation as an employer then has to "man" the organization. It does so, in principle, by seeking persons of the proper qualifications for each of the multitude of positions to be filled. To secure them, it must offer wages or salaries at least equal to the "going rate," that is, at the labor-market price. If the employer pays "too much" he (or it) presumably suffers in product price competition because of high labor costs. If the employer pays "too little" he presumably suffers in labor-market competition, so that either he cannot get employees at the price offered or more probably he gets poorly qualified workers with resulting losses in efficiency.

The principles of a competitive market can be found in elementary texts in economics. To varying degrees, they work. But perhaps less in the labor market than elsewhere in the economy. Wages are usually subject to collective and not simply individual bargaining. Salaries often represent "administered prices" rather than a market price, partly because of the great diversity of job specifications and the consequent difficulty of determining what the market price is. And there is very good reason to suppose that income differentials reflect organizational considerations, such as the number of echelons or layers of authority from bottom to top, rather than any precisely tested market value.

The basically economic criterion of corporate membership is not impaired by these determinants of the amount of income it provides various members. Lacking the charitable appeal of hospitals and educational institutions, which may get unpaid assistance from supporters, and lacking both the prestige of public service and the power of governments to require service in crises, the corporation secures services by paying for them. Whether the price is adequate or "fair" is another question, the answer to which depends upon such conditions as general and special levels of employment which will affect the bargaining power of various employees, on the willingness and ability of the employee to respond to alternative opportunities, and on the degree to which wages become a matter of public control.

This economic view of corporate membership is also not impaired by the fact that it is incomplete. Employees are likely to have multiple motives at the work place and employers are likely to seek something more than bribed performance. It is, in short, difficult for either party to be "pure." (To speak of economic incentives and rewards as "pure" shows the lengths to which abstract analysis may carry one away from conventional wisdom.) Yet no amount of sophisticated search for the hidden wellsprings of human motivation, no amount of pedantic discourse on the corporation as a social organization can evade the elementary circumstance that employment involves money changing hands, whereby the employer meets his payroll and the employee, hopefully, meets his living expenses.

Order, Discipline, Hierarchy

Going to work in a corporation is something like a marriage. Like marriage, the relationship is formed by a "contract." Like marriage, also, the relationship results in a "status." Even the legal analogy is incomplete, however, as the contractual elements of marriage disappear once the relationship is formed, but they persist in the employment relationship. It is more accurate to say that the contractual conditions of employment involve the acceptance of relationships that are not themselves contractual in character. These relationships, summarized as "order, discipline, hierarchy," can be made to appear comparable to the ideology of an authoritarian church or state. Two corporate characteristics save the situation from being as restrictive of the individual's freedom as either marriage or authoritarian control imply—the rules, sanctions, and power are limited strictly to the work place and its technical tasks. This limitation in turn is one of the persistent contractual elements in the relationship.

Any administrative organization pursues its mission and provides a livelihood for its participants within a more or less elaborate set of rules of behavior. These rules go far beyond virtuous platitudes; they range from the general expectation of such disci-

plined regularity as punctuality to such minutiae as the number
of invoice copies and receipted bills required to claim reimburse-
ment for expenses in line of duty. Administrative rules may be
more common in public agencies, where they are a major source
of the taint in the word "bureaucracy," than in private ones, but
it is more likely that governmental rules are simply more open to
view by clients and casual observers. The principal incitements to
rule-making are sheer organizational size and internal diversity of
people and jobs. As human memories are frail, and human ingenuity in evading rules strong, regulations are commonly reduced
to writing. This fact alone adds to the "formality" of the whole
austere business of maintaining order. The result is a kind of
"private law," complete with specified penalties for infractions.
The corporation, being less majestic than the state, which always
retains a monopoly on final coercive power, must use dismissal as
its ultimate sanction—a kind of organizational equivalent of capital punishment.

The individual who accepts employment commits himself to a
system of rules. He also submits himself to a system of authority.
Thus corporations and other administrative organizations are said
to be hierarchical, that is, they have several distinct grades or
levels of position and power. The just powers of governors derive
from delegation by superiors, not by representation of the governed. Neither benevolent nor despotic in principle, administrative authority is rather functional and restricted, and thus also
disciplined by rules.

In our non-working model of corporate organization, rules are
sensible, discipline equitable, and authority just. In working
models the situation is slightly more complex.

Rationality

The Freudian revolution in psychology, especially, has almost de-
stroyed the picture of man as a rational creature. Hidden, sub-

conscious motivation now constitutes a major component in our constant quest for explanation of human conduct. There are in fact many social circles in which the language of psychopathology must be acquired if one is to participate in conversations. The man with a big appetite clearly had an insecure childhood, possibly bottle-fed rather than breast-fed. The woman who thinks another woman is no more virtuous than she should be is "projecting" her own real or desired sexual misconduct. The man who grumbles about his boss has of course made his boss a father-figure whom he therefore wants to kill as the successful rival for his mother's love. If the neophyte to the game of parlor psychoanalysis wants to learn to play, he can no doubt find several teachers who learned the hard and expensive way by undergoing analysis, which may in fact still be going on. If his psyche bruises easily, he may not want to play, but that too has its simple explanation—he wants to flee life's cruelties by returning to his mother's womb.

I do not mean to poke fun at people's emotional disturbances or at the psychiatrists who attend to them. I do mean to suggest that the popularity of Freudian psychology has tended to make us too suspicious of human motives and much too cynical about man's potential rationality in facing life's problems and dilemmas.

We do not in fact need any very elaborate psychological theory for first-order explanations of human behavior. People commonly behave as they do because they act in ways that are "expected" in the situation. Whether these expectations are also largely internalized by the individual, and thus self-animating, or largely responsive to group pressures and sanctions, will matter for some purposes (will he misbehave when the opportunity occurs?) and not for others. And his really deep-seated motives may be consequential only when they lead to his emotional disturbance or to action that is not "expected."

This small psychological discourse has been prefatory to the troublesome question of rationality of human action in complex organizations, where the demands of efficiency, cost calculation, and a multitude of decisions seem to require it. The answer from our "model" is clear. Wherever there are optional courses of action, the "expectation" is that the decision will be based on the best available information and appropriate logical inferences, that is, approached rationally. Another way of saying this is that countless situations are viewed as presenting "problems," and thus requiring "solutions." The alternatives to rational conduct are many. "Decisions" may be made on the basis of pure precedent (the way it has "always" been done), a rule of thumb that avoids new thought, by sheer unexplained intuition, or even on the advice of astrologers. Or decisions may not be made at all, and everything that happens simply attributed to fate (usually expressed in explanatory, disarming messages such as "circumstances beyond our control," which often should be read as "we failed to take the proper action at the proper time").

Now the impressive thing about the organizational environment of corporations, although not unique to them, is the extent to which rationality is expected, encouraged, and even enforced. Indeed, substantial resources are devoted to developing information and to discussion of its implications for action. Where rationality becomes "institutionalized," that is, becomes a socially sanctioned rule of conduct, the psychology of the unconscious is useful only for explaining deviations from the rule. To use an analogy, the deep reasons for a mathematician's interest in his subject may be such as to be properly left out of polite conversation, and yet not affect his disciplined use of the rigorous logic of his trade. The divisional general manager may be a bundle of aggressions that sharpen rather than dull his judgments. His subjective neuroses thus enhance his objective rationality. Who could ask more?

Immortality

Many organizations are in principle immortal and in fact achieve a life span that far exceeds that of their mortal, human components. The harsh realities of competition may force a small company into bankruptcy or absorption by another concern. This is quite unlikely to happen to the giant corporations, not only because of their greater resources for meeting adversity but also because their importance in the economy is such that they cannot be allowed the privilege of dying. Even in the United States, with its principles of private enterprise, if large and strategic corporations, like the Eastern railroads, are sick, they will be given "transfusions" of public funds, forgiven their taxes, or as a last resort taken over by public authorities. For large corporations, not even death and taxes are certain. Their future, though indefinite, is interminable.

This curious condition has a number of significant consequences. The organization is likely to endure beyond the retirement or death of founders and newcomers alike. It is thus not surprising that the individual is viewed as being "fitted in" to the corporation and not the contrary. And the organization itself must be able to withstand turnover, which is sooner or later inevitable even if no one changes employers and no one moves up, down, or out, because, obviously, everyone retires or dies. All enduring corporations thus face the "succession problem," the replacement of current officials by others who are hopefully qualified.

It would be ridiculous to suppose that a change of officers is unimportant for the ordinary transactions of corporate life. Yet our model can tolerate no such homely wisdom, for the model is not greatly affected by people. Rather, the inevitability of turnover is one of the major reasons for the clarity, formality, and specificity of job descriptions; continued operation depends upon insuring against the vagaries of life, death, and human differences.

Often the corporate manager is supposed to pick and to "train" one or more potential successors to insure the organization against emergencies. Occasionally this obligation to participate in "executive development" is also used to be sure that the incumbent keeps on his toes, or he may be removed by executive order without waiting for his death or retirement. I have been told of a department store in New York where the policy of threatened replacement by subordinates is made so explicit that turnover is speeded up by the increased incidence of ulcers and cardiac conditions among the threatened managers.

Such situations tempt one to the metaphor of cellular replacement and metabolism in the organism, high activity requiring high energy and thus high metabolism. In other words, life feeds on death. It is, however, not at all clear that rapid turnover in corporate offices does indeed signify vitality, for disease also commonly uses up cells to a dangerous degree.

Corporate immortality also encourages planning for a future that will never come for the planners. Since there is a certain reasonable expectation that executives will reach policy-forming levels on the basis of experience, and therefore age, the future time horizon that exceeds their own life expectancy need not be very long. Yet these men are expected to plan for posterity. And they do.

The most extreme case of long-range corporate planning that I know of is the 100-year cycle of timber planting and cutting adopted by large lumber companies in the Pacific Northwest. The transition from the exploitation of timber as a wasting resource, like coal, to its management as a replaceable resource coincided with the transition from individual timber barons to corporate business.

Planning or saving for posterity is not, in individual psychology, an "economically rational" action. One is reminded of the benighted Wisconsin farmer resisting the missionary efforts of the agricultural extension man. The farmer's reasonable response was, "Why should I worry about posterity? What have they done for me?" Yet we do know and expect concern for the material welfare of lineal descendants, despite the sacrifice of current hedonic enjoyment by the accumulators of wealth and despite the unequal advantages for those children and grandchildren wise enough to choose rich progenitors.

The motivation that prompts corporate executives to commit disposable resources to the corporate future rather than to their or the stockholders' present enjoyment is puzzling. Since the question has not been examined by the probers of the executive psyche, we can only speculate. Perhaps, as in the case of rationality, we need no explanation but the "expectations" on the corporate community to whom executives pay attention. If, however, we want to push further it appears probable that senior executives do in fact become sufficiently identified with "their" companies (actually, their employers) that the organization's future welfare becomes the moral equivalent of the private estate for their own dependents and descendants. The motives are not very important for our model corporation, but the action predicated on an indefinite corporate future is important. Plunder may still occur, but it is distinctly unfashionable.

I I I

THE WELL-OILED MACHINE

WHEREIN *complex work organizations are viewed as social machines with almost-human parts, finely finished but not otherwise useful.*

IN CORPORATE life, organization is nearly everything. The complex array of jobs, of positions and duties, can be pictured as standing apart from the temporary human inhabitants, a kind of social landscape that provides a setting little affected by the petty affairs of transients. Such a picture would be more impressionistic than photographic, more like the studio portrait emphasizing character than the "mug shot" that highlights unflattering details. Yet the picture is similar enough to what the untutored eye sees to be recognizable. For there is a sense in which the homely aphorism, "organization is people," represents a greater distortion than the view that organization is either super-human or non-human.

The model administrative organization has been likened to a machine, and that analogy can be pushed pretty far. Like the machine, the organization involves the assembly of finely tooled and highly specialized parts, and operates in terms of both reciprocal and sequential actions, with a temporal discipline and rhythm, and all sorts of opportunities for breakdowns.

The machine-like character of corporate organization is enhanced by the importance of real machines. And real machines provide the proximate specifications of the kind of people who work with and for them and determine the rate and rhythm of action for production workers and also for all sorts of people at considerable geographical and social distance. Naturally, real machines, being inanimate, do not in fact do any of these things in any ultimate sense. They are the agents of real people acting out their several parts in a machine-like organization. But the mechanical metaphor is almost unavoidable.

The organizational equivalent of the engineering drawings that precede the construction of a machine is the tree-like diagram with circles or squares representing positions or functions, connected by lines representing flows of materials and messages and the paths of power. I shall yield to the temptation to add that many circles represent essential working parts and a few represent rather inconsequential, external ornaments; most are standard equipment, some are optional extras.

The design of the corporate machine, and thus the first prerequisite for its operation, is represented in these diagrams. And the diagrams are never far from the hand and the eye of the individual component with any administrative responsibility, for they tell where he and others fit into the grand scheme of things.

Mechanical Cooperation

The first requirement for "getting along" in an organization is to do one's job. In principle, although not always in fact, it is also the last requirement. To "do good," without reference to the love of God or neighbor, is the sum of the law if not of the prophets. Affection for one's employer or fellow worker is not required; in fact, sentimentality may impair rational judgment, impersonal performance, and orderly procedure. Devotion to duty has only a remote or negative relation to devotion to people.

The greatest single advantage of the model administrative organization over other forms of human interaction is the capacity for inducing strangers and even potential enemies to cooperate in accomplishing the collective mission. This is accomplished not by brainwashing or conversions in character but by the single process of employment. Cooperation consists of persons performing tasks that are related to other tasks and to goals set for the unit, the department, the division, the company. The goals are achieved without anyone trying to achieve them. Cooperation is accomplished without anyone being cooperative.

These minor miracles are the result of organization, which of course does have to be planned and manned, and occasionally led and disciplined. The model, then, is somewhat more than life-size, and our normal perversity prompts us to seek out the discrepancies rather than the perfections. Yet the ideal standard is remarkably approximate to actual behavior. In large organizations persons who are unseen by and unknown to one another are caught up in webs of reciprocal or sequential dependence. Officers, whose names may be known by subordinates who never see them, perform about as they would if they had any other names, that is, about like their predecessors and successors. Workers quit, are fired, retire, or die and are replaced by others of similar qualifications. Filing clerks get married, get pregnant, quit their jobs, and become part of the inactive files. Persons working together who take a distinct displeasure in one another's company still do their jobs, hoping perhaps that someone will get transferred.

The model components of model organizations are not exactly nameless and faceless, but they are far less than whole people and they are in particular emotionless. They are, to exaggerate, creatures of the organization, mere replaceable parts. The grand task of planning an organization is to identify the necessary parts and to arrange them in such a way that they mesh with minimum friction and, when put in operation, move the machine in the planned direction.

This mechanical cooperation permits the use of radically divergent personality types and trained skills, allows the organization to go on while its human components are being shuffled and replaced, and achieves collective goals out of the efforts of individuals who perhaps couldn't care less. It is really remarkable what money, in the form of wages and salaries, can do in dissolving human apathy and antipathy. I do not say that money alone makes the world go around, or that our mechanical model powered with money is precisely a true one, but it is true enough for enough people to be taken very seriously. It is a noteworthy social invention, a testimony to human ingenuity in the almost non-human use of human beings.

Jurisdiction

To the outsider seeking information or a redress of grievances, the most exasperatingly "bureaucratic" feature of administrative organizations is the difficulty in finding someone who takes his problem seriously and proceeds to solve it. Chancing on a salesman in the field, a salesgirl behind a counter, or a receptionist in a business office, the information or justice-seeker is "referred" to someone else. The first referral may or may not be accurate, and in any event is not likely to be final if the problem is serious enough to require referral to higher authority. One is reminded of the cartoon showing a man holding a very broken fountain pen approaching the offices of the Acme Lifetime Pen Company. The pen, though not our man, is referred in successive panels to successive echelons of power, until it is taken by the president to the board of directors. The final panels show the president returning with pen in left hand, pistol in right. He kills the plaintiff and thus upholds the company's lifetime guarantee.

This story, in turn, reminds one of the real, not facetiously fictional, habits of the primitive inhabitants of Australia. For these people, kinship organization and relations were the sum total of significant social position. A man visiting a neighboring group had to establish a kinship tie with some member of the group, and if he could do this he was accepted in peace and harmony. Failing this, he did not socially exist and the group he was visiting proceeded to kill him just to keep the system tidy and clearly superior to any mere troublesome individual.

Such drastic measures for handling problems are of course rare and usually unnecessary, for in the normal course of events, the troublemaker will either be sent away finally satisfied or will have given up his quest as hopeless.

Buck-passing, as referral is called, may at times be a way of evading responsibility and wearing out the outsider, but it has an eminently sound organizational foundation. All semblance of internal order would rapidly disappear if everyone were in charge of everything, or if any person the unknowing outsider buttonholed promptly handled the problem. The parts of the corporate machine may be replaceable, but they are not interchangeable in either structure or function. The determination and maintenance of jurisdiction, "sphere of competence," are thus essential specifications for the operation of complex organizations. The appropriate question is, "Who's in charge of what?" and one of the principal purposes of organization charts is to answer just such questions.

The answer may not be altogether easy, even for the employee who is knowledgeable, or willing to find out, and blessed with a happy disposition and a modicum of good will. Jurisdictions and functions are organizationally established for organizational purposes, not primarily for the peculiar problems of outsiders. And even within organizations the "unusual" situation may arise in a most annoying and unmechanical way. Yet this is a realistic insight that we must not indulge in too freely, for it would be disruptive of our model. Nor can the organization plan precisely for the unplannable, so it must somehow adjust, however haltingly, to handling cases that require solution but do not precisely fit the established jurisdictions of competent functionaries. Such cases are pregnant sources of organizational change, along with the everpresent (but non-model-like) tendencies of officials to expand their powers and evade their responsibilities, thus leaving jurisdictional boundaries as dotted and wavy lines. If this leaves some people uncertain and some problems unsolved, it is simply the way the organization hangs together and avoids crumbling with every emergency. In civilized society it is impolite to kill troublemakers. The function of established jurisdictions is to make this inviting possibility unnecessary.

Matching Men and Jobs

The degree of supremacy of the organization over the individual, although not total, is impressive. This can be seen in the transformation of organizational charts into manpower. Positions or functions are first translated into job specifications. Those specifications are then translated into the qualifications of persons. Finally, one hires the persons with the qualifications to comply with the specifications in filling the positions.

The "supremacy" of the organization derives partly from the power of massive size, partly from the intricate specialization made possible and necessary by size. The man must fit the slot, for the slot cannot be changed without changing several or a great many other job descriptions. And, aside from new organizations or positions, the company has temporal priority. Its recruiters and personnel officers are seeking a man just like the man who had the job last. They may expect a little more, or a little less, but not much.

This assumes the existence of an organization, however, and perhaps we should start from the beginning. Determining total manpower requirements then becomes a fairly complicated affair. The two principal variables needed for calculation are *function* and *scale*. The former determines the kinds of jobs to be done and the kinds of people to do them, and the latter determines how many of each kind. The "economic base" of a corporation is comprised of the array of goods and services to be produced for the market. Without manpower concerned with production the organization becomes something different, and we are no longer interested. The kinds of workers needed are determined mainly by the product (manufactured goods, retail sales, bank transactions, insurance policies) and the technology used. Scale, however, interacts with function, since scale permits labor specialization and thus a narrower description of jobs. The closer we are to a corporation's economic base, that is to production, the easier is the rational solution of manning the organization. We thus neglect for the moment non-production workers ranging from charwomen to chairmen of boards, from plant guards to public relations men. Job specifications derive from product, technology, and scale. These are matched with people capable of doing the jobs and the two are joined by a financial bargain.

If people and jobs cannot be matched at the offered prices, clearly "something has to give." The jobs have to be redefined to match the people, the people have to be changed, say by on-the-job training, to match the jobs, or the financial inducements have to be increased sufficiently to lure qualified people into employment. Cases can be found to illustrate all three strategies, and possibly all three may be used simultaneously. However, if one were betting on any particular case with very little prior information, one would win on the average by betting against organizational change, for the relevant variables are simply less flexible than are persons and pocketbooks.

I have the impression, which I cannot systematically substantiate, that demand takes precedence over supply even within the corporation. By this I mean that technological decisions and organizational charts are made without consultation with personnel departments. The duty of personnel directors is thus not to advise on the state of the many labor markets that will have to be entered in order to fill the positions. Rather, their duty is to deliver the people in the needed dimensions and numbers. Severe labor shortages at the "going" wages and salaries may result in changes in the shopping list, but as far as I can see the list is revised if at all only after a trip to the market, not before. If my impression of the subordinate position of the personnel function is right, it would appear to be an organizational consequence of a common and long-standing assumption that labor is always in excess supply. That assumption when challenged is commonly admitted to be wrong for many varieties of jobs, and sometimes for nearly all jobs. Nevertheless, corporate organization may not exactly reflect available wisdom, which in this case would seem to indicate that prior study of labor markets might offer advantages over trial-and-error shopping.

Wherever job specifications can be made fairly precise, selection procedures may be as simple as trying out the applicant at the jobs as a simple test of his honesty in reporting his experience or his capacity to judge his own competence. The matching problem grows in precise proportion to the vagueness of the qualities sought or duties to be performed. Qualities of leadership, initiative, and creativity may be difficult to define precisely or to detect in applicants. And for such jobs one is unlikely to be able to say, "just step right over to this group, Mister Brown, and show us how you lead your men," or "sit right down Doctor Smith and be creative." Success or failure may still be hard to judge at the end of a trial and in either case may have been more the result of circumstances beyond the man's capacity to control rather than of his special virtues and shortcomings. (A colleague once spoke perceptively of the arrogance of business managers assuming the blame for failures they could not have prevented.)

The selection of persons for positions hard to define in terms of simple operations, requiring performance hard to judge over a brief period, must then rest upon appraisal of the candidate's experience in related work or upon expert testimony. The promotion of a man to a position carrying somewhat wider responsibilities than those he is carrying already, but of the same sort, is the common method of selecting managers. Non-managers such as chemists or lawyers are likely to be selected on the recommendation of members of their own clan, for who else can judge?

The risks and uncertainties in selection, abetted by uncertainties as to the qualities sought, lie behind the attempt to find some rational formula for identifying the right kind of talent. In a social order permeated by puzzles and tests it is not surprising that managers and personnel officers should have recourse to batteries of tests. Some tests may be designed to identify aptitudes for types of occupations and may come close to doing so. Other tests may be designed to test traits of character like initiative and imagination, or emotional stability under stress or attitudes appropriate to getting along in the business community. Aside from the ethical questions aroused by the attempt to probe into the individual's subconscious—Thurber, one recalls, warned people to "leave my old psyche alone"—one may wonder what are the proportions of rational and magical components in so-called personality tests. The sharp operator may learn how to give the sought-for responses without subjecting his soul to search, as Whyte has suggested in *The Organization Man*. Or success on the test may assure success on the job because the job performance cannot be conveniently appraised and test results are simply used in a self-confirming way as the equivalent of job results. This would be like the teacher who knows Johnny is bright because she has seen his I.Q. score in the principal's office, so she gives Johnny an "A" for being smart, not for doing his work.

The general emphasis on rationality and the particular emphasis on "professional" management in the corporation lead to a continuing quest for improvement in specifying qualities sought and in identifying those qualities in selecting persons. If, once more, magical solutions—gimmicks—get a temporary cachet as rational until proved otherwise, this should not surprise us. The more urgent the felt need for solutions to problems, the more likely are critical faculties to be impaired when solutions are offered by promoters wearing the aura of "science."

We can confidently expect that the quest for improvement in matching men and jobs will lead to an expansion of mechanical substitutes for human judgment. Individual qualities and achievements, coded for punched cards or electronic memory keepers, may be sorted to match a set of demands put to the machine. This may be a new form of "servitude to the machine," to the nostalgic regret of those who remember the days when people were not reduced to punched cards. The trend is not likely to be delayed by the critics. It is doubtful, however, that in the near future divisional general managers will be selected because theirs is the only personnel card left in the last slot in the sorting machine. What instructions could one give the machine?

Separate: Equal and Unequal

One of the principal "economies of scale" afforded by the corporation is the division of labor, the specialization of performers in an interdependent network of tasks. Lauded by economists since Adam Smith, division of labor has the presumed advantages of higher proficiency over a narrower range of action than that achieved by the all-purpose craftsman and the additional advantage of shorter training. (If jobs thus become less interesting and challenging, that is a different problem.) The literal division of labor, the dilution of skill combinations into several component parts, is one historic and contemporary aspect of specialization. This process, however, is relevant only to products that already exist, say mass production of clothing, and not to new products and services, which usually require new skills and often new skill combinations. Much of the specialization characteristic of corporate organization arises from *diversification* rather than *division* of labor.

The splitting-up of jobs is often discussed exclusively in terms of wage laborers in manufacturing. No occupation, however, is immune to such specialization. We need only compare the dermatologist with the general practitioner in medicine, the expert on wills in the "law factory" with the all-purpose attorney, the modern manager and his corps of advisers and assistants with his omniscient and omnipotent forerunner. Yet, again, some specialties are new, not just fractions of old ones, and the growth in the total range of human knowledge and techniques requires diversication as well as mere division of labor. Organizational size clearly encourages both forms of specialization, that is, extension of the total range of functions and the fineness with which that range is parceled out to persons.

The number of distinct occupations is likely to be very large in the giant corporations. Many job titles convey to the layman no meaning, unless he has at hand the thick *Dictionary of Occupational Titles* issued by the United States Employment Service. Other titles may be misconstrued. In occupational language a "necker" for example, is not one who indulges in mild sexual play but a clothing worker who operates a knitting machine that supplies neck-bands to sweaters. The game of specialization clearly cannot be understood without a program.

A complete array of corporate positions would be virtually impossible and in any event hopelessly tedious. We can settle for far less, and thus gain in general understanding, by identifying a limited number of "classes" of occupations. A functional classification of cogs in the corporate machine will not provide the personnel man's inventory or shopping list, but it is likely to correspond to the types of departments or markets he must enter.

Starting from the corporation's economic base, our first class of workers is those involved rather directly in physical production. Here it is useful to distinguish three sub-groups. The first, and still the largest sector of the industrial labor force, may be called "machine tenders." That is, these are workers who labor in close coordination with mechanical processes, and in many instances (such as in continuous assembly) are paced by the machine. In other cases the worker's rate is determined by managerial rule or by management-union negotiation, but he still "serves the machine" as the man who feeds a molding machine or a drill press. A second sub-group, of growing importance, are the "machine supervisors." These are men whose "mastery of the machine" has been restored by high degrees of mechanization. This sub-group may be illustrated by the man who guides a fairly complex productive process by moving levers and pushing buttons or the man whose main responsibility is not a manual one at all but one of "monitoring" an instrument board and taking only corrective action. A third sub-group of workers provides auxiliary services for direct production, such as construction and machine installation, transportation, and materials handling. It includes the rapidly growing breed of "maintenance men" who are increasingly the newer version of the skilled craftsmen.

A second functional class of workers provides for custodial services and plant and office security. Of these, the security officers are the more interesting, as like policemen generally they tend to have authority exceeding their rank or prestige. To these men fall the tasks of preventing unauthorized persons from entering company property and unauthorized materials from leaving it.

The large class of workers who share with many machine-tenders the threat of technological displacement is comprised of clerical staffs. Clerical staffs function as communicators (writing and talking) or as memory-keepers (filing and searching). Although many secretaries combine two legitimate general functions (we shall not inquire at the moment about others), the duties should still be distinguished.

We now come, perhaps tardily, to managers. The essence of the managerial function is coordination, the integration of specialized activities of subordinates in fulfilling a mission for which his organizational unit is responsible. Leadership, training, and the tender care of subordinates' psyches are either irrelevant in our ideal model or incidental to the coordinating function.

The most rapidly expanding occupational category in the American corporation is comprised of "staff" functions. This is in fact a very heterogeneous class of occupations united only by two general functions—supplying information relevant to decisions and, less uniformly, instigating innovations.

Finally, reaching the organizational summit, we may distinguish executive functions as comprising policy formation and final decision. The latter function obviously extends executive responsibility over other occupational categories. Yet it is useful for some purposes to keep executives, with their company-wide responsibilities, separate from lesser members of the corporation. These are the men concerned with operation of the machine as a whole. As President Truman noted by a sign on his executive desk: "The buck stops here."

Our social machine now, finally, comprises people, and has someone in the driver's seat. It is not frictionless, but is, one can hope, in operating order.

I V

THE GEOMETRY OF POWER

W HEREIN *the crude fact of the existence of
bosses is noted and the possible justification for their
power in a society of unequals explored.*

No one in his right mind would mistake an administrative organization for a society of equals. On the contrary, position and
rank at the work place provide about the most elaborate and finely
graded system of "social stratification" known to man. If, as in the
military services, seniority in grade is added to rank itself, the
"pecking order" observable in chicken yards is obviously a feeble
imitation in nature of the art of fine discrimination. The typical
corporation does not reach military extremes of precision in assign-
ing relative position, but it does include enough strata to provide
the social geologist with ample raw materials for his chipping
hammer.

The Human Pyramid

Organization charts are commonly portrayed in two-dimensional
space as triangles, sitting solidly on a base, and proceeding up-

ward to a point. But it is the three-dimensional pyramid that gives the best visual representation of the distribution of rank in an administrative organization. Although organization charts are primarily made to be looked at from the top down, their dimensions as a matter of fact are determined from the bottom up. This point can be established by an exercise in simple arithmetic.

Coordination in corporations is achieved by the exercise of authority (legitimate power). That authority is derived from delegation of powers from higher authority. Authority is delegated for a very simple reason: the limited possibility of direct surveillance of vast numbers or vastly different tasks. We come, then, to an essential concept for the understanding of the pyramid of power. The "span of control" may be defined as the number of direct subordinates whose work is supervised by any power-holder. That span of control is restricted by the limits of human vision, time, energy, and knowledge.

Let us suppose that the span of control is restricted to ten subordinates. If then we have one hundred production workers, we must have ten foremen and one chief executive, giving us a neatly shaped but relatively low pyramid. Note, however, that if the limit of ten is absolute, as few as eleven workers require a three-layer pyramid, as the two first-level coordinators must also be coordinated. Note also that this kind of ratio does not run up "overhead costs" with great rapidity, as a ten-fold increase (a thousand workers) would require only one additional echelon, and a million workers would require only seven layers of authority. A doubling of the work force from a half-million would require more managers, it is true, but no more echelons of managers. Some "under-employed" coordinators would simply be brought up to full performance.

This small hypothetical exercise is wrong in several respects, all of which may be summarized as the fault of simple-mindedness. The "proper" span of control cannot be set so arbitrarily as we have done in our example. The span of control can be broadened if the tasks of subordinates are highly homogeneous—for example, railroad track workers, masons setting in place the brick walls of a large building, weavers in a large textile factory. It can also be broadened if the tasks of subordinates are highly routinized, even if specialized—for example, workers tending metal stamping machines in an automobile parts plant.

The administrative converse of routinization is an organization of work in which problems must frequently be referred to the manager for decision. Such a work situation clearly narrows the effective span of control for coordinators.

The combination of these principles results in an organizational pyramid with somewhat concave sides. Duplication and extreme routinization of tasks are most likely at or near the bottom of the structure, giving rise to width without substantial height. The decision-making power of coordinators is likely to increase as one moves to higher levels. At the same time the number of direct subordinates decreases. In fact, there is strong reason for supposing that the span of control will become steadily narrower as one approaches the apex of the pyramid. But that requires additional echelons of authority and thus postpones the final ascent to the summit.

The manager, or his wife, may brag about the hundreds or thousands of men he has "under" him, but all but a very few of these will be rather far under. The number of steps from bottom to top may be fifteen or twenty or even more, if one counts the tricky half-steps represented by such titles as "assistant to" the general manager. Even if the steps are short, and some of them are not, this is not the sort of ascent to be lightly undertaken by a man with a heart condition.

The standard organization chart tends to identify single officers or at least single offices (with hidden clerical staffs) at middle and upper levels, groups of workers at lower levels. This practice tends to coincide with differences in span of control. On the chart, this minimizes the lateral extension at lower levels and somewhat arbitrarily makes the shape of the pyramid appear more rectilinear than it really is.

The size of an organization, and particularly the width at its base, are clearly relevant to the number of echelons of authority but not exclusively so. Thus a highly diversified company is likely to have a steeper power structure, because of heightened problems of coordination than one which has expanded into "more of the same." A sharp reduction in labor force through mechanization will not necessarily reduce direct administrative costs. This is not because of managerial over-staffing but because the new organization of production probably requires less supervision but more coordination.

The decision-making power of administrators is crucial to the size and shape of the pyramid of power. Where foremen can have rather large constituencies, the reason is that the workers have virtually no decisions and thus none to refer to the boss. At higher levels, the extent to which problems move up and decisions move down is not a merely mechanical question. It is a question of administrative policy. "Decentralization" means the location of decisions at or near the place where the problems arise; in other words, less upward referral. Such a policy may achieve a substantial "flattening" of the structure of authority as higher administrators are relieved of problem-solving for subordinates. The manager can thus handle more people "reporting to him" if in fact they do not report very often or if they confine their reports to information without questions.

"Flattening" of administrative structures through decentralization is enhanced by a pronounced lateral extension that is a sort of by-product. This lateral extension arises from the addition of staff experts supplying information relevant to decision. In a highly centralized organization, advisory staffs are concentrated near the top of the organization and might be thought to resemble a kind of Byzantine dome on the edifice. Where authority is decentralized staff functions are likely to be added at lower levels, so that they push out the otherwise concave sides.

By now the architectural form of our structure is sufficiently complex to be faintly confusing, as indeed it can be to the hapless inhabitant who gets off on the wrong floor. Yet sensible people can tell the difference between up and down and will be generally correct in the assumption that the higher you go the fewer people you encounter.

The Excuses for Bosses

Why does one need bosses anyway? Why cannot an organization operate on a single plateau of interdependent specialization, unmarked by any promontories of power? Since sharp departures from the ideal of equalitarianism appear also in productive organizations of communist countries, we may suppose that managerial power has some basis other than simple Marxist notions of exploitation.

To answer our questions, let us take an indirect route, namely, a specification of the conditions for dispensing with bosses. A purely static (and wholly unrealistic) model of an organization in a benign environment, ideally planned and ideally staffed with participants perfectly motivated leaves no room for managers, as there are no goals to be determined, no hostile forces to be counteracted, no plans to be made, no routes to be selected, no personnel to be recruited, no incentives to be invented, and no discipline to be imposed. Perhaps not even any bells to be rung or songs to be sung. In two words, no problems.

Authoritative decision is of course not the only way invented by man to resolve issues. Under a different set of unrealistic assumptions one could imagine a corporation as a self-governing body with no governors, a kind of town meeting that would debate measures and take votes. The success of this procedure would rest on a fairly uniform distribution of appropriate knowledge and technical skills among the membership, or at least a fairly clear understanding of the issues and proposed solutions. Such direct democracy has been abandoned in most of our governmental organization, mainly because the citizen cannot be a universal expert. We have thus maintained a political accountability to the electorate along with executive and administrative responsibility for carrying our programs. This brings us to the second major problem in the notion of corporate democracy, the circumstance that the electorate—corporate employees—are not likely to be properly representative of the interests to which the company must be attentive.

The power of property will no longer quite justify the authority of executives and the delegated authority of managers. Yet it remains true that the corporation is accountable to investors, suppliers, customers, and public agencies. That accountability centers on executives. They may delegate powers as an aid to fulfilling their obligations, but they cannot thereby evade responsibility. This external responsibility of the executives is an insurmountable barrier to representative government within the firm.

If we look upward in the organization, bosses are the coordinators of the work of subordinates toward the accomplishment of objectives; and these objectives are not determined by subordinates. Looking downward, managers exercise delegated authority appropriate to their rank and function. Policy-formulation, adaptation of the corporation to changing circumstances, and decisions on innovations are responsibilities not likely to wander far from executive country. Managers are likely to have other kinds of problems to solve—the redefinition of means for achieving constant or changing objectives; selection and motivation of subordinates; adjudication of disputes; and enforcement of rules. It is partly because our model falls short of inhuman perfection that managers are necessary. They are, in a sense, organizational maintenance men. Managers and executives are also necessary, however, because the organization's mission, its policies and foreign relations, are essentially determined from the top down, not from the bottom up.

If any particular manager is not entrusted with the entire range of functions—goal setting, goal implementing, fighting fires, and putting down insurrections—one can be reasonably sure that someone else is, usually a higher authority or a specialist responsible to a higher authority.

Control Devices

Morality is a quality unevenly distributed in human, including corporate, populations. In fact in the lives of individuals morality is a standard to be approximated, not fully achieved, and in action it becomes a variable, a question of time and cricumstance, of more or less—not an attribute or a question of all or none. Canons of conduct are not self-enforcing, moreover, and we have noted that rule enforcement is one of the functions of authority in corporate organization. If this duty occupied a major part of the time and energy of the manager, he could scarcely get his other work done, and the situation would be a kind of moral morass that would prevent anything approximating a "normal" operation of human affairs.

Fortunately for the maintenance of order, most people obey most rules most of the time. Much of this moral behavior is thoughtless and habitual. Some of it is deliberate and conscientious, resting upon "internalized" convictions concerning propriety and rejecting attractive but immoral alternatives. Some of it is constrained and fearful of punishment. These people and these actions are so normal as to be, for the moment, uninteresting. It is the universal potentiality for sinning that challenges the maintenance of order and discipline.

Misfeasance, malfeasance, and nonfeasance constitute a handful of legal terms less redundant than some beloved by lawyers. They may be translated as doing the proper thing in the wrong way, doing an improper thing, and doing nothing. In combination they pretty well cover the delinquencies of men. Each, however, requires a definition of the standards to be applied, the degrees of departure from standards, and the penalties that will match the crime. The ultimate sanction available to private organizations is dismissal, the least, the subtle sign of disapproval. The manager may exercise his right of dismissal or recommend it, if he does not have unqualified authority to use it. He may impose other disciplines covered by rule or precedent—pay-docking, demotion, official reprimand, and probation ("Don't let it happen again"). He may enter an adverse note on the offender's service record, a note that will appear when the man is considered for another position. In theory, the discipline is stern but just.

A corporation is of course concerned with the maintenance of public law wherever its interests are affected. Most of the offenses in the State's criminal code are capable of being committed on company time and company property, and possibly with the company or one of its members as victims. The company can scarcely affect indifference to the fact that a boss has killed his secretary in a fit of rage over a misspelled word, even though there may be no company rule expressly forbidding the killing of secretaries having more than two years of service with the employer.

Corporations, as other organizations, also have a system of "private law," and its enforcement is primarily the responsibility of constituted private authorities.

Open and flagrant violation is not the kind of misconduct that is likely to challenge the maintenance of morality. Secret sinning is. Meting out punishment is a simple matter compared with discovery of the crime and identifying the culprit. Because many of the offenses that are to be detected are directly relevant to job behavior, and because much of job behavior takes place in rather confined areas, detection of wrong-doing suggests surveillance. But detailed personal surveillance by supervisors is administratively expensive. What is involved is a radical contraction of the span of control in order to oversee all operations, requiring still more managers to do other managerial duties.

Labor-saving technology may reduce the administrative costs of close watch, for example through the unblinking eye of the television camera. Some companies already use such equipment. This calls up the disturbing picture of George Orwell's 1984 and the efficient imposition of a regime of terror. Avoiding for the moment ethical issues, monitoring the screens would scarcely reduce surveillance costs by more than three-fourths or four-fifths, as four or five pictures are the probable limit of the observer's span of sight and attention. Besides, who oversees the overseers?

Less extreme and more indirect methods of detection are the rule. As with the solving of crimes in the outside world, methods of detection may require rather specialized skills. The checking of numerical totals of performance units may be a simple matter, but quality of performance will be somewhat more difficult. Inspectors and quality-control services are of course installed in part to protect the company from customers' complaints, but they may be used also to identify the workers responsible for excessive rejects.

The principal specialized control device in corporations is the accounting system. Financial operations in business may be used as a measure of performance as well as for preserving honesty with other people's money. All units within a corporation that produce goods and services for the market may be subjected to scrutiny in terms of costs and returns. Since both sides of the ledger are subject to accounting conventions, the judgment of success or failure may rest in part on complying with the standards adopted by financial officers. Those officers thus become a set of impartial judges of managerial excellence.

The appraisal of business results in financial terms can never be far separated from questions of the propriety of financial transactions. The line between the unwise and the improper is at times thin, and the differences are best seen at the extreme. A purchase of materials at prices well above the competitive market may simply indicate poor business judgment or a failure to require competitive bids. Suspicions of conflict of interest or downright gouging are aroused if the man making the decision has a financial interest in the supplying company or if his bank account reveals a rather unusual deposit around the time of the transaction. Embezzlement, a crime that by its nature can be committed only by persons who are thought exceptionally worthy of trust, is perhaps most common in strictly financial corporations such as banks. It is not unknown in other companies. The man who simply pads his expense account may have the same excuse—that of living beyond his means—as the embezzler, but he rarely thinks of himself as a thief. He may rationalize that he is simply getting paid for overtime which cannot be directly recompensed under company rules.

The procedures imposed by controllers and the examinations made by accountants and auditors constitute a network of barriers to misappropriation of funds. Rules of course constitute challenges to conscientious evaders of rules, with a resulting battle of wits between the bad guys and the good guys.

Because of their special function as agents of moral control, it is not surprising that accountants and auditors seem to have an especially distrustful character. Whether this is a matter of selection or training of a personality type, the bookkeeper is commonly and often correctly pictured in fiction and popular lore as a man with a small, exceptionally tidy, and habitually suspicious mind. Cast in the role of keepers of the corporate conscience, their jobs, like those of policemen, do not yield an encouraging view of human nature.

Leadership

The exercise of authority involves something more than discipline and control, and exclusive emphasis on restraint would indicate an unhealthy preoccupation with evil. Corporate managers are also supposed to be positive, to display leadership. Leadership is a virtue rather more widely subscribed to than understood. And many of the qualities listed as desirable for leaders, such as conscientiousness and solicitude for the welfare of others, we should also like to find rather generally.

The legitimate occasions for leadership in corporations largely involve change. Only routine management, not leadership, is needed in stable and secure organizations. The leader then sets new goals and justifies them, sets performance standards, and encourages followers to new effort. He is an innovator, moralizer, demonstrator, teacher. And as such he is a dangerous man.

Almost everything we know about complex organizations points to order, devotion to established and limited duty, and finely specialized interdependence. Under the guise of leadership, the intricate machine may be crudely upset. The leader who extracts heroic performance from his followers may be thereby interfering in their normal involvements in all sorts of non-occupational but proper uses of time and energy. His leadership may involve imperialistic forays into neighboring territories and consequent border disputes. If the loyalty of his followers is personal and emotional, the relationship violates the sound organizational principle that authority rests in the office rather than the man, lest all become demoralized with the departure of the loved one.

The German sociologist, Max Weber, identified one form of authority as *charismatic*, resting upon the rejection of traditional values, the espousing of the leader's new ones, with authority resting on the personal allegiance of his followers. A friend, somewhat innocent of the language of sociologists, tells me that he encountered the term "charismatic leadership" in his reading. Knowing that his secretary held a proper Bachelor of Arts in sociology, he asked her the meaning of the term. Her quick reply was, "Think of Jesus." Now this type of authority, in Weber's view, was in sharp contrast to that appropriate to "bureaucratic" (that is, administrative) organizations. As usual he was right.

Leadership of the type and quality that corporation executives sometimes like to attribute to themselves as "great leaders of men" is usually, and fortunately, the product of a mistaken ego. Real crisis situations may provide opportunities for truly individual leadership. If the crises are manufactured, the strategy is likely to wear thin. And in the ordinary course of events such individual qualities must be severely restrained for the sake of organized and orderly action.

The Power of Knowledge

Authority, in the sense in which we have applied the term to managers and executives, is legitimate power. It is the capacity to get others to comply with orders and suggestions, to obey rules and do their duty, but it is a capacity exercised with restraint and within a system of values and rules that are binding on the power-holder as well as on his subordinates. In the administrative organization, managers generally exercise delegated, legitimate power.

Popular speech affords another meaning of the term "authority," however, exemplified by our reference to an acknowledged expert in some field of knowledge as an authority on his subject. This second sense of the term is appropriate for understanding the corporate power structure. The emphasis on rational decision-making in corporations encourages the quest for authoritative knowledge on subjects relevant to decisions. Thus managerial power is passed out not only to other, lesser, authorities of the same general type, but also to persons who command information. In the conventional language of administration, these latter persons are "staff" officers. In the conventional diagrams of power, they are represented as advisory to "line" officers. Clearly line officers, having responsibilities to those who were the source of their delegated powers, are "in charge." But they are also somewhat at the mercy of their advisers, for after all their advisers *know*. The interdependence between inconsistent bases of power is an intrinsic source of tension in administrative organizations. This is not our present concern, which is the effect this "staff authority" has on lateral extension of our geometric structure and the more significant effect it has on reducing the autocratic power of managers. The lawyer, the industrial engineer, and the marketing manager, for example, control essential knowledge and skills beyond the competence of mere executives. Their positions may be advisory, but the advice is of the sort that executives neglect at their peril. The powers behind the throne, soothsayers though they may be, still affect the judgments of corporate minds.

V

NOW HEAR THIS

*WHEREIN some people talk and some people
listen and some people do neither as messages take
indirect routes and occasionally reach their destinations,
and WHEREIN the power of knowledge,
maintained by secretiveness, is viewed
with some misgivings.*

MAN is not the only animal who communicates with his fellows, but he alone is capable of doing so indirectly, of establishing contact with others who are out of sight and earshot but not out of mind. Man alone can communicate with the past (and with the future if there is one) by the written word. Only because of print and other "media" such as radio and television do concepts like audience and public have more than local significance. Without indirect and distant communication the modern corporation, like the modern state, would be impossible.

Communication is a link as essential in social systems as gravity is in the solar system. Communication, however, is a more complex, more multi-dimensional force than gravity, and thus it is less capable of reduction to the elegant simplicity of the mathematical formula. Words divide as well as unite, appeal to sentiment as well as convey meaning, distort as well as represent reality. Small wonder, then, that the builders and operators of large-scale social systems have attempted to understand, harness, and use this complex and ambiguous force in human life. Good managers believe in good communication as an article of faith so basic that the qualifier "good" would almost seem dispensable as redundant. I shall suggest, however, that this qualifier and many others are necessary before the corporate communicator's attempt to reach the mind of another can be understood or communicated.

Going Through Channels

Communication in our unreal model of corporate organization follows simple principles to achieve complex results. Policies established by executive officers are communicated "downward," to subordinates. These policies become programs, combinations of objectives and methods for achieving them. In their downward course, messages are differentiated according to the various functions necessary to accomplish objectives. They also become particularized, so that when they reach any person who is supposed to *do* something beyond interpreting messages, what is communicated is a set of instructions rather than a policy or an objective.

An executive committee, let us say, has decided that the company should embark on the manufacture of a new product or product line. This policy may be communicated relatively intact to a vice-president or divisional general manager. All subsequent steps in the communication chain may or may not start with the original message, but they will certainly add to it information designed to elaborate and implement the original. A plant site must be selected, land acquired, buildings constructed, machinery and power installed. Suppliers must be located and contracted with, distributors selected, and salesmen hired. Superintendents and supervisors must be selected along with the workmen who will make the products.

This synopsis dwells on actions or results. A full and faithful report would require the recording of enough dialogue to fill several novels of normal length and fill the reader with boredom if he were required to read it. Incidentally, the letters, contracts, memoranda, and forms would fill several more books, but one fears that as contributions to literature they would lack something in plot, style, and development of character. If, with a novelist's sense of drama we can imagine the short pungent message ("Hell, no! Tell the bastard we'll buy the plot across the river!") we should also try to force ourselves to imagine the endlessly trivial sentences necessary to complete the transaction. Although executives are not immune to trivial thoughts, noble and evocative prose fits best with generalities of policy. By the time this gets both filtered and elaborated, when the messages reach their several ultimate destinations, the sentences are likely to be short and dull.

If executives were both omnipotent and omniscient—qualities that they may attribute to themselves but that we are not bound to take seriously—there would be no need for upward communication at all. Having enunciated a policy or issued a sweeping command, they could then turn to the next problem with complete assurance that the first matter was settled. Or, if some failure or uncontrolled accident should occur, the all-knowing executive would take the necessary remedial action without awaiting a report.

Upward communication, then, consists of at least two classes of messages: word that the message reached its destination, and information on the "current state." Neither class of messages reaches the top in pure and original form. A steady flow of "yes sir's" from all parts of the empire might give the executive a special sense of power, but if he attended to them they would in fact make him impotent. Similarly, instantaneous or even daily reports on purchasing transactions, units of production, sales made, absentees, papers filed, and memoranda issued would inundate the hapless executive who "likes to keep his fingers on the pulse."

Upward communication, it is clear, must reverse the process encountered by downward messages. Information becomes generalized and integrated as it travels upward. Both the particularization and the generalization processes are accomplished in stages, and the operation of these stages is insured by "going through channels." Unless messages "touch all bases," there is substantial danger that they will not get through at all or the greater danger that they may get through in a too concentrated state going down or a too undigested state going up.

Critics of executive policies have had much fun with the insistence of senior officers that written proposals be reduced to one page or less. Some university professors in particular, who live much of their lives in the environment of the written word, are likely to consider the condensed memorandum as fairly conclusive proof that executives are an illiterate lot. Whether or not policy-forming officials are great readers, the point here is that abbreviation is essential to the operation of a communication system that does not swamp the executive with details. If the executive were to know more about small matters, he presumably would have to know less about large matters, for even an exceptionally brilliant and well-organized man has limits on his capacity and on his time. Generalization loses information, and application requires that it be added back. This logical principle applies in administrative communication as it does in science and technology. The trick is to do it right.

Too little information in the appropriate details makes proper action impossible for want of knowledge. Too much information is equally discouraging; consider the person who makes the mistake of asking a neurotic "how are you?" and gets a full reply.

If communications moved only up and down in organizations, becoming particular as they move down and general as they move up, our rather idealized picture would be incorrect only because of human frailty—the link in the chain that fails to do the right thing at the right time. This "ideal" state, however, depends on an assumption consistent with the theory of the executive as source of all initiative and inconsistent with the actual state of corporate organization. "Going through channels" is the counterpart of the "chain of command" as the principle of power. Functional specialization must somehow get coordinated, and that requires communication. If all initiative were an executive matter, then all other messages flowing through the organization would be confined to those confirming the system and those reporting the current state. In fact, however, initiative arises at many points and particularly among functional specialists of all sorts. How these specialists communicate with other, different specialists and how coordination takes place introduces a slight modification in our model and a serious modification in everyday behavior.

Direct "lateral" communication is not consistent with going through channels. A supervisor in one department should have no direct dealings with a supervisor in another department. If coordination between those designing the productive process (industrial engineers) and those responsible for staffing the operations (personnel directors) is to be achieved, it should not be by direct negotiation. The only procedure consistent with the standard "principles" of administration is to effect the communication through the "lowest common administrator." Going through channels means that messages must go up and down, clearing through the common administrator, in order to get "across." Actual censorship or the "pocket veto"—simple failure to relay the message—is a theoretical possibility on the part of every coordinator in the extended chain. The further apart the initiator and the intended recipient in the organizational structure, the nearer each is to the lower, outer, and opposite boundaries of the pyramid, the longer and more hazardous is the route that any lateral message must follow. By comparison, letters sent by Pony Express, with only the risk of Indian attacks, had a safe and reliable journey.

The flaw in this arrangement is easily seen. If transverse communication is rare, the problem is small. If it becomes very frequent, the lowest common administrator, the critical coordinator, is likely to lose all initiative as he fights with his "in-basket." For, to repeat, the system is simply not designed to tolerate widespread initiative in lower and lateral positions or negotiations between widely separated peers.

What happens, of course, is that the system is violated for its own good. Negotiations are carried on directly, and the coordinator is called only if there is disagreement or if a matter of "policy" is involved. Often all preliminaries and even agreements bypass the administrator, but a memorandum is prepared for his eyes or his files or both as a piece of paper that preserves the principle that has been violated by unrecorded conversations. It seems to me that the modern corporation would be helpless without the telephone, not only because of its near-erasure of space and consequent saving of time, but because it permits conversation without written record and with minimum if any human intervention between the communicators. The tendency to record telephone conversations should be viewed with deep suspicion not just because of some abstract concern over invasion of privacy, but because it may encourage overly conscientious coordinators with a passion for eavesdropping to try to monitor the direct flow of messages and create a major constraint on sensible operations.

Communication Nets

The elaborate specialization characteristic of corporate organization stands as a clear challenge to coordination, the meshing of interdependent parts for the achievement of collective objectives. Our earlier mechanical model rather neglected the circumstance that the parts are human and their interaction social and dependent on communication. Small wonder then that communication should become, among managers and managerial consultants, a kind of talisman for achieving integration.

But what is to be communicated and to whom? At times as I read the hortatory literature designed to uplift the practice of management, I get the impression that the reformers would answer, "Everything to everybody." Of course this is ridiculous; the attempt to get all messages to all hands could only result in undecipherable noise. Even at a much lower level of intensity where the messages are clear but continuous and mostly irrelevant to any single listener, he may miss the critical one because he has the habit of not paying attention. And at the point that the message cannot get through at all because the system is saturated, some specialization of the communication net must be developed.

The ideal communication system in a complex organization is the one that gets proper information from proper sources to proper recipients expeditiously—that is, with the fewest possible relay points—and without distortion. This "hi-fi" system does not need such esthetic embellishments as stereophonic sound, for fidelity is a question of accuracy rather than tone. The routes that messages are supposed to follow, and part of what happens to messages in transit, we have called "going through channels." We need, however, to add a little more detail to the picture to bring it closer to reality.

The first complication is that there are many different kinds of information to be transmitted, and this is not just a question of being general or particular. A manager could know the contents of an encyclopedia save for the one article relevant to his problem and be as effectively ignorant as the untutored savage. The differentiation and routing of messages therefore must be highly accurate.

Information often does not convey meaning in its raw state, particularly if it has been supplied by experts for use by laymen. Although the messages may give a first impression that they are expressed in English, the vocabulary and even modes of expression may be substantially alien to the recipients' ears and eyes. Where languages differ, no communication is possible without interpreters and translators.

The net of communication then must rely on several different types of connecting links. The simplest is the relay point that passes along messages without alteration, possibly adding a monitoring or record-keeping operation. More difficult are the responsibilities of coordinators at various levels, for they must particularize messages directed to subordinates and generalize messages bound for superiors. Translators must stand as intermediaries between mutually non-communicative specialists or between specialists and managers. If we may draw a distinction used in international diplomacy, we encounter interpreters who eschew literal translation and favor paraphrasing that conveys tone and context. This may be a more accurate form of transmission of meaning than mere substitution of vocabulary. When meaning is not self-evident, interpretation is essential. We do not of course need to go to the psychiatric extreme of detecting hidden meanings, illustrated by the psychiatrist who, following a cheery "Good morning," from a colleague, went off wondering aloud, "Now what do you suppose he meant by that?"

Transmission failures and distortions are of course possible at every point in the network. One is reminded of the cynical, and often accurate, aphorism in the armed services, "Someone always doesn't get the word." Even if every communicator had no perverse interest in silence or misrepresentation, the sheer number of intermediaries may multiply rather than simply add to the potentialities of mischance.

It is the possibility of failure or confusion in communication that requires "feed-back" or "secondary information," that is, confirmation that channels are open and messages received. Feedback, as used in the special and somewhat uncommunicative language of experts on communication, actually combines two or three notions we have dealt with: confirmation of receipt, repetition of message to confirm accuracy, and possibly "current state" of operations. The purpose of feed-back is to permit identification of failures and correction of errors either of original instructions or of their perception and application.

Like any other aspect of social systems, a communication net relies on, and must continuously confirm, *expectations*. The use of the proper route, such as going through channels, is a way of confirming that the system operates, more or less. This is closely related to authentication of source. Where communication is indirect, as most of it is in the corporation, the recipient of a message must be assured that it comes from a proper source, and that in turn is ideally accomplished by using channels. The research chemist who is told by a fellow worker, "Say, I just ran into J.B. (the president) and he told me to tell you to start working on plastics," has reasonable ground for maintaining that he has not received the message, is not bound by it, and indeed doubts its source and accuracy. The use of the network is as binding on superiors as on subordinates. The plant manager who not only boasts that he knows every man in the plant but also likes to settle operating problems on the spot is likely to be completely subversive of the "normal" system of communication and of the authority of all intermediate grades of managers. If his boast is accurate, it is a confession of grave guilt.

Expectations in communication include timing and sequence. Delays in messages raise anxious doubts concerning the operation of the system. The longer an expected reply to a question or request is delayed, the more uncertain is the initiator concerning the "reception" of the message in the full ambiguous sense of its being apprehended and of its being accorded favorable attention. Silence may be terrifying. The adage that "no news is good news" is clearly a brave but vain attempt to suppress the mounting conviction that all is not well. The most extreme example that has come to my attention was the communication system established for guards in a prison. Each guard was to report to a central office within a ten-minute period every hour. A guard's failure to communicate spoke volumes.

Undue speed can be as disruptive as needless delays and awkward silences. An immediate reply to a request that is more than routine may indicate lack of "adequate" consideration. Immediate approval of an unusual request somehow implies that it was expected and overdue. Immediate disapproval somehow implies that no request from that source would be approved regardless of intrinsic value.

There are obvious limits to the frequency with which even appropriate messages may be transmitted and understood. Beyond some point, the "circuits" become overloaded or the messages become pure noise. One strategy of sabotage, therefore, is to follow rules of reporting exactly and fulsomely rather than exercising sensible restraint. Unlike the Biblical heathen, "who think they will be heard for their much speaking," some people may understand too well that rapid chatter may conceal as effectively as does silence. If excessive communication arises from zeal rather than malicious mischief, the organizational consequences are no less disruptive. It is simply harder to correct the situation, for how does one suppress virtue?

All of us have probably at some time received a supplementary or countermanding message before the principal communication arrived. The story is told of one practical joker who would send friends a single telegram, reading with nerve-wracking simplicity, "Disregard previous wire." One can imagine that the curiosity thus provoked was nearly intolerable. In a complex communication net, substantial disorder in the sequence of messages is likely to make them misleading or incomprehensible. If a production order reaches the plant manager from headquarters before he has heard the outcome of his request for permission to install the machinery, it would require considerable bravery for him to take this message as cryptic approval of his request. He may rather reasonably suspect a lack of communicative coordination at headquarters.

I have often been impressed with the extreme fragility of communication nets. The error potential is very high and only partially offset by devices for checking on the receipt and understanding of messages. The cumbersome complexity of indirect discourse had sound organizational foundations; and salvation does not lie in dismantling the system. Rather, the working system becomes even more complicated by the addition of secondary networks that by-pass channels, expedite messages and confirm arrivals, and suppress "required" but irrelevant information. As communicators are not thereby exempt from use of the overt system, some dissemblance and subterfuge, a kind of "double-think," are required. At the very least the man who "leads two lives" needs to know at any moment which is which.

Knowledge, Secrecy and Persuasion

If knowledge is power, then differential knowledge is likely to enhance the position of its possessors. Among highly trained technical and professional specialists the situation ends up in a kind of balance of power. The abstruse and exotic information monopolized by each occupation is balanced by the equally exotic and monopolistic knowledge of others. And none can gain ascendancy except by successful appeal to generalists, to managers, who exercise power that does not derive from technology. Between specialists and managers, we have noted, there is a kind of coercive interdependence, since the powers they claim are different in type and source, and neither can go it alone. Since any system of balance of power is subject to competitive attempts at imbalance, we have here a guaranteed strain within the organizational elite. In this society of equals, as in Orwell's *Animal Farm*, some will attempt to be more equal than others.

What of those who are clearly unequal, the unknowing and unmanaging? What protects them from being subjected to absolute, and therefore corrupt, power? The authority of managers, we have noted, is limited and constrained by principles of legitimacy —confined to job-related matters, subject to consent by subordinates, and guided by rules of the organization. The powers of the knowledgeable are subject to similar restraints, since they are exercised through the intervention or consent of managers. In the case of professionals, their awesome superiority over their clients is additionally restrained by codes of ethics and possibly by publicly sanctioned licensing arrangements to insure both clients and honorable practitioners against charlatans.

The abuse of power then should be not much different from other forms of human sinfulness. Some special problems and uncertainties arise, however, from two conditions in the contemporary corporation. The first is the rapid rise and expansion of new "professions" with rather vague and uncertain codes of responsibilities. The second is the temptation to maintain power by restricting knowledge, that is to keep potentially common knowledge uncommon so that the power that it gives is not dissipated.

The question of secrecy cuts across both of these problems, but emerges traveling in several different directions. The salaried professional who deals with corporate employees as individuals, as physicians do, is caught in a curious predicament. His employer and his clients are different, unlike the situation faced by the private practitioner. What then happens to the "professional confidence" or the "privileged communication"? Company physicians appear to have worked out a code whereby both the patient and the employer are informed of physical conditions directly relevant to the individual's capacity in his employment. The employer, however, is not given information that *should be irrelevant* if he were as tolerant and dispassionate as the physician but that might be harmful to the patient if publicly known or even privately known to his all-too-ordinary superiors.

Even for the physician, however, the line is not easy to maintain as one approaches psychosomatic difficulties and especially as one gets into psychiatry. Who has legitimate access to the diagnosis? If the employer does and the patient does not, the patient is denied the opportunity of deciding anything for himself on the basis of professional advice, and his sensible and proper approach to the physician is as a potential adversary. His fate is being decided on the basis of knowledge that he does not share. He may not even be given the opportunity of seeking a review of evidence by another qualified professional of his own choice. I recall with outrage the case several years ago of the honors graduate at my university who was nearly barred from continuing his intended career in graduate school because as a first-term freshman he had been noted as an "anxiety case" on the basis of a half-hour interview with a staff psychiatrist. The intervening objective evidence of success meant nothing as against the supreme arrogance of the psychiatrist. The professional persisted in his folly to the end, but he was fortunately overruled by a physician who was not a true believer in quick judgment and intransigent wrong-headedness. The near victim had not been told why he was in trouble and was rescued only by outside intervention.

I have used the situation of medical and psychiatric practice because it illustrates difficulties that may be immensely greater where the professions are new and meagerly disciplined by standards of either quality or ethical conduct. The layman is ordinarily not in a position to question the professional's judgment. The professional does not have to be right to be believed. All he needs to do is to exude complete confidence in his opinions. The layman's only recourse is to seek verification of judgments, either by objective test that he can appraise or by seeking the opinion of another expert. The latter tactic will work only if "his expert" is not tied to the first one by close bonds of mutual protection in their incompetence. A challenge to the power of knowledge can only be made if one is armed with equal or superior knowledge.

The problems of secrecy are tactical as well as ethical. Secret knowledge is suspect knowledge. The expert's customer—his employer or client—may have many motives for wanting the advice he gets, or even the fact that he is getting advice, kept "confidential." The advantage of expert knowledge is dissipated if this knowledge becomes a free good. But secrecy may also be equivalent to unreliability of alleged information. This problem is particularly acute, as I have indicated, in the newer specialties that do not have a well-established body of principles and a long record of practice. This is especially so in applied psychology and various fields of the social sciences where experts, virtuous incompetents, and charlatans may be difficult to distinguish unless the client "takes evidence" from several witnesses independently and also attempts to check the results that the advice was supposed to produce.

Ethical questions keep intruding, however. The employer, let us say the corporate manager, may not care much about quality and accuracy of "expert" testimony as long as it is to be used manipulatively in dealings with others, such as subordinates or outsiders. My present concern is with communication, and secrecy as

its opposite, inside the organization. Calling on "scientific management" in setting job standards for production workers or on a
"scientific attitude survey" to inform workers what they think may
be an attempt to put the judgment beyond the ken of the worker,
and thus hopefully beyond successful challenge.

We are really dealing with two kinds of secrecy here. The one
is knowledge inaccessible except to experts. No special pains are
necessary to preserve the differential. The other is readily understandable information that is kept from common currency by
deliberate blocks to communication. But I have suggested, and I
meant the suggestion seriously, that the second kind of secrecy
may be used to fake the first. The aura of mystery, aided by the
magic of "science," may give occult powers to those whose privileged position could not withstand full disclosure.

The point is sharpened if we turn to expert strategy on communication itself, which gives a peculiar irony to the whole business. If there are special "techniques" of communication, not
generally known and perhaps not generally knowable, then communication is not intended to equalize information but only to
disseminate *some* ideas or bits of knowledge. Poor performance,
errors, misdeeds, tension, and conflicts are blamed on poor communications, and serious effort is devoted to improving the flow of
information. Not information alone, of course, but also persuasive
and uplifting messages, and thereby hangs our tale.

"The purpose of communication is persuasion." I heard this
aphorism in one of those management improvement sessions (at
a resort hotel) that the contemporary corporation uses so extensively, to "improve communications" among other reasons. It
has haunted me ever since. For what it says is that there is no
point in mere transfer of cognitive knowledge of information, no
point in journalistic or scientific reporting. Communication becomes a strategy of power, a model of "winning friends and influencing people." Its enemy is not misunderstanding or ignorance
but improper attitudes and values.

If this point is grasped, the managerial enthusiasm for "good
communications" becomes more understandable if not more lov-

able. The goal is shared values, but perhaps not shared information. Indeed, completely shared information, including information on what the communicators aim to accomplish, might well
defeat the "appeals to reason" that are really appeals to sentiments.
Perhaps the most interesting feature of communication as persuasion rather than as transmitting information is the use of sentiment and emotion. Fact and logic are the essential ingredients of
rational action, but this may be thought insufficient to secure
cooperative agreement. The impersonal, money-mediated appeals
to self-interest give way to warmly personal appeals to fundamental verities. The communicator must watch his facial expression and gestures, his tone of voice, and choose his words with
careful attention to their emotional nuances and overtones and
not just to their meaning. At the extreme, the communicator practices the "calculated use of affect," that is, an unemotional strategy of appealing to others' emotions.

Once more questions of strategy and ethics become entangled.
If expert knowledge, including expert methods of "communication," become devices for manipulation, the power of knowledge
is probably being misused. This issue has been chiefly discussed
with reference to irrational appeals in advertising and particularly
appeals to subconscious motivation as angrily depicted in Vance
Packard's *The Hidden Persuaders*. Interests and attitudes are also
pretty variegated among the constrained cooperators within the
corporation, however, and this provides an open invitation to
manipulation.

Manipulation, including manipulation by communication, depends upon concealment of intent. No manipulative strategy
can survive its identification as such. And such identification tends
to arouse suspicions and make the next strategy more difficult to
bring off and its "useful" life even shorter. No wonder, then, that
there is such a demand for abstruse, expert knowledge hedged
about by the intrinsic secrecy of inaccessibility by laymen rather
than by mere concealment of the poor cards one is holding in a
gigantic bluff.

Manipulative, secretive communicators should not be uniformly viewed as mere gamesmen or cynical power-seekers. The attitudes they seek to persuade others to accept are often genuine. Real rather than simulated conviction aids persuasiveness. But by what objective standards is it possible to say that their subjects' values are wrong? It is simply not true that all rational and reasonable interests are alike among corporate employees or that manipulation is "for their own good." There are all sorts of vital matters that modern man cannot judge for himself, on which he must rely on advice. He has, however, some reason to hope, if not confidently to expect, that the advice will be "disinterested" and not simply designed to enhance the advisor's power and position at his expense. Management, including the management of "communication," will not be able to claim full "professional" standing until it can reasonably meet the test of disinterested advice to its several relevant clienteles, including fellow employees.

The uses and misuses of secrecy are also evident in other contexts. Corporations having military contracts will be required to maintain security regulations to guard against leakage of information to unauthorized (potential enemy) inquirers. Detailed costs and more particularly new market strategies or planned product innovations will be concealed from competitors if possible. And shady and outright unlawful practices will be hidden from prying eyes of government agents. The circumstance that not every employee can be expected to respect a confidence leads to caution in the internal dissemination of such kinds of knowledge. Of course some "security" regulations are carried to ridiculous extremes, and the value and novelty of the guarded information may be grossly exaggerated. Since these restraints are primarily matters of the corporation's external relations, they are of significance for internal organization only as access to secrets may come to have symbolic value, both because it indicates that one can be trusted and because practically no one is immune to the heady sense of importance in being able to say, or preferably to think and not to say, "I know something you don't know."

What remains of strictly internal importance is secrecy on salaries. At first glance one would think this was simply a matter of respecting personal privacy. Yet that will scarcely stand a second glance. All public officials have known or at least knowable salaries. Many private organizations such as private colleges and universities announce salary ranges by commonly accepted ranks, if not individual differences within the range. Corporate officers serving companies with registered stocks have readily discoverable, if occasionally outlandish, salaries, bonuses, and tax-avoiding stock options. I think the answer is devastatingly simply. Secrecy is designed to obscure an inequitable system of rewards and to protect those who determine salaries from the crude force of competition among subordinates. The man who is given a salary raise or bonus that is not given to his peers is commonly sworn to secrecy or at least told that "this is confidential." There is no reason at all for this if the difference in rewards reflects differences in merit by commonly accepted criteria. It is the uncertainty of the criteria of merit or the patent unfairness of income differences that prompts deliberate concealment or obfuscation of the factors in the judgment of individual cases.

If the man who is favored, let us say because he has an attractive competing offer of employment, feels he deserves his absolute income (and who doesn't?), he has little to gain by keeping the confidence. If he is nervous about the envy of colleagues, that is something for them to worry about and do something about. I may be reflecting the sentiments of the underdog, but I doubt if secret salaries have ever had a really defensible justification. They are perhaps designed to insure "individual bargaining," but any market system that deserves any ethical support depends upon full knowledge by all participants. I sometimes doubt that corporate executives believe in the labor market at all.

Besides, secrecy of all sorts, and particularly on so basic a matter as the system of rewards, is virtually impossible to maintain. Either one of two alternative consequences of attempted secrecy is equally destructive to confidence in the equity of the system. Either the confidential salary is known accurately, and the attempted secrecy gives rise to suspicion of attempted fraud, or the differences are exaggerated by rumor, and that gives rise to suspicion of gross injustice. Neither suspicion is totally unfounded; probably neither is totally justified. My impression is that the "conspiracy of silence" on salaries will not benefit all of the conspirators, and possibly none of them. What are they trying to hide?

The Argot of the Upper World

One barrier to communication that easily slides over into secrecy or imposed ignorance is the use of somewhat different vocabularies within the corporate structure. I am not now referring to the substantial quantitative difference in command over words which has a high correlation with education and intelligence and a somewhat lower but still positive correlation with rank and power. The anti-intellectual intellectuals who are enthusiastic over "basic English" do not in fact use it, for as basic English issues from the mouths of its real practitioners, it is distinctly lacking in taste, to say nothing of style. No, I am commenting here on the cultivated mutual unintelligibility of equals.

Occupational languages abound at the workplace. For the production worker the vocabulary includes tools and processes, machines and machine parts, types of materials and types of product. Virtually every occupation or occupational group uses a tongue that is distinctly alien to the untutored ear. And woe to the one who tries to sham familiarity with the language, for he is certain to choose the wrong word at some point. The reaction of pain or hilarity is likely to exceed the Parisian's response to the American's schoolbook French.

Special occupational languages serve the communicative function of technical precision in discourse, calling things by their "right" names. They often serve as a kind of shorthand, with a single word or phrase conveying meaning that would otherwise require several descriptive sentences that might still be cloudy or ambiguous. The expert, regardless of his type or status level, is likely to insist that he cannot understand unless the technical terms are used.

Special languages serve two additional, more symbolic, functions. They identify the "in-group" and outsiders, they admit and exclude, they unite and divide. The proper use of language signifies that one belongs. This is not of course peculiar to occupational specialties, as any parent of a teenager can testify. Regional and "class" accents and vocabularies serve similar functions of identification.

The other side of this coin is at least equally important. The uninitiated are not only excluded symbolically by their failure to display the proper identification, but they are excluded actually. If they do not understand, they are not parties to the conversation, they are not even part of the audience. Messages to insiders are noise to outsiders.

The ignorant outsider may be either intimidated or annoyed by his exclusion, and often he is both. His defensive reaction is likely to be the suspicion that he is the victim of double-talk. His querulous query, "Why can't you say it in plain English?" may be reasonable or unreasonable, but in either case it is understandable. Plain English, however, will simply not serve a specialized and highly technical civilization. Yet the expert is inclined to defend his own vocabulary as essential, and view all others as "jargon."

Unquestionably the symbolic and communicative functions of language are often confused by insiders. Verbal virtuosity may be needlessly substituted for plain English or plain thought. In medicine, for example, simple translation is often substituted for diagnosis. The patient who goes to his physician with the complaint that he has a bad cold may be told by the physician, after suitable examination, that he is suffering from acute rhinitis, that is, a bad cold. But then, why single out physicians? What of one's gardening neighbor who knows her plants only by their "scientific," that is, Latin botanical names? To Gertrude Stein, "a rose is a rose is a rose," but not to the rose fancier.

The linguistic landscape of the contemporary corporation is thus about as confusing as the languages of India or Africa. In both cases, discourse across linguistic boundaries requires a common tongue, a *lingua franca*. The corporate equivalent of Pidgin English or Swahili is a kind of managerial argot known generically as the language of Madison Avenue. Although linguistic inventiveness is surely not confined to advertising agencies, there can be no doubt that the copy writers and account executives must be given the lion's share of praise or blame.

These masters of prose live in a largely verbal environment. And the language that penetrates the midtown New York skyscrapers housing corporate headquarters has the ring of an authentic tribal dialect. That language is not altogether abstruse, but it is undeniably different.

The Business English spoken in big business is not the Business English of the high school commercial courses. In the living vernacular, nothing is ever finished, completed, or terminated. It is *finalized*. A group assembled to discuss ideas and plans is, aptly enough, a *brainstorming session*. If more information is needed, the matter is not investigated, it is *researched*. Since we want to be thorough, we "research the hell out of it." Mottoes abounded until a few years ago, but now one shows his sophistication by a spoofing sign, "Thimk," "Avoid misteaks," or "You can help stamp out research." The one motto that, to the best of my knowledge, had avoided the corrosion of wit is an oral, not a written admonition. "Think upstream!" This says, in translation, "Try to see things the way the boss does, and someday you, too, may be a boss."

A glossary of useful terms for finding one's way around the business world would not be appropriate in a book intended to have some modest durability. The words that identify, the language of belonging, change too rapidly, and yesterday's slang is worse than none. Like the language of the young, business argot is fickle. Yet in a system that believes in good communications, it is at least as important to "say it right" as it is to "say it often."

V I

RULES OF ORDER

*W HE RE IN the mass of rules that hem about
organized behavior in corporations is viewed as the
law of a private state, but the absence of an
independent judiciary to protect the subject
from arbitrary discipline
is regretfully reported.*

C O R P O R A T E social organization operates to a remarkable degree "by the book." The book may be referred to as "the Bible," but the reference is faintly sacrilegious, as the document is quite secular. The book is the assembly of rules of conduct, of rights and duties, privileges and immunities, rewards and punishments. The matrix of our model, the cement that bonds together disparate and discordant parts, is a body of rules.

Work organizations may provide a hospitable environment for warm human relationships, but these relationships are not required. Indeed, they may be mischievous if they interfere with duty, encourage slovenly performance, and provide protection for friendly fools. What is required for corporate continuity is order, the use of SOP (standard operating procedures), behavior by the book. Despite our growing insight into the vagaries of human discourse at the work place, the best single predictor of human behavior in organizations is an accurate answer to the question, "What is he supposed to be doing?" We should be quite improperly cynical if we did not expect a fairly high correspondence between expectations and observed reality and quite improperly naive if we expected the correlation to be perfect. Rules are not made to be broken but to be followed. Yet the fact that they may be broken is a principal justification for making procedures and penalties explicit. Explicit they are in corporate organization, explicit well beyond the point of tedium.

Human Predictability

Critics of the social sciences make much of the unpredictability of human behavior. The criticism has some slight merit in view of the degree of uncertainty in human conduct, but is ridiculous if carried to the extreme of denying the facts of continuity and regularity. If they took themselves seriously, the doubters could scarcely dare to get out of bed in the morning. Indeed, the uncertainty in their minds should be so great that they should become catatonic schizophrenics, incapable of any voluntary movement at all. The economist, Kenneth Boulding, speaks of the "miracle that Tuesday follows Monday," but this is surely a routine miracle that one can count on occurring again next Tuesday. Only in the Broadway musical "Camelot" does the king determine the weather and seasons by royal edict, but all sorts of lesser rulemakers successfully establish the nature, timing, and sequence of human activities.

A principal function of any system of rules is to make social interaction orderly, that is, predictable. Often rules are lacking in real moral content, in investment with emotional value. I have been unable to find any moral superiority in driving on the right as compared with driving on the left, but there are considerable gains in efficiency if one settles on one or the other. The alternative would be a rather intolerable chaos, with drivers involved either in a constant game of "chicken" as played by teen-age hot-rodders and by Latins at unmarked intersections or else stopping to settle the matter by flipping coins, debate, or fisticuffs. Likewise there seems to be no very moral virtue in having a carbon copy on blue flimsy paper take precedence in the rank of its recipient over a copy on yellow paper. It is simply more orderly, less provoking of needless decision and consequent uncertainty.

The basis of human predictability is behavior in accordance with "expectations." Much of this behavior is habitual, but it will be generally governed by rules that are commonly known and commonly followed.

Most rules have qualities and justifications beyond mere convenience. Rules serve to delimit and indeed to determine the proper means of attaining desired or prescribed goals. Some alternative means may be as inconsequential as the color-precedence of carbon copies. Many alternatives, however, will be regarded as downright bad, not simply untidy or disorderly. They are contrary to morals, despicable, or dangerous. Human conduct then is not only regulated, but it is also overlaid with values. The values justify the rules, give them a rationale in terms of goals and moral verities. For rules of mere convenience, the answer to the "why" question may be merely, "Because that's the way we do it," or the desk motto that disarms questioners by declaiming, "There's no damn reason for it; it's just our policy." For most rules, however, the answer must be, "Because that's the right (meaning both correct and virtuous) way to do it."

Nothing I have said so far about the functions of rules is peculiar to corporations. These homely truths apply equally to garden clubs or debating societies. What is peculiar to corporations and other administrative organizations is the number, complexity, and detail of the rules of conduct. Little is left to imagination, habit, or common sense. The corporation binds together a myriad of specialized occupations performed by persons with highly dissimilar backgrounds and probable attitudes who may be here today and gone tomorrow. The corporation must somehow survive both heterogeneity and turnover, must keep the drama moving with a tremendous and constantly changing cast of characters, each playing a "bit part" that is nevertheless essential to the plot. A drama of character, to pursue the metaphor, would be unthinkable under such conditions, but a drama of action can be essayed if the players will simply do their parts, that is, do what they are supposed to do.

Fixing Responsibility

Knowing who is supposed to do what is the first requisite of order in complex organizations. This knowledge is not only essential if one is going to follow the game, but it is even more important for determining the causes of misplays or errors. The duties of offices constitute positive prescriptions for the incumbent. They also, and thereby, constitute negative prescriptions for others. Aside from general rules of conscience or convenience, such as honesty and punctuality, job duties are highly specific and therefore highly differentiated. It is thus not enough to say that the duties demanded of one man are not demanded of others, that others are in a sense exempt. Others *must not* assume our man's duties, for this is not only an attack on his competence and the power appropriate to his duties, it is a preface to chaos. Order and predictability require that the duties be performed, to be sure, but by the right person at the right time.

I am speaking here of normal not emergency situations, the character of our organizational model not the occasional vicissitudes of practical operation. Some emergencies such as illness may be sufficiently common to warrant additional rules for handling them, such as a prior understanding as to who steps into the duties. Others may be sufficiently uncommon and unpredictable to require extraordinary action. My concern here, however, is with the ordinary, and the words "ordinary" and "regular" both derive from Latin words relating to rule. To achieve the ordinary, the corporation must contend with three additional words, or rather with the qualities and actions signified by those words, which are *competence, performance,* and *responsibility.*

The criterion of competence sets the procedural rule for selection of persons to fill jobs. For this purpose, all sorts of admirable or regrettable qualities and achievements of an individual are irrelevant unless they bear on his capacity to meet the demands of a particular job.

The rule of competence is more easily stated than applied to particular cases. The precise requirements for general education, specific training, and experience may be debatable although presumably only within fairly narrow limits. More serious difficulties arise from the relevance of various personal qualities. Is the race or national origin of a salesman irrelevant if his customers do not think so? Is a college education necessary for a job simply because others expect it, because peers and subordinates will not take a man seriously who does not have the proper stamp? Is the circumstance that a man's political sympathies are with the Democratic Party sufficient indication of poor judgment to bar him from a managerial position? To answer these questions with a resounding "no" is perhaps unduly idealistic in a partially irrational world. Yet ideals are at least relevant to standards. They shift the burden of proof to those who would condone violations.

One of the most pervasive problems involving competence is the "family connection." Arrayed in defense of family influence in placement are two principles that are generally unchallenged. The most general one is that it is eminently proper for a father to assist his son's welfare, including his career. The second is that wealth, including business interests, may be handed from one generation to the next. The son entering his father's business is therefore scarcely guilty of scandalous deportment. The problem does arise, however, where the father is a manager, not an owner. He may be able to secure special consideration in employment and promotion for his son or some other close relative. This violates the rule of competence, of selection on the sole grounds of merit. For this situation I have found a phrase very common in

business; the favored kinsman is said to have "high relative ability," and one is supposed to be sharp enough to catch the pun.

On the question of nepotism or favoritism, as with most moral
problems, there are gray areas between virtue and sin. Many of
these gray areas occur where it is not clear whether there is any
real favoritism. The son may be highly competent but denied recognition on merit by those who envy success and can seize on
nepotism as a way of denying that it is deserved. The son or
relative may have to be especially good to offset the handicap of
a family connection. With the exception of a few giant corporations where the founding family still exerts strong influence on
company affairs (for example, DuPont and Ford), employment
of close relatives is in fact very rare and in some companies contrary to explicit rule. (Such a rule, of course, is an example of
"falling over backward" in the attempt to achieve rectitude, as it
may violate the principle of competence. Just as there is no assurance that competent fathers will have competent sons, there is
no assurance of the contrary.)

The criteria of competence are also muddied by consideration
of the qualities of wives in determining a man's fitness for appointment or promotion. The discussion of this practice in Whyte's *Is
Anybody Listening?* and in his *The Organization Man* has stirred
up a lively controversy, mostly over whether Whyte's treatment is
exaggerated. I have no way of settling this question with statistical
accuracy and can only testify that it is not rare. The possibly more
interesting question is, when is it justified? Again one cannot
safely adopt a grim line that holds that any such consideration is
an invasion of privacy, an improper extension of competence
into irrelevant qualities. If, for example, "official" entertaining is
a part of the job by the ordinary ways of doing business, as it
seems to be particularly in marketing and sales, the "entertainer"
needs to come equipped with a proper hostess, to whom by common convention he should be married. An even clearer case can
be made for the manager of the branch plant of a large company
in a small community. The man, and his wife, simply cannot di-

vest themselves of corporate identification. Their every activity with persons outside the immediate family is likely to be tinged with a recognition of the man's position. He represents the company willy-nilly. His area of privacy, and that of his wife, is very narrowly restricted. Whether his wife is in a position to do him much good, as when social contacts become business contacts, she is clearly in a position to do him much harm. If she flouts local convention, ranging from dress and speech to matters of moral belief and conduct, the manager will be held to blame.

The moral shades grow darker, however, when we approach questions of intracompany entertaining, for example. Meeting the wifely test of having the boss and his wife to dinner has vicariously tormented at least two biological generations of readers of women's magazines. Surely a smaller, but still appreciable, number of anxious women have met the test in real life. Let us hope that most of them passed, for the greater glory of happy endings. But why should such tests be necessary? I feel that the excuse of convention, of being unable to get other businesses or the community at large to accept the narrow view of technical competence of the breadwinner as uniquely relevant, carries little weight within a corporation. Policy-level corporate officials have the power to inhibit if not prevent "extraneous" considerations if they want to. And they should want to.

Again, I do not mean to be naively righteous. I can imagine situations in small communities or in newly established operations where company personnel have little choice but to behave as a kind of community and not just as a business organization. But I should regard such situations as exceptional and sufficiently dangerous that positive effort should be made to divorce the family from the office.

From this point of view I think it is fortunate that large company headquarters are mainly located in New York or in other large metropolitan centers. With suburban life the norm and with optional choice of residence, it is very nearly impossible for the company to behave improperly in attempting to extend its criteria of competence to reach into a man's family or his pattern of social activities. Morality by default may not be the highest virtue, but it is surely preferable to wickedness.

I believe that large companies that have moved to suburban areas or contemplate doing so run a substantial risk of gradually establishing "company towns" in their immediate environs. "Making the grade" by irrelevant social manipulation, a constant quest and danger in military installations, could well increase the proportion of incompetent but friendly managers and block the careers of men whose wives may be too bright for their own good. The question of the place of wives is whether a corporate employee's competence must include that of his wife, whether the man's duties need to include being forehanded enough to make a suitable marriage, to fall in love with a wonderful girl who will fortunately also help her husband in his career.

The rule of competence is a necessary but not sufficient condition for the rule of performance. The desired performance is the basis for determining the skill and talent sought, but this does not insure against laziness or evasion. Thus most corporate rules are in fact performance rules. They specify actions, that is, duties. Duties are allocated to persons or, more properly, to offices. No work organization could operate long on the principle that "someone ought to handle that problem" and then await volunteers, draw lots, or conduct an election. Order and predictability demand that responsibilities be fixed and, by the same token, delimited so that several people are not trying to do a one-man job.

The principle of responsible performance is, like competence, easier to state than to apply. One critical question is whether delegated responsibility is thereby dismissed. The case of the conspiracy among electrical manufacturers, which aroused anew the old popular suspicions of big business during the winter of 1960-61, involved two unanswered questions. First, did the highest corporate executives in fact know what their conspiratorial vice-presidents were up to? Second, were they in any event responsible? General Electric, the company having the doubtful honor of drawing the heaviest fines and the largest number of executives sent to jail, had a highly specific rule against collusion with other companies, as we know from reiteration of the rule in press releases. But we also know that rules are not self-enforcing, and it is not at all clear that those responsible for formulating the rule also carried the responsibility for checking on compliance. No evidence of legal culpability on the part of the chief executives was found by the Federal investigators. In strictly organizational terms, it appears that the corporations failed as self-regulating enterprises that could insure responsible (that is, rule-abiding) performance. In fact those held responsible by the courts were attempting to follow out company directives that demanded that they simultaneously maximize profits and market position in a chaotic market (see *Fortune* magazine for April, 1961). They could, they held, comply with one performance criterion only by violating another, the rule against collusion. I do not mean to condone their conduct, but this kind of moral dilemma is not unique to corporations. The responsibility still seems to me to have been partly that of those who set impossible demands to be fulfilled according to rules that were not in fact enforced by their promulgators. In short, the chief executives either knew of the violations or should have, which at best is not an ideal choice.

Cooperative Strangers

An organization's network of rules, followed with reasonable reliability, insures against all sorts of personal preferences, interpersonal likes and dislikes, and rampant uncertainty as to courses of action. Persons caught up in this official network behave toward one another "correctly." Since the rules define the proprieties of official interaction, personal friendship of the participants is not necessary and often not desirable. Friends are very likely to permit relationships to get informal and sloppy, to condone or forgive errors of conduct, to protect one another against just discipline. Like the etiquette of polite social discourse, the rules permit strangers and even personal enemies to behave correctly, to avoid both uncertainties and unseemly scenes.

Etiquette is for enemies, one is tempted to say. At least, it is not for friends. One of the surest signs of a rift between friends or a falling-out between lovers is that they begin to treat one another with punctilious politeness.

This cool austerity is of course difficult to maintain in close, continuous working relations. Suppression of emotion and filtering out irrelevant subjects and personality traits call for exemplary role-playing. The rules will, in fact, be observed in their purest form precisely with strangers, not with enemies or friends. But the call of duty is also a very considerable force. The network of performance rules extends far beyond any small coterie of employees, and compliance with those rules will be expected and enforced by literal strangers. Thus to expect a friend to protect one in poor performance may be placing an intolerable burden on the friendship, as the friend then joins in culpable conduct.

If official interaction tends to be impaired by durable relationships, it is buttressed by turnover. To repeat, duties and rules of interaction apply to "offices" or positions and not to particular persons. The worldly immortality of the organization insures turnover quite apart from hiring and firing, transfers and promotions. The solid substance of survival is the predictability of personal behavior given by compliance with rules.

Decontamination of Power

A final function of rules in complex organizations is the containment of power. Given the fact that coordination of specialized activity is achieved not simply by interdependence but also by the exercise of authority, some people are in a position to give orders that other people are in a position to obey. But what orders? In our model of corporate organization the answer is clear:

those orders, and only those, consistent with performance of tasks related to missions and according to rule. The rules, binding on both governors and governed, produce presumably a government of laws, not of men.

Because power is delegated by chief executives, who represent interests besides those of corporate employees, it cannot be argued that managers "derive their just powers from the consent of the governed." That consent is assumed, however, because of the voluntary contractual character of corporate employment.

Of course it has long been recognized that the mutual dependence of employers and employees may be asymmetrical, that is, lopsided. The employee's job experience, for example, may have little transferability to another employer, so that he may be virtually "entrapped " by his employment if he wants to maintain his earning capacity.

The knowledge that subordinates have few escape routes and perhaps slight inclination to use those that may be open can easily lead to abuse of power. Most corporations rely only on the restraints provided by superiors in the complex gradation of authority as a check on an irresponsible manager with a tyrannical disposition. Many administrative organizations provide for a kind of judicial process whereby the subordinate can make an appeal against a superior on a rule of law. This is especially true with respect to dismissal "for cause." In the corporation this protection is afforded only to those employees covered by a union collective bargaining contract and grievance system. In the course of time this gives rise to new bodies of rules and interpretations. The codes of professional societies give a somewhat similar protection even to the individual professional employee, for his value to the employer may depend upon his maintaining his professional recognition and standing. To take an extreme example, a disbarred attorney is not going to be very useful in handling a corporation's legal affairs.

Other employees, lacking such external support, must rely solely on the internal regulative system and its enforcement from on high. Concretely this means that an employee may generally go one step "over the head" of his immediate superior if he feels that his boss has transgressed the rules. As a practical matter, he is safest if he obeys the illegal order and then appeals the matter if he wants to prevent a repetition or to exculpate himself for what he regards as wrongful action.

Because in fact the administrative guardians of the rules are not always sufficiently watchful to detect the abuse of power by subordinates or may themselves be parties to collusive subversion of the rule of law, I am convinced that corporations must move toward the establishment of judicial processes. That is, judges are needed who are neither rule-makers nor rule-enforcers but rather available as courts of appeal against arbitrary acts. The alternative will, I believe, be an increasing use of the public courts for enforcement of what amounts to private law. For rules function to contain power only if they are enforced, and if the enforcement rests with those who are abusing power, the system suffers from a functional weakness.

The question is not exactly one of "equality before the law," but rather one of an orderly and restrained inequality, so that the corruption of power, noted by Lord Acton, does not become that absolute power that "corrupts absolutely." For the classic question, far older than Lord Acton's famous aphorism, remains: "Who guards the guardians?" When the answer is, "They guard themselves," the rule of law is likely to be a feeble defense against tyranny.

Part Three

COUNTERPOINT

VII

THE UNEXPECTED IS ORDINARY

W HEREIN *the official program is shown not
to include all essential information concerning what
is to be done, who is to do it, who matters
and who does not.*

P ERFECTLY organized corporations are imaginary. The relationship between ideal organizations and real ones is, however, somewhat more than "purely coincidental," to use the legalistic and libel-evading phrase employed by novelists. Ideal organizations constitute the "model" or "standard" that actual organizations approximate.

What accounts for the difference between the ideal and the actual? One is tempted to attribute shortcomings and deviations to simple human fallibility or to ordinary human cussedness. There's no denying that corporate organizations comprise real people, with real weaknesses. But many features of complex organizations are designed precisely to restrain or prevent the mischievous effects of human frailty. That they fall short of perfect success is not in itself surprising. All social institutions do. What then becomes interesting is the nature, the sources, and the consequences of departures from the ideal. If these are entirely individual, "accidental," unique, and therefore unpredictable, there is nothing of a general nature that can be said about them. The situation, however, is not that chaotic.

Paradoxically, many of the departures from the ideal prescriptions of organizational charts and manuals arise from the ordinary characteristics of organizations themselves. For example, persons caught in face-to-face relationships for 40 hours a week and for week after week and even year after year are extremely unlikely to treat one another with the proper punctilio, the distant distaste of dutiful strangers. Even military etiquette, which is the most austere regulatory system to be found in any administrative organization, is likely to be eroded and softened by sheer frequency and durability of interaction. When officially correct relations are about to be reinstated, the change is heralded by some such priceless prose as, "That's an order!"—a bit of drama probably originated by the art of motion picture writers and now dutifully imitated in nature by real officers.

Behavior that is irregular in the strict sense of deviating from rules is not necessarily disorderly in the usual sense of mischievous or unexpected. The line between virtue and sin, itself a hazy boundary, is not the same as the line between the predictable and unpredictable or order and chaos. What is officially unexpected may be quite ordinary in life experience at the work place.

Informal Organization: A Basket of Unwritten Scraps

During the late 1930's a number of books were published reporting on an extensive program of social research at the Chicago Hawthorne plant of Western Electric. That research program, under the general guidance of the late Professor Elton Mayo of the Harvard Graduate School of Business Administration, marked a major transition in the understanding of work organization and more particularly in the treatment of the subject in textbooks on "business administration." The key concept in this small intellectual revolution was "informal organization." The Western Electric researchers found that production workers developed their own codes and standards, their own patterns of interaction. These standards and ways of behaving, having little to do with the "expected" behavior delineated by formal charts and manuals, were taken as manifestations of informal organizations.

The Western Electric researchers studied production workers, not managers or staff technicians. By their silence in their reports concerning these other components of business organizations, they left the impression that informal organization was a peculiar feature of the lower orders, whereas the managers and their technical counterparts among the higher orders could be assumed to follow "the book." This assumption, or inference, combined with a number of bits of advice to managers, led to criticism of the "Mayo School" as biased in favor of managerial manipulation— the philosopher kings tolerantly preserving and exploiting the quaint tribal customs of the untutored natives. This controversy need not detain us at the moment. Other observers have taken the insight developed from the Western Electric studies and extended it to all types and varieties of human relationships in organizations. No occupational group or rank is exempt from the principle that part of the behavior at the work place cannot be accounted for by the official or formal organization. Even the ruling tribes have quaint customs. This "unexpected" behavior has been covered by the blanket term "informal organization."

It is perhaps not too cynical to suggest that the great popularity of the term informal organization derives from its vagueness. The concept rather literally covers a multitide of sins—and virtues. Being defined negatively—all behavior not in conformity with the official model—the term represents what logicians would call a "residual category." In the ordinary language of discourse, this is to say that informal organization is a scrap-basket concept. And because the official procedures tend to be written while the actual procedures are communicated by word of mouth, I have referred to the concept as a basket of unwritten scraps. Since the term comprises any departure from formal procedures, specified duties, or minimally necessary interaction, examples are not hard to find. I shall illustrate how informal organization modifies each of the four principal components of the administrative model—division of labor, hierarchical authority, indirect communication, and codified rules.

Specialization of tasks is often carried very far in corporations, particularly among manual workers in mass-production industries. The angry treatises of social critics and the jocular settings for popular humor alike abound in illustrations of the hapless automaton whose calling consists of firmly attaching Nut 19 to Bolt 19 on an endless succession of heating units for two-slice toasters. Jobs of that sort can of course be found, but where that degree of specialization exists there is a very high probability that its stupefying effects on the workers will be partially offset by an "informal" bit of social machinery—the work exchange. With jobs so routinized, a man can readily learn his neighbors' tasks as well, and groups of four to eight workers trade jobs from time to time. Regular job trading is likely to occur where tasks are routinized and readily learned, such as on the assembly line, in a "typing pool," or among retail clerks. But emergency arrangements, particularly to do the essential tasks of absentees, must exist in all parts of business organizations.

A boss can demand compliance with a legitimate order, and even an occasional illegitimate one, but he cannot demand deference or genuine esteem. Thus the real leader in any work unit may be someone other than the official superior. If the leadership is exercised toward achieving the unit's mission, and the unofficial leader does not display his influence too blatantly, the body may survive with two heads. Occasionally a talented subordinate "carries" his incompetent boss. More commonly a power struggle sets in, not usually with pistols or insults at twenty paces but with subtle moves and counter-moves, often through third parties. Open insubordination is rarely feasible. The strategy of the challenger must always stay within the letter of the law in order more effectively to subvert its spirit, which is to support constituted authorities. A pattern of informal leadership often divides an organizational unit into two mutually exclusive factions. As in the great world of power politics, however, the independent or neutralist position is often a very favorable one, as the uncommitted individuals may well continue to receive favors from both sides. From this point, any reader of business novels can fill in the characters and plot details to suit his own taste.

The most commonly recognized type of informal organization in business and industry is the grape-vine, a communication network that works with extreme rapidity and occasional accuracy. How rumors spread and what determines the accuracy or distortion of the messages in transit are still imperfectly known, but part of the psychological mechanism is fairly clear. Possession of secret knowledge may give very little personal satisfaction. If the secret is to become public later, the early possessor's claim to prior knowledge may be met with disbelief. The value of the secret can thus be realized only by sharing it and making it less secret. In a sense, the purveyor of secrets or gossip or rumors always gains a temporary ascendancy over the recipient. Children, who torment one another in quite uncivilized ways, recognize the principle by the taunt, "I know something you don't know," a claim that can only be substantiated by sharing the information and thus abandoning the original claim. To share a secret on the condition that it go no further preserves its value as privileged information, a value that can only be validated by further, circumspect, revelation. Thus the true secret may very quickly become an open one, the message having been sped on its way because the value attached to its confidential character has assured both attention and repetition. Anyone who stands revealed as not sharing in an open secret will attempt to rectify this embarrassing social isolation as quickly as possibly by plugging into the circuits at as many places as he can.

Although informal communication is a game that any one and indeed any number can play, the finger of suspicion points strongly to official communicators as being the chief unofficial ones as well. I mean secretaries. They have knowledge without official power, and they constitute a kind of "shadow" organization by their extensive dispersion in physical and social space. The fact that secretaries are also commonly female has, in my opinion, very little relevance. I doubt if a fair case can be made for the special proclivity of women to gossip, except, as with secretaries, when gossip is one of the few available ways of exercising some power. Gossip, whether benevolent or malicious, accurate or distorted, is simultaneously a way of bypassing formal agencies of communication and of enhancing the power of the individual over a system he does not control.

Once a grapevine is well established, it may be used of course not only to speed communication but also to avoid some hazards of formal discourse. One tactic is the "trial balloon," which consists of "leaking" a rumor concerning some policy about the reaction to which the instigator is uncertain. If the reaction is favorable, or at least not dangerously unfavorable, the rumor (and the efficiency of the grapevine) can be simply confirmed. If, however, the reaction is very unfavorable, the rumor can be denied officially, through channels, and no one has lost face because no official policy has had to be withdrawn or amended.

Administrative rules may be less often broken than bent, to use an old quip. In most organizations practices grow up that soften the full effect of official rules. In his book on *The Wildcat Strike*, Alvin W. Gouldner refers to such practices as "indulgency patterns." They are not rights but privileges, yet privileges that persist gradually assume the qualities of rights, as in the common law. One such indulgency pattern is the doctrine of the "second chance." For many offenses such as an unexcused absence or reporting to work intoxicated, the rules commonly specify outright dismissal as the penalty. In practice, the offender is commonly reprimanded and warned on his first offense. Now it is difficult to write such a practice into the rule, for it would seem to encourage one misdemeanor as a "right." Yet the rule itself may be viewed as too harsh for full enforcement and factual "expectations" differ from official ones.

All of these illustrations of deviations from the charted course of conduct have in common a certain order or patterning of activity sufficient to think of them as examples of organization. They are not simply random bits of idiosyncratic behavior. The danger in the loose and residual use of the notion of informal organization is that it can be made to include behavior that is not in the least organized, since such behavior patently passes the simple test of not conforming to official expectations. For most purposes of understanding what goes on, it is much preferable to try to identify the scraps in the unsorted basket and to do so by name, so that a work exchange can be distinguished from a grapevine or a leadership struggle from an indulgency practice. Informal these are because they are not formal, but they have little else in common.

Details and Ornaments

The scraps so far identified do not come close to emptying the office waste basket. Many types of orderly behavior that qualify as "informal" because unwritten are absolutely essential to the conduct of the enterprise. This comes about because of the impossibility of complete planning. Although organizational experts, "scientific" managers, promoters of efficiency, and other zealots may attempt to leave nothing to chance and human ingenuity, they are quite unlikely to succeed. Wherever and whenever there is occasion for decision (and at least microscopic traces can be detected in any job), the action resulting from decision must be regarded as an "unplanned" but essential supplement to the formal structure. The actual way duties are carried out, the way decisions are implemented, the way officeholders define their roles and play their parts become in effect the detailed ingredients of the organization. No manual could specify these in advance, and their specification after they are developed would make the guidebooks even thicker and more tedious than they are now. The new recruit needs this detailed information, of course, but he fortunately needs it only for the parts of the organization that matter to him in his work assignment. For the rest, the maps may not show the side roads and local landmarks, but such details could only obscure the main routes by an excess of information.

Not even in unplanned details does the individual have open options, however. Organizations persist, and persisting they accumulate precedents. An option once exercised with apparent success tends to be followed when similar circumstances arise again. Many "occasions for decision," as seen by the outsider or the one who finds no guidance in the recipe book, turn out to be reduced to habit or tradition. Organizations operate according to "the law" but also according to "the lore." The lore tends to be binding even with succession in office, although as long as it remains unwritten it can be challenged somewhat more easily by a heroic performer who thinks he can show cause. As with any other context of social life, the longer a precedent has gone unchallenged the more persuasive must be the argument in favor of abandoning it as unsatisfactory. The quixotic enthusiast who attempts to challenge all received doctrine is likely to find himself, like the famous and frustrated original, ineffectually tilting at windmills.

Other unwritten elements in organizations are more ornamental than essential, although the line is not a sharp one. Here I refer to the rich variety of symbols of rank and function. Perhaps the most pervasive but increasingly flimsy distinction is that between the head and hand workers, symbolized by designations of "white collar" and "blue collar." A slightly more accurate distinction is whether the expected garb at the work place includes a jacket and tie. Supervisors of all grades and technicians with equivalent managerial ranks are expected to wear ties and usually have a jacket on display, if not actually worn. The shop foreman's clothes may be rumpled and not recently cleaned, but they are not to be confused with manual workers' clothes.

For more distinctly managerial types, the mandatory uniform of the day is, with only slight exaggeration, the "gray flannel suit." Now experts are supposed to be able to tell the difference in the cut and quality of the Board Chairman's uniform and that of the junior manager, but this is mostly a carefully cultivated myth on the part of high-cost merchant tailors and the more expensive shops. The young hopeful, in fact, may be sufficiently deceived by the assumption that price correlates with quality that he spends more on his clothes than his superiors who know better.

The managerial uniform, bearing no really reliable insignia of rank, identifies membership in a "class" or social category, not in precise position. But it does tend to distinguish between genuine managers and persons of assimilated rank like engineers and other professionals. The manager is likely to be strongly, and if necessary explicitly, discouraged from wearing jacket and trousers that do not match or any tie other than a "sincere" and conservative silk with subdued diagonal stripes. The more "individualistic" technical or professional people are much more likely than the manager to assert their individuality in "sportier" clothing.

Symbols of pure rank, being unreliable on the person, are easy to note in his setting: shared or private offices, shared or private secretaries, the location and size of offices and desks, the accoutrements of carpets and draperies, and, at lofty levels, the number of outer offices and guardians that must be cleared before the inner sanctum is at last reached. Automobiles, too, signify position, whether the cars are official or private. The story is told of the manager of one large corporation who, upon his elevation to the executive committee, failed to trade his large Buick for a Cadillac and thus inhibited the "status mobility" of managers all down the line.

I have found in buildings housing the central headquarters and corporation executive offices that there is a marked correlation between physical and social altitude. The top floors are usually "executive country," whether reached by private elevators or not. In fact, if one rides the elevators in the skyscraper office building of a corporation directed from New York, he will find on the lower floors (there may be twenty or more) that he emerges from the elevator to plastic tile floors and must consult a wall directory and signs painted on doors to find the office he seeks. At higher levels the carpeting comes right to the elevator door and a receptionist wearing a charming smile alongside her vase of flowers will start the necessary negotiations to get you to your destination, if in fact you have any business being there at all.

Many of these differences are well known and indeed taken for granted. But what is their point? Clearly the symbols of status constitute part of the nonfinancial rewards for success. Note, however, that few of these symbols are without cost to the company, even if they are not disposable income to the individual. The key to the officers' toilet is almost purely symbolic, but custom-designed furniture involves substantial amounts of money. The fact is that many managers cannot afford at home the kind of opulent comfort that they enjoy at work. It is doubtful that this inequality of environment is what keeps men working late at the office, an excuse that novelists have led us to believe often signals an illicit love affair. Yet in the covert struggle between the employer and the home—an intrinsic feature of industrial civilization—the corporate employer often holds the higher cards.

The economic justification of corporate luxury has never been seriously examined. A case can be made for offering the incentives and rewards necessary to attract and hold the right people in various positions, but to my knowledge there has been no experimentation on executives and managers, comparable to the endless study of manual workers, to determine which if any of the luxuries are in fact necessities. The plain fact is that the costs of gracious living at the office are portrayed in the company's accounts as genuine costs, like raw materials, factory buildings, and power for turning the machines. Until their utility has been demonstrated, the more tenable hypothesis is that such expenses represent a polite way of having one's hand in the till to benefit by the custody of other people's money. The loss to each shareholder may be trivial, and on balance the business provided to the suppliers beneficial to the economy as a whole, but it does seem appropriate to distinguish between costs and luxuries in corporate expenditures.

There is a further difficulty about status symbols and that is that they are subject to rapid deterioration. In fact, the degradation of status symbols is one of the most solidly established laws of social change. If the copy cannot be distinguished from the original, then the original is degraded and no longer useful as a symbol of excellence. This has clearly happened with clothing, which has thus lost its capacity to place the wearer by rank. Although the control of direct corporate expenses, such as furniture and assistants, may prevent the manipulation of symbols by the unworthy, even there the manager seeking to placate a discontented subordinate may "buy him off" with a symbol of higher position. Such cases are extremely unlikely to remain isolated, and the symbol thus becomes rapidly extended and cheapened. If a proper order is to be restored, new or more luxurious symbols must be created for the true elite. This kind of evolutionary process may help to account for the seeming excesses in the conspicuous display of opulence that corporations accord to their higher-ranking employees, at company expense. The Rolls Royce Company, manufacturers of the world's most expensive "standard" automobile, has published a series of advertisements asking if it is not "economical" for every corporation to buy its president a Rolls Royce (or the faintly less conspicuous Bentley with its attendant inverted snobbery). Their argument is that the president will do better work if he knows he is appreciated, and besides he will arrive at work in the morning rested from his comfortable commutation in quiet splendor. Economical it certainly is not, but symbolic of eminence, difficult (and costly) to degrade it certainly is. On the other hand, the Bigelow carpet manufacturers, in a series of clever cartoon advertisements, suggest that "A title on the door deserves a carpet on the floor," an appeal designed to degrade (and spread) the symbolism of carpeting where titled doors are the rule rather than the exception. We may shortly expect wall-to-wall carpeting on some of the cleaner factory floors, with executive carpets distinguished by depth and unique designs. This will unquestionably make shops and offices cheerier places, but it remains to be proved that they will also be more productive or that the inhabitants will be happy with the actual distribution of creature comforts.

Cliques, Claques, and Clutter

Of course not every chance bit of human action, including conversation, deserves to be regarded as "part" of the organization. Yet some "informal" patterns are sufficiently regular to be a predictable component of life at work. A considerable amount of social interaction in shops and offices is neither essential to the conduct of corporate affairs nor antithetical to official requirements. This may simply be regarded as the "enrichment" of social relations among persons in continuous official contact. The work place actually provides the necessary if not sufficient conditions for the formation of groups—continuous, face-to-face contact among small numbers of individuals. Enthusiasts for the concept of informal organization have gone so far as to characterize industrial structures as networks of these "primary" groups. This is clearly an exaggeration, as the formal structure still exists as an ideal model, and without its existence there would be no occasion for the individuals to be assembled where and when they are. Such groups, however, do exist, and the commonest basis for their formation is in fact geographical proximity.

The biological term "ecology," meaning the relationship of the organism to its environment, is useful here. Work organizations involve spatial concentration and dispersion of human individuals and their activities. The ecology of work is thus likely to have a strong influence on the sociology of work, the group behavior that represents an enrichment of the minimally required, "mechanical" relationships.

We must be cautious, however, about the character of "informal" groups or the individual's relationship to them. The notion of a "primary" group is a rich one, and it is not at all clear that groups at the work place will qualify. Primary groups (for example, families and play groups) tend to treat their members as whole persons, not as narrow role-players. Strong sentiments attach to the preservation of the group as such, and the individual so identifies with the group that he thinks of his participation as voluntary and spontaneous. Now few groups formed within corporate organizations match these qualifications in any high degree. For the individual, and especially for the newcomer, the informal patterns he encounters may be at least as binding and constraining as the official handbook of duties. The pressures to conform may be unwritten, but as any one who has been brought to heel by a raised eyebrow realizes, informal sanctions are not to be taken lightly.

There is a further difficulty in the conception of the "group structure" of business organizations. The implication is that the person's group identification is unique and preclusive. No evidence to this effect has yet been adduced by the assiduous students of human behavior at the work place. They simply assume it. But the individuals who trade jobs may or may not be those who eat together, congregate in the men's room for a quick cigarette and a dirty story, or bowl together after work. I have the impression that the worker, whether manual or managerial, is actually a member of a number of informal "cliques," with some individuals common to all of them and some not. Perhaps the common units in any one worker's "social field" may take on some of the rich attributes of a "primary group," but even this remains to be established. The occasion for the appearance of such social units is still the fact of employment, and it is not at all certain that the units will carry over to other contexts of human activity. Do they live in the same neighborhood? Do the families entertain one another socially? Do they join the same voluntary associations or enjoy the same recreational activities? I do not deny that friendships may be formed at work, but I think we should not assume that people who do things together at work have a very extensive or abiding friendship. Man's capacity to separate out his life into rather distinct segments, a capacity that is fully developed and even stretched in an industrial society, is clearly great enough to permit him to leave his "friends" at the shop when he starts for home.

A number of years ago in an argument with a fellow scholar also interested in industrial organization, but more fascinated by informal groups than I, I proposed a wager. On the assumption that the object of our endeavors was to predict the patterned behavior of individuals at work, I offered to lay out on a table all sorts of bits of information about workers' private lives, their informal associations, even their personality traits. But one bit of information would be the answer to the question, "What are they supposed to be doing?" That information, I suggested, I would choose and bet against the field, expecting to win on the average. The point I wish to make is that the knowledge of informal associations may extend and deepen our understanding of work organizations, but it is not to be taken as a substitute for knowledge of the "formal" structure as such.

The Outside World Intrudes

Perhaps the strongest basis for social "solidarity" and division, for cohesion and exclusion, in the "informal" part of industrial organization is imported rather than domestically produced. Although I have suggested that many individuals leave their "job friendships" behind as they leave the company premises, I am not so confident that as they enter they leave behind their social origins, their nationality identification, or their institutional loyalties. In the case of ethnic or racial identification, they may not be permitted to do so. But often exclusiveness is two-sided, enforced by the group itself as well as from outside. Many a plant manager in a multi-national, urban setting must proceed with exquisite caution in placing workers where they will cooperate rather than fight with their fellows and select foremen whose authority will not be rejected for deeply emotional reasons of ethnic antipathy.

If this behavior were peculiar to manual workers it might be dismissed as simply indicative of low educational levels and only partial incorporation into the institutional features of an industrial society. This view has some faint merit, but it must not be accepted too completely. One must also recall the defensive truculence of the self-made manager when he encounters "those college kids," the barely tolerable arrogance of Ivy League products toward graduates of state universities, and the rather fine discrimination that alumni of one Ivy League college, if sufficiently numerous, show with regard to other, but lesser, Ivy League alumni. One is reminded that the military officer who has not attended one of the service academies can scarcely live down the taint on his record.

The usual rule in an "open" society that religion and politics are to be avoided in conversation is commonly honored in the case of religion but not politics. The hapless Democrat in managerial circles is likely to find his other qualities viewed with considerable doubt.

The significance of social origin has its anomalous features. I recall a visit to a steel mill in the early days of World War II. Some twenty women, dressed in company-supplied blue smocks, were tin-plate inspectors at an average wage of about 85 dollars a week. At the plant cafeteria for lunch a similar number of secretaries and clerical workers were on hand, dressed in "heels and hose" not supplied by the company. Their average wage (or rather salary) was 35 dollars a week. Not only did the two groups not intermix, but they were not recruited from the same sector of the community. A "factory job" was only suitable for the daughter of an immigrant. The secretary might well come from a quite proper family. Of course we have intermixed here the prestige of the white-collar job but also and therefore the persistence of community distinctions on the job.

Conscientious managers attempt with varying degrees of heroism to insist solely on criteria of merit in selection and judgment of individuals. The scarcity of what are sometimes called the "ethnics"—that is Negroes, Jews, and the descendants of late im-

migrants from Eastern and Southern Europe—in higher managerial circles raises the suspicion that the success of the merit
principle is somewhat less than complete. Pure merit criteria
are, however, more closely approximated in large companies than
small ones.

The Strategic Use of Deviance

No insight as revealing and persuasive as the notion of "informal
organization" could be expected to endure solely as an academic
curiosity. The first use of the notion in business was in "labor
policy," that is, in the managerial strategy of dealing with production workers. The irrational, sentimental character of workers
came to be accepted as a fact of life, but a fact of life capable of
use rather than passive acceptance. Indeed, some of the more extreme followers of the "Mayo school" felt that the studies had
demonstrated the low importance to the worker of wages as compared with prestige among his fellows and praise by his superiors.
Now this is the kind of notion that managers find very appealing
when applied to workers, but not to themselves. I think it can be
fairly said that experience and further research have now clearly
demonstrated that workers will not be bought off by Mayo's
"techniques of cooperation" in lieu of money. In the real world
the choice is not so clear. They want both.

The same is true of managers. The gradual recognition that
some friendly warmth in human discourse is a pervasive characteristic in industrial organizations has reduced the tendency to think
of feigned warmth as something managers practice on manual
workers. It is now something managers practice on each other
also. The late Dale Carnegie was the highly successful author of
a book, *How to Win Friends and Influence People*, which carried the strategy of forming "friendships" for ulterior purposes
into the reach of every ambitious reader of self-help literature.
The doctrine of "human relations" in industry, once a tactic for
keeping employees loyal and out of unions, has become the style

of life everywhere in the corporation. First names are the proper form of address. To address an administrative superior as "Sir" is positively archaic. The work unit is the "team," and the whole managerial group is the "family." Bosses are instructed to be solicitous of the private problems of their subordinates and at times to practice, within limits, lay psychotherapy in getting them to talk out their problems. In effect a kind of "bureaucratic kinship system" is established with the older generation nurturing the younger, and cousins properly attentive to their common heritage and mutual needs. Indeed, in this predominantly masculine society, we may push the metaphor to its absurd extreme. The corporation seems to seek an arrangement which is surely an anomaly in human society, that of homosexual reproduction, with the necessary counterpart that the "father image" is rampant. The boss is, with at least partial affection as well as partial accuracy, "the old man." Lesser managers are "junior," regardless of age. Some of them are simply retarded, which can happen in the best of families.

Is this simply a kind of harmless nonsense, perhaps copied from universities where it is at least equally prevalent? I think, rather, that it is a mixture, in proportions difficult to determine, of rather crafty and manipulative use of sentiment in an otherwise cold-blooded environment and of a rather genuine quest for making the inevitable "enrichment" of social relations at the work place overt and honorable.

What started, then, as a kind of extended supplement to the traditional and idealized theory of administrative organization has become an integral part of both theory and official practice. There is a lesson in this experience, although I am not sure I am happy about it. The lesson is that you cannot discover some scientific principle, whether about inanimate nature or human behavior, without some fool coming along and finding a use for it. I still count on human ingenuity in inventing forms of conduct in corporations that have not been fully expected, but I do not expect any single unanticipated regularity to go along unnoticed or unused.

V I I I

COMPETITION

WHEREIN *vying for preference and position*
is recognized as an important component of
behavior within the nominally cooperative organization,
and some curious strategies for staying in the game
are recorded.

EVERY right-thinking American believes in competition. As a
practical matter, however, the abstract belief is tempered and
modulated. Competition is often a virtue earnestly wished for
other people but somewhat less earnestly expected of oneself. The
rigors of competition, and particularly the possibilities of failure,
may lead both the sharp and the timid to avoid its full force,
either by finding other roads to the rewards or by leaving the
game.

Competition is a social invention that probably ranks with the
invention of the wheel in age, and possibly in importance. It is a
social form that encourages individuals to effort by rewards according to *merit*. Merit is determined by the object of the game
and rules of procedure. Although the difference between competition and conflict may be one of degree, competition generally
permits preservation of the system as such, whereas conflict tends

to be destructive of the system. Of course individual competitors may be eliminated temporarily or permanently. If, as in some types of economic market competition, all players save one are eliminated, the resulting system is no longer competitive even though it survives as a way of producing and distributing goods. One essential rule, therefore, in any system that is to be kept competitive is that the game must be stopped short of its full course.

Unlimited competition is a contradiction in terms, for competition without limits is in fact conflict and will destroy the system. An absolutely essential feature of competition is a set of rules—how the game is to be played—and if the game is to be continued or renewed, the rules have to be regarded as more important than the outcome of particular contests. Generally speaking, the most efficient ways of winning contests are by use of force or fraud, either one of which is likely to wreck the game. A contest is "fair" only if these otherwise effective tactics are prevented or strictly controlled. The legitimate deceit by poker players does not include use of marked cards, and legitimate bodily contact in American football does not include all sorts of "dirty play."

Recreational games constitute something more than a playful analogy to competition in the real world of affairs. The social principles are the same, whether the rewards be trival and temporary or elevated and enduring. In all competitive systems, rules occupy a paramount position. They constitute a static or defining principle of the social form. We can, however, go much further. One of the most general of the "dynamic laws" of social systems, that is, the predictable course of social change, is that in any enduring competitive system there will be an increase in the number of rules. The reasons for this are not hard to find. Competition encourages innovation in tactics and strategies, but this great virtue has correlative dangers. If the rewards for success are highly desirable there is corresponding pressure on standard procedures. Some competitors may adopt illegitimate tactics already recognized in the rules and punishable by conventional penalties. Short of perfect foresight, however, some innovations are likely not to be covered by existing rules. The innovation may be accepted, modified, or rejected by upholders of the system, but in any case it must be accorded a place in the body of regulations.

Any competitive system thus carries the seeds of its own destruction, or, more properly, of its own destruction-and-reconstruction. The rapidity of change is likely to be correlated with the importance of the issue to the participants as well as with the number of players (which is a kind of numerical test of importance). The large administrative organization and particularly the contemporary corporation qualify on both scores. To its many participants the corporation offers the opportunity to vie for preference and position, for prestige and power, and to the winners go also the spoils of real money.

Competition *within* productive organizations is a notion largely alien to classical economic doctrine, for in that doctrine participants in the market were supposed to be individuals or at least singular entities, not large assemblies of diversified and partially contentious job-holders. The older textbooks did, it is true, permit the "outside" market to intrude within the factory, but only in a kind of impersonal way—the bargain for services (labor) reached by employers and individual employees. With workers assumed to be pretty interchangeable and usually in excess supply, *their* competition could be expected to keep the price for services at a minimum, tolerable level. Neither the extensive gradation of positions nor the extreme, non-convertible diversity of skills figures much in economic theory and, it must be added, not much in fact prior to the late Nineteenth Century. The competitive market for goods within the firm simply could not be contemplated before the appearance of the diversified firm that manufactures different but functionally equivalent products. If changes in economic theory have not kept pace with changes in economic fact, this is a matter that need not long detain us. Although the rewards to the worthy within the corporation are usually in part economic, that is, financial, the rules of play have only slight resemblance to impersonal markets, and it is not at all clear that it is the business of economists to analyze them. It is, however, surely somebody's business and we shall make it ours.

Playing the Game

Competition within the corporation is both individual and collective. Individual competition is in fact an essential if often implicit characteristic of the ideal model of administrative organization. The matching of individuals and jobs in terms of qualifications by merit and performance clearly requires a selective process that somehow permits evaluating and grading potential claimants. Were differential qualities of no consequence, selection might be accomplished by any procedure at all—for example, seniority of service, favoritism by superiors, or simple chance by, say, drawing lots. The presumption of merit requires the presumption of competitive testing. Yet pure theory may in fact be violated in each of these and several other ways. But if the presumption of merit exists among aspirants, a lost competition may be more tolerable than selection without contest. For if it is difficult to maintain belief in the fairness of a competition among losers, it is impossible where the game is rigged or simply not played at all.

A competitive system of selection and promotion provides a kind of counter-melody to the grand themes of cooperation in complex organizations. When the purity of impersonal selection from any source is modified by a regular policy of "recruitment from within," existing employees are given a protected position. This seeming advantage may be counterbalanced by the very ease of identifying the probable candidates. Some corporations try, as a matter of policy, to keep lines of succession as fluid as possible not only to expand the pool but also to reduce the pinpointing of personal rivalry. Yet the most probable successors to an administrative position are usually to be found among the incumbent's immediate subordinates, and these are few, visible, and often constant if constrained companions.

Frequent transfers in personnel may reduce the force of directly personal competition. The official reason for transfers at managerial levels is to broaden the man's experience, season him, groom him for future and greater responsibilities. Transfers, however, also serve to break up excessively close-knit informal cliques and to create some uncertainty as to the pool of competitors for various positions. Usually the succession to the highest office permits of little obfuscation of this sort. If executives are picked who have many years of service left before retirement, active competition for the position may occur only once, if at all, in a top manager's life. Several business novels have used such a dramatic interlude in a career as an effective plot device. It must be assumed that the contestants who are entered in the "finals" have survived a number of preliminary rounds of strenuous competition.

In a "pure" market, success or failure in competition is the result of many actions by individuals largely unknown. The judgment is impersonal. A managerial employee of the corporation is somewhat affected by the impersonal labor market for administrators but usually much more affected by the personal judgments of colleagues and superiors. This situation places a maximum and often excessive strain on the rules of merit and performance. Particularly in the hazy areas of desirable "personality characteristics," dispassionate judgment may be difficult to achieve and difficult to maintain. Ingratiating manners may be substituted for outstanding performance, and the shadow of dedicated duty may conceal the substance of extreme self-interest or vindictive intentions toward unsuccessful rivals.

Extreme personal rivalry is in fact a social situation very difficult to maintain as an enduring form of relationship. From a strictly organizational standpoint the situation is somewhat paradoxical. Personal competition for preference is supposed to operate within a framework of cooperation and even collective identification—the unit, the division, the company. Although rivalry is conceived as a way of eliciting high performance, it must be very sharply contained if it is not to destroy the organizational system and loyalty to it. Whenever defeat of a rival takes precedence over getting on with the job, the organization and its mission are in danger. The feelings of individuals add point to the dilemma. Personal ambition may be tempered by the strain of having to watch every step, of being always on the alert to one's own tactics and those of every rival.

Here once more we encounter the instability of competitive systems. Novel tactics are likely to appear, and although the competitive advantage to the innovator may be rather temporary if tactics are quickly matched by other players, the benefits from that advantage may be of lasting value to him. If he has taken a trick with his new tactic, he still has the trick even if he cannot repeat the coup. The first volunteer for extra work shows qualities of "leadership" that other and seemingly reluctant volunteers lack.

Extra work, in fact, is one of the most troublesome of competitive strategies. Deliberate restrictions on output and the quick condemnation of the "rate-buster" are commonly attributed only to manual workers with or without union organization and support. This is a comforting, patronizing, and carefully cultivated myth. Notions of a performance standard, a "fair day's work" or its equivalent in task or time units are absolutely common in every occupational category. It is a fair, although not absolutely sure, bet that the loudest complainers about the norm of mediocrity themselves resist what they regard as excessive demands on their time and energy on the job. There are, no doubt, elements of protection of the weak in these performance restrictions. I am convinced, however, that the much more basic factor is the protection of all participants against the danger of having to maintain a vigorously competitive stance and a steadily increasing rather than constant set of expected duties.

Were extreme personal rivalry to prevail, unit by unit, throughout a corporation, every individual would be in a constant state of "rational paranoia." That is, he would fear that every man was his enemy, and he would be right. Now such a state does not lose its pathological qualities by being general and therefore "normal." The psychological qualities of human individuals are such that they have a rather limited capacity for tolerating uncertainty. If "the system" fosters uncertainty, individuals or groups will ordinarily find means of reducing it. One way in a competitive system is to restrict the permissible tactics and discourage tactical innovation.

Competition within the firm has more enduring and less harrowing qualities when conducted between units or divisions. Manufacturing divisions may have products that have the same function if not design, and in such cases their salesmen may behave like representatives of independent businesses. As in most other situations, a little competition may well be a good thing and a lot of competition may destroy the position of the company as such with the customer. Running down the products of a competing division may simply send the customer to a supplier who presents a more unified, if slightly exaggerated, picture of his wares. Soap companies, it is true, seem to survive and thrive and support large advertising budgets designed to sell myriads of competing cleansers, each better than all others. Cigarette and automobile manufacturers play the same game with fewer players. In these cases, however, company identity or "image" is not greatly emphasized, and numerous brands may be necessary to "cover" the market. This still does not settle the character of the intra-company competition, which may be fairly severe. The in-fighting between proponents of soap and adherents of detergents may make the daily cliff-hangers of the sponsored soap opera rather pale dramatic fare by comparison.

Market competition between company divisions is a kind of explicit sharing of jurisdictions. Most other jurisdictional disputes are unintentional, troublesome, and therefore somewhat lacking in tactical rules and restraints. The basic reason for jurisdictional problems is that the ideal of a perfectly planned organization is never realized. Thus some boundaries between functions or "social territories" are likely to be hazy and the claims on them overlapping. Where, for example, does product development end and regular production begin? Who should set production standards: engineers with their highly trained skills or supervisors with their long practical experience? Who should cultivate stockholders: the controller's office because the stockholders' interest is in company finances or the public relations office because of its skills in communication with laymen?

Perfect plans would in any event not last long. Changes of all sorts, whether initiated by the company or adapted to changing conditions, will alter functions and their relative importance. Perhaps the most interesting problems arise with the decision to produce a substantially new product. Several existing product divisions may desire to capture control. One division may argue that the major raw materials or components are like those it is already purchasing and that this familiarity with the supply market is critical. Another may argue that the prospective method of production (for example, a "batch process" in chemicals or sequential assembly in appliances) is one that the division has perfected and that efficient production is critical. Another may argue that the type of customers and channels of advertising and distribution are like those it knows and sales are after all critical. Naturally, if substantial pessimism prevails over the product's prospects, each division may assiduously espouse the cause of some other one.

In the case of a new product, some decision is likely to be made, and the losers rearrange themselves for the next contest. In other situations, such as competing products or competing services— for example, lawyers and accountants as tax advisors—the sore may simply stay irritated and the patient survive a chronic low fever.

When outright conflict occurs, some settlement is necessary. I am impressed with the generality of "collective bargaining" in corporations. The term is usually reserved for management-union negotiations, but the restriction is scarcely justified. Within the corporate "state" disputes over jurisdiction are either settled by negotiation and agreement or else appealed to a "higher court," ultimately to the top executive powers. When decisions are reached they are commonly reduced to writing, since memories may be short and individuals may be transferred. If direct negotiation is successful, a "memorandum of agreement" is prepared, in other words, a contract is drawn. Otherwise, a policy statement is circulated to all interested parties, in other words, a court decision is announced.

If opposition to a policy is foreseen, or a jurisdictional conflict is likely, a precautionary counter-strategy may be used. One such strategy I should call "marrying the opposition." Like dynastic marriages when kingdoms still counted, the prospective opposition may be neutralized or actually turned into allies by making them partially responsible for carrying out the policy. The tactic must be employed with extreme care; its success depends on "loyal" participants with conscientious differences of opinion. Under these circumstances the differences are more likely to be composed or constrained if all parties have at least an "advisory" role in the operation than if some are left outside to nurse their wounds and grievances. The tactic will not work with uncommitted participants or with die-hard objectors, if unanimous consent must be obtained. Then stalemate rather than positive participation is ensured, and the strain of face-to-face opposition is set up in lieu of the somewhat more impersonal rivalry among contenders at a distance.

Sharing the Wealth

It was about two decades ago that a book emanating from the Harvard Graduate School of Business Administration first hinted that there might be a division of interest among managers. (It is probable that the "case studies" widely used in actual instruction, which I have not carefully examined, contained conflict situations much earlier. Since the cases are commonly treated as problems rather than reduced to principles, the probability of contention among managers did not reach the publications intended for the non-classroom reader.) In fact, most textbooks on administrative principles treat divisiveness as abnormal, a failure of the organization. This is rather odd if one simply thinks for a moment about money. Corporate resources for internal allocation are never inexhaustible, and wherever scarcity exists relative to claims, some vying for position is virtually certain. The preparation of budgets and their defense in budget hearings takes on much of the quality of the taxation and appropriation process in government, which indeed is what it is in the "private" sphere.

Budget-making normally starts among units in production and also among various staff services and divisions. Budgets go "up the line" as recommendations. But at each stage of budgetary coordination a small scale tournament is likely to take place, since the total of the requests at that point is likely to exceed the amount that the coordinator dares try as his "first offer" at the next higher level. Where the expectation is that initial requests will not be honored, and this is usual, there exists the maximum temptation to start impossibly high in the hope that what one *really* wants will be preserved after deflation. In this kind of a game, the honest man is a fool. The reduction of excess claims by an across-the-board cut rewards the least moral contestant, the one who makes the most inflated demand. Other procedures, including the extremely hazardous group discussion of the relative merits of proposals, may well have the same effect but to a lesser degree.

A major source of the competitive spirit in budget-making is that budgets have symbolic as well as "real" significance. Even if an increased budget carries no direct financial benefit to the manager or to any of his present personnel, being entirely intended for new faces and new furniture, the increase is a sign of success, a reward for well-doing, a mark of approval. To ask for a repetition of the previous budget, to say nothing of less money, may raise questions concerning the man's ambitions and other attributes of managerial virtue. To ask for more but get less, except as part of a general economy edict applied with some uniformity, may be taken as a sign of some unhappiness about the value or quality of the unit's work.

Budgets are commonly made on an annual basis, and only rarely can savings be carried forward and accumulated. This seemingly sensible rule of flexibility, of keeping resources relatively liquid, has some curious consequences. Because of budgetary strategy in the first place and the possibility of general reductions owing to business conditions with consequent errors in estimated revenue, the seasoned budgeteer will have a more or less concealed "pad" or a "contingency fund." His success in getting and keeping his surplus may prove embarrassing. If he does not spend it, he not only cannot keep it, but he has revealed his strategy. At his next budget review, the reviewer will start bargaining from the previous sum actually spent, making an honorific increase in amount allocated extremely unlikely. In this peculiar economic situation, nothing fails like success—that is, frugality in the stewardship of other people's money. When the company fiscal year coincides with the calendar year, a peculiar kind of "Christmas" spending occurs. Managers buy rugs—or advice—in December in order to preserve the formal honesty of the budget.

Large corporations normally expect to finance much of their expansion by "retained earnings," net income not distributed to stockholders. The principle, modified and adapted, is also likely to apply within the firm. For all units that have "profit accountability," meaning that they have revenue as well as expenditures, a favorable balance is clearly a mark of success and an unfavorable balance a mark of failure. The unit that is more than self-supporting has a much greater chance of getting a favorable hearing on budgetary increases than one that is living on relief. Thus, unless very explicit steps are taken to protect and rehabilitate losing endeavors, there is a notable tendency for the rich to get richer and the poor poorer. Here, at least, the old aphorism stands restored: nothing succeeds like success.

The claims presented by units without external income, ranging from scientific scholarship to psychiatric services, provide a situation of nearly "pure" competition, as none can prove its case in current fiscal terms. But they do make claims.

Proving Merit

The rewards for competitive excellence within the business firm are often easier to identify than is the nature of the contest. Individual promotion, a successful jurisdictional claim, an expanding divisional budget may be easily confirmed, objective results. The paths leading to success may be so different as to defy comparison. How does one compare the skill of a foot racer, a football lineman, and a tennis player? One can compare each with his own kind, but not with other kinds. This is precisely the problem presented by persons and units who are at a considerable distance from production and sales and not measurable by the common yard-stick of cost accounting.

Some staff services may attempt to approach financial measurement. Accountants, the measurers of others, may also attempt to assert their own measure by claims to costs saved, wastes detected and corrected. Whether they save more than they spend in the process is a nasty-nice question. Advertising units may attempt to take credit for increased sales volume (or a smaller relative decrease in sales compared with competitors) and thus prove the net value of the advertising dollar. Even attorneys may cite the number of suits settled as plaintiffs, with damages collected, or the number of suits settled as defendants at values below the original claims. All of these cases are, at best, somewhat partial and unconvincing. It is doubtful that any of the practitioners of these services would be willing to rest his claim to employment on directly measurable financial grounds. Others cannot do so.

Since merit is rewarded if only it can be determined, a perfectly natural thing happens. Various occupational types develop standard symbols and measures of worthwhile activities but without basic and incontrovertible demonstration of worth to the primary mission of the organization. For some, the standards may be sufficiently common to be compared from one company to another. In other words, the players are being compared with their own kind. For scientific and technical personnel, patents and publications in professional journals are marks of merit. For public relations men the number of column inches of company news releases ("free advertising" except for the substantial expense of maintaining the program) may be determinable and comparable. Now this does not determine the relative merits of foot racers and tennis players, and most assuredly it does not determine whether there is any excuse for employing a tennis player. It does permit an approximate standard for judging the tennis player's standing if one is going to have one at all.

Patents, at least, may be of actual value to the company. Favorable news releases are unlikely to harm the company relations with customers and legislators, and they may do some good. Other "demonstrations" of merit may approach pure irrelevance. Chemical engineers, for example, may demonstrate their virtuosity by filling their laboratories with spectacular displays of complex and utterly useless blown glass. This is designed to impress the laymen, particularly if accompanied by an unintelligible explanation of its use. Besides, to some it may have an aesthetic appeal and brighten the day for the workers.

The more sedentary and intellectual types of staff workers may be hard pressed to prove activity. Report-counting will work for some, mail volume for others. Some persons with largely advisory functions, finding their advice not actively sought, may take the initiative. One way of doing so is to run a kind of clipping service, specialized for the officer's field of unsought advice. These clippings can then be reproduced and, accompanied by moralizing memos from the advisor, circulated to those who might otherwise forget him. My examples by no means exhaust the competitive strategies developed for dealing with an essentially noncompetitive situation. The only common element, in fact, is the attention of the decision makers and dispensers of rewards. Even for those occupational groups poor at blowing glass or writing homilies, all is not lost. The final advice must be, "If all else fails, draw charts, preferably showing a rising line of progress." Progress, after all, is a many-splendored thing.

I X

CONFLICT

W HEREIN *the struggle for existence and*
especially for power results in occasional
insurrections against constituted authorities and more
frequent border skirmishes between
adjacent enemies.

IN THE organization of contemporary culture, most social relationships have been nominally sterilized of emotion. Except
within the family and among very intimate friends, the stage directions to the actor are to "play it cool." These directions are
especially emphatic when the scene is in the office or shop. One
would vastly underestimate the strength of social codes if one
supposed that these directions were simply disregarded. One
would underestimate the essential wholeness of human individuals if one supposed that they were uniformly followed. Individuals have values and beliefs as well as calculated interests, specialized life-views as well as those shared by most of their
contemporaries, convictions about rights as well as conceptions
of duty.

It is the dual circumstance that individuals differ and care about
their differences that provides the basis for both love ("Vive la
difference!") and hate, affection and anger. The administrative

organization of the business corporation never quite succeeds in eliminating these and other elementary human emotions. In fact, it provides some conditions that encourage their appearance and display. Membership in such organizations provides no assurance of common beliefs and convictions or even of a coalescence of interests. When interests, however coolly calculated, fail to coincide with other interests, the quality of the inconsistency is likely to take on a distinctly emotional tone, and the language of discourse is apt to feature liberal references to rights, to justice, and to high moral principle.

To speak of the prevalence of conflict within the corporation may itself constitute an exaggeration. Outright physical combat is understandably rare. A dispute between an engineer and a foreman is rarely settled by a fist-fight behind the boiler room, and rival divisional managers customarily walk around unarmed. The use of coercive physical force as an instrument of policy is strongly discouraged, except when exercised by the state. In all other circumstances the destruction of enemies must be accomplished by other, subtler methods. And destruction may not be the goal, but only restriction, containment, or subordination. Although "pure" conflict is destructive both in intent and in result, there are various approximations where there is no desire to destroy the system as such, or even the opposition, but only to alter the system and the position of people in it. The shading from highly regulated and overtly sponsored competition at one pole to anarchical conflict at the other is extremely gradual. My concern here is with the many situations that have as a prominent feature a basic lack of agreement on ends and means, on worth of efforts and value of results, and a high likelihood that the disputants will put off the mask of cool sophistication to reveal their underlying human emotions.

Opportunities for Conflict

Reasonable men may reasonably differ on all sorts of things, including matters of goals and policies. And not all men, when they differ, remain reasonable. In principle, corporations have clear-cut objectives and a set of priorities among them if they cannot all be simultaneously achieved or "maximized." In practice, even such central objectives as profits provoke disputes between adherents of short-run and of long-run considerations, and some, while admitting the importance of avoiding loss, regard high profits as of less consequence than maintaining a "position in the market" and cultivating other virtues.

The various objectives of corporate policy—profits, harmonious working relationships, attributes of good citizenship like support of educational and benevolent activities—are not achieved without human effort. In a small company the executive officer may be all things to all men, but the president of a large concern cannot "operate the company out of his hat." Specialized staffs are developed to implement company policies and to represent those policies in company councils. It is this manning operation that virtually assures that uncertainty over priorities will not remain abstract and inconsequential. Policy priorities get translated into precedence of persons. Principles get entangled with partisan interests. Spokesmen for policies enter into contention for recognition of the importance of their function and tend to view the corporate world as having one promontory, which they occupy, and a number of lesser foothills occupied by other, somewhat misguided, captains.

The arena, to shift the metaphor, becomes more crowded as we admit other contestants. The objectives of corporations, even when clear, may not be easily or automatically achieved. And certainly they require the effects of quite differentiated operations. Success in the manufacturing business catches up design, production, and sales in an interdependent but not necessarily harmonious system. Behind these functions stand financial operations, personnel recruiting, management and organization, and expediters "not elsewhere classified." Again, job specialization ensures that these functions will have protagonists, that their several contributions to the operation as a whole will not pass unnoticed. Since *all* are probably necessary, a kind of uneasy peace may prevail as long as conditions remain relatively stable. Any attempt to change or expand the objectives is likely to produce as many procedures as there are vocal participants.

Suppose a company wants to increase its unit sales of a product by 10 per cent. How is this to be achieved? The advertising department may advocate an intensified advertising campaign, perhaps with a new and more vigorous agency. Their solution, in effect, is to achieve the goal by increasing distribution costs, in total if not per unit. The sales manager, impressed with the vigor of price competition, is likely to maintain that the goal is impossible without a price reduction. If this view is accepted, the advertising manager will still want to get the message across, to send out the good word, to potential customers. If price is to be cut, will this be at the expense of profit margins? (The price-setters are required to protest that this is impossible.) Or by cutting costs? (The production manager is required to say that they are already cut to the bone, and, because of exceptional efficiency, well below those borne by competitors.) Sooner or later someone will suggest that "overhead" costs are too high and that the real place to look for cost reduction is in the non-contributive, non-profit making, and in a word, useless charges. Since those are the thrones on which other influential kinglets sit, a certain air of defensive hostility sets in. If the challenger keeps it general, he will incur no personal wrath and will also be assured that his view is understandable but mistaken. If he names names, he must expect personal anger and counterattack.

Let us understand, this is a discussion among gentlemen, not a barroom brawl. The decor and the demeanor require restraint. This is civilized combat, not the law of the jungle. But let us not confuse it with a church supper. Reputations ride on outcomes, and battle formations are in a stance of readiness, even if the weapons are words and statistics rather than cross-bows or atomic missiles.

Credit for success is easier to share than blame for failure. The customary quest for extending jurisdictions may be quickly reversed if the disputed function appears to be the one that must bear the onus for failure or misconduct. One is reminded of the joke about the crowded car pulled over by a policeman because of reckless driving. In answer to his request for the driver's license he was told, "There wasn't none of us driving, officer, we were all in the back seat singing." Where responsibilities are ambiguous, it is quite possible that no one has been in charge. The loser in a jurisdictional dispute would be somewhat less than human if he totally concealed his satisfaction when the successful claimant ran into trouble.

I have called uncertainties over objectives, procedures, and responsibilities the "opportunities for conflict" rather than causes. The causes may match the occasions if the alternative courses of action have conscientious adherents, that is, adherents solely concerned with pushing the cooperative endeavors in the best possible way. This no doubt happens, but it is very difficult to disentangle from rather more self-interested action in building careers or extending empires. Actually the cross-currents of interests and convictions may make the distinction nearly meaningless.

Although for illustrative purposes I have discussed conflict primarily in personal, face-to-face terms, it should not be supposed that battles involve only hand-to-hand combat. Since the match between individual and collective interests is rarely perfect, individual struggles can and do occur. But individuals are often representative of and spokesmen for lesser collectivities—organizational divisions and functions. The morale, and sometimes even the power, of individual contestants will be influenced by the number and loyalty of their supporters. Whole units may be diverted from their normal "civilian" tasks to prepare ammunition for a prospective battle. Defensive as well as offensive weapons must be kept in repair and possibly improved, and espionage and counter-intelligence must not be neglected. It may even be appropriate to have occasional displays of power to exhilarate adherents and intimidate enemies. Such partial patriotism, which is also encouraged in national military establishments, may encourage beneficent rivalry in excellence. I do suggest, however, that divisional rivalries within corporations may have little to do with the "real enemy," that is, other, competing corporations and much to do with changing the internal distribution of power and rewards. If this view is approximately correct, its significance is that the large corporation is spending some portion of its man-hour resources in internal war and its containment rather than in furthering its various stated objectives. For this problem there is no ideal solution, the difficulty being one of degree. The old principle that the ranks tend to close when there is a real external enemy would suggest that the rigors of market competition, which large corporations often appear to avoid, might be very useful in maintaining internal peace and order.

The Class Struggle

The common, and indeed exclusive, meaning popularly attributed to "industrial conflict" is the division between capital, or management as its representative, and labor, or unions as its representative. Clearly such a division does exist, and it is formalized by explicit organization of the contending parties and recognized by law and custom. Its foundations, however, are remarkably ambiguous.

Application of the Marxian notion of an inherent class struggle between those who own the means and instruments of production and those who own only their own labor leads to some rather curious consequences in the contemporary corporation. The "separation of ownership and management" makes the formal position of managers precisely that of employees. Except for managers who are given stock as part of their compensation, and thereby gain some slight "ownership" interest, the manager is clearly a proletarian in Marxist terms. The stockholding corporate employee is in an ambiguous and possibly ambivalent position with regard to the struggle between capital and labor.

The formalization of the management-labor division and their relations in collective bargaining and labor disputes has served to institutionalize one type of inconsistent interests and obscure others.

Management, we have seen, is by no means a cohesive body of men all practicing the same group-think. It is not even clear that management is united with regard to its opposition to "labor." Reduction of direct labor costs will of course benefit the company's competitive position, and the benefits may redound more to the advantage of managers than of workers. Yet labor cost reduction is advantageous only as long as it is consistent with quality of performance. The credit and rewards for successful competition are as a matter of fact likely to adhere to top managers only. By this view, the proper place for a "class" division is at the point where the clear benefits of restrictions on labor costs or other labor-relations policies stop.

Managerial salaries, it should be noted, are also labor costs. Depending on circumstances, managers may either gain or lose by restrictions on the wages and salaries of others. They may gain if savings in one sector become expenditures in others, thus changing relative income distributions. They may lose if their salaries are directly a function of those "below" them. Managerial representatives cannot be expected to bargain too keenly over a union wage demand if their own salaries will be increased as a consequence of a higher base for the lowest wage category.

Even in cases of industrial disputes and strikes, there may well be pro-union factions in management, because of direct financial interest, because a strike will hurt the company's market position, or because an amicable settlement is easier to live with in subsequent day-to-day operations than a bitter one.

What I am suggesting is that the solidarity of management with regard to "labor" is either spurious or irrational. The basis of identification of the opposing groups is extremely shaky, since all parties are employees and many persons conventionally identified with management—for example, professionals, technicians, and salesmen—do not in fact manage anyone except, from time to time, themselves.

The circumstances differ if we look at the other side, but not the conclusion. Workers have at least four reasonable bases of loyalty and identification and therefore of division from other, competing interests.

Workers do, in fact, have a stake in the employer's success, not only for security of employment but possibly for higher wages. This supports the views ardently advocated by such spokesmen for business as the National Association of Manufacturers. This interest, however, is valid only for those workers who genuinely benefit, and not, for example, those who lose their jobs or their skill ratings as a result of technical change.

Workers even have some basis of identification with an entire industry, as when they seek to retain or expand its position in the national economy. American automobile workers do not like the competition of foreign cars any more than do their employers, carpenters dislike the shift to glass and aluminum in construction as do lumber companies, and coal miners regret the shift to oil as do the owners of mines.

Workers share many interests with others in the same occupation. They are likely to have similar backgrounds in education and experience, common income and relative status, and similar career expectations. They especially share an interest in maintaining and if possible improving whatever advantages in wage differentials they have. The degree of occupational identification is likely to increase with skill levels because the bases of like interest are correspondingly heightened.

Finally, workers may have a common "status" identification, and this is the principal basis for the organization of industrial unions. But the criteria of status are, we have seen, exceptionally difficult to define. And such a basis for identification dispels none of the others. Most particularly, it does not get rid of differentiated occupational identification, a problem that is a major source of internal conflict and consequent fragile solidarity of the industrial union.

None of these four sources of identity corresponds at all neatly with the distinction between "management" and "labor." The first two operate independently of relative rank, the third divides up ranks "horizontally," and the last could operate at any rank. One can conclude that the supposed solidarity of labor is also spurious or irrational.

My personal belief is that the power of industrial unions is on the wane, because two trends are running in the same direction. The one trend is the technological displacement of the semi-skilled workers who, with his low occupational identification, was the mainstay of the industrial union. This displacement not only reduces the unions' numerical strength but shifts the skill distribution upward to include a higher proportion of skilled and technically-trained workers. The second and correlative trend is the resurgence of occupational identification even within the industrial unions as presently constituted.

I do not think that these trends presage greater ease in personnel management or in negotiating labor agreements. On the contrary, I expect a great proliferation of occupationally oriented groups, many of which will call themselves "benevolent and protective associations" or "marching and chowder societies" but will behave almost exactly like unions in pressing their members' common interests. On particular issues such organizations may form temporary coalitions and coordinate their interests and pressures. On other issues the groups may form different coalitions or stand alone. This seems to me simply an extension of the current situation where the national labor confederation is an extremely fragile coalition except on limited issues like some (but not all) national labor legislation.

I do not mean to dismiss status considerations too cavalierly. Status distinctions do exist in the corporation, and they are important. Their very number, however, discourages neat divisions into conflicting groups. The one division that has a considerable coincidence with the conventional distinction between "management" and "labor" is that between managers and the managed. Again, the fit is quite imperfect. Persons may be found at the end of a "chain of command" in positions that are otherwise fairly exalted (assistant legal counsel, laboratory scientists) or at least are at "white collar" levels such as secretaries and computer programmers. It is perhaps the number of echelons separating the originators and ultimate recipients of orders, together with other indicators of relatively low rank, that partially distinguish the customary candidates for union organization. I suggest, however, that it is not status as such that is troublesome, but more precisely the system of authority. I believe it is extremely difficult to establish a system of authority so completely that the people who have "none" concede the justice or equity of their position. Terror, if consistent and durable as in concentration camps, may in fact lead the victims to "identify with" their tormenters. Any other, more lenient system is likely to exhibit signs of discontent among the powerless. This, however, is more apt to lead to grumbling compliance than to revolt unless the sense of inequitable power is linked with other perceptions of "relative deprivation" such as wages and conditions of work. But that, surely, is a long way from the class struggle in which so many neo-Marxist managers seem ardently to believe.

Doers and Thinkers

A division that rests on more reliable foundations than that between management and workers is that between "line" and "staff" positions. Although this distinction may also become blurred, as when managers are themselves highly differentiated by function, it operates with very high reliability.

The essential, pragmatic basis of the distinction is between those whose primary responsibility is to coordinate and supervise the work of others and those whose primary responsibility is to supply information and advice. Since the functions are complementary, the basis of conflict does not readily reveal itself from the job descriptions. A partial key is provided by the distinction between the authority of delegated power and the authority of specialized knowledge. The distinctions run both wider and deeper, however.

The way in which line and staff officers lay claim to competence tends to be different. The staff man will ordinarily have achieved his major training by formal, advanced, and specialized education prior to appointment. The line man, and particularly if he is of the newer breed of "professional" managers, may have a somewhat comparable claim, but much of his competence is likely to be based on experience with the company or another like it. The higher his position and prestige, the larger the part that is to be credited to experience. The staff man, on the other hand, acquires his initial recognition from outside the organization, and pretty much continues to do so if he is successful. His administrative superiors, being laymen or ex-professionals becoming laymen as they gradually lose their professional standing, are simply not competent to judge him on technical grounds. For that, only his technical peers, wherever they are employed, can be relied on. If one wants to be a little Freudian, the manager's "father figure" is likely to be his boss or the company president, whereas the technician seeks to emulate an older successful colleague or some college professor back at his school.

The staff man's relative immunity from direct responsibility for the "main show"—production and profits—is accentuated by his lack of identification with his administrative superiors or with managers in general. His loyalties tend to flow outward, not upward, to peers and not to superiors. This can only heighten the line manager's unease or antipathy for the "thinker," the "egghead," the impractical and irresponsible dreamer or misguided adviser. To questions of competence and worth are added questions of loyalty. The low suspicion on the part of the manager that a technical or professional colleague is "disloyal" may be very well founded, for the professional is likely to have more in common with his counterpart in another company or on some college campus than with his non-professional associates. The line man's identification with the hard realities of profit-making, while the technical specialist performs duties difficult to justify in strictly instrumental terms, heightens the "doer's" conviction that the "thinker" is biting the hand that feeds him.

Attempts to reduce the line-staff friction by job transfers are generally impractical, because highly trained skills are unlikely to be acquired quickly by the amateur, and the professional may be a fairly poor manager who will lose or interrupt the real basis for his presumed value to the employer. It is true that continued tenure by the staff man tends to lead to increasing identification with the company and just possibly to decreased mutual misunderstandings with the administrative mind. But I am inclined to think this is more likely in small organizations than in large ones and with moderately rather than highly prestigeful staff people. The higher the professional's rank among his peers, and this is most likely in the large company that can afford him, the less likely he is to become "socialized" or "assimilated" into the main stream of management belief and behavior.

The most rapidly expanding occupational category in modern industry is precisely the non-managerial component of "management" and particularly researchers and "relations experts" of all varieties. This has meant not only a kind of relative "downgrading" of junior and middle managers but also, in many instances, a reduction of specific managerial job scope by assignment of tasks to specialists. A manager may be unable to set job specifications for subordinates, hire them, or fire them. That is the function of the personnel department. He cannot rearrange his budget without approval of the accounting department. He cannot change a production process without consulting with the engineering development boys. And his proposed speech to the local Rotary Club will have to be rewritten for both "corporate image" and style by the word merchants in public relations and possibly cleared with corporation counsel—by which time it is too late.

I do not mean to imply that staff officers always make common cause, since every man is a layman outside his own field. Various staff units may contend with and harass one another. But with respect to relations with "pig-headed administrators" the information-suppliers have much in common. I find the line-staff division the single most reliable one in any administrative organization— it exists in government, armies, and hospitals, and to an extreme degree in universities. The generalists may still exercise final power over the specialists, but they do so with a shaky hand.

X

PRIVATE SOCIALISM

W HEREIN *corporate collectivism is seen as
an attempt to keep the peace by appeals to company
patriotism, while the rich support the poor and welfare
services are provided for all.*

T H E modern corporation is a profit-making organization. Its aims in life include making money for itself and its investors. The wry humor of the wall sign, "This is a non-profit organization; we didn't intend it that way, it just happened" is a kind of thin joke that cannot remain eternally funny. Profits mean not only economic survival, but in a crude way they are taken as a measure of success in a competitive economy. Yet the contemporary corporation often uses gross profits in curious ways. As public bene-factors they make various contributions to public welfare, like the "good citizens" they attempt to be. And within the organization, their budgetary behavior does not exactly coincide with the hard-headed calculation attributed to the canny producer or trader pic-tured in textbooks in economics.

I think the internal economics of the contemporary corporation cannot be understood without reference to the management's rela-tive freedom from detailed accountability to the "owners," that is, investors in corporate equity stocks. A "hired" manager representing an owner alive to his financial interests would scarcely behave in the way that the semi-independent "trustees" of pooled wealth do in fact behave. The trustees, though perhaps as conscientious as their more strictly accountable counterparts in business management, are clearly sensitive to additional interests, including their own.

The freedom of corporate managers is only relative. Power without responsibility is always unstable. It is more accurate to view the responsible executives as operating within a sphere of autonomous decision-making but limited beyond that sphere by counter-pressures or actual veto powers. Limits are set by competitors and customers, by administrative agencies and courts, and notably by suppliers of materials and components, by suppliers of labor, organized or not, and by suppliers of capital, including financial institutions and stockholders. Extreme mismanagement is likely to be met with effective vetoes, exercised in ways appropriate to the interests affected. Competitors may capture markets, and customers may buy other brands. Civil and criminal actions may be instituted by public authorities. Suppliers may sell to higher bidders. Workers may quit, strike, or conscientiously withhold efficiency, that is, operate within the tolerable range of sabotage. Financial institutions may refuse loans, and stockholders may sell shares in such numbers as to depress the market price with adverse effects on new stock flotations. In extreme instances they may exercise their reserve rights and through a proxy battle "throw the rascals out." It seems safe to predict that even the American Telephone and Telegraph Company, the model of independent management, would not dare pass its quarterly dividends for more than a few quarters.

It is, however, because of the autonomous sphere of corporate action that giant corporations depart from traditional theories of business organizations and market behavior in a number of ways, all of which challenge our conception of corporate conduct. Two areas of relative independence provide the basis for some features of internal corporate organization that I plan to examine here.

These two elements of freedom are the capacity to withhold earnings and the protection against many of the rigors of extreme competition because of a firm position in the market.

Earnings are withheld nominally to expand the enterprise, with presumably future benefits to the stockholders who are thus caught in a situation of "forced savings." Since the saving decision is made for them, by their betters, they can only hope that the investments will indeed have future values at least equal to the present value of the dividends that were not declared. If all investors could be counted on to reinvest all or a major part of their earnings instead of indulging themselves in frivolous consumption expenditures, corporate executives would not need to exercise their discretionary power to make these decisions "for the investor's own good."

This tender protection of the ordinary individual from his own foolishness has strong overtones of a kind of "managed economy." The rate of investment becomes a predominantly centralized decision, not one trusted to the haphazard whims of individuals. "People's capitalism" this may be, but some people are clearly more equal than others in determining the individual's economic welfare.

The disposition of declared earnings is somewhat challenging to traditional notions. The financial behavior of corporations becomes even more interesting, however, if one looks not at official earnings but at various "costs" of operation that scarcely meet the common criteria of essential expenses. Management's relative independence from detailed scrutiny by the financially interested parties, the "owners," permits some rather frilly luxuries. These include not only the elements of gracious living accorded to the captains of industry and petty officers too but also some welfare practices within the organization. Like the chauffeur-driven Rolls Royce, these internal indulgences show up in the financial reports as part of operating costs.

Some features of the internal economics and politics of corporate organization invite the metaphor of "private socialism," or, perhaps more exactly, the "welfare state." Analogies are always hazardous, and these will not be pursued rigorously. They may, however, give us an initial stance from which to survey phenomena otherwise neglected or hidden from view.

Three internal policies that justify the metaphor are the protection of the weak by the strong, a system of benevolent taxation, and the cultivation of collectivism.

Protection of the Weak

Most large corporations have numerous products and even whole divisions that operate at a loss. This is most understandable in conventional terms if the product is new or the company has entered an unfamiliar market. Risk-taking is an honorable element in business competition. Development costs may be very high, and the time to recover the investment may be very long, or, risks being what they are, the costs may never be recovered. As a practical matter, however, corporations that invest heavily in research and development do not and probably could not allocate costs of development retroactively, or repay those costs out of profits in any precise budgetary fashion. Research units normally do not operate on a cost-accounting or profit-and-loss basis. Rather, research investments tend to be viewed from an averaging point of view, often intermixed with considerable irrational faith. The long-term future when research investments are expected to pay off may in fact never arrive.

The more challenging situations, however, are those in which losses persist, but the company does not withdraw from the market. Here several types of rationale are developed, representing varying mixtures of reason and rationalization. The doctrine that most closely approximates economic rationality is that of the "full line." This argument runs that the company's salesmen, calling on distributors, dealers, or ultimate customers must be prepared to offer the full range of related products including unprofitable items, or the business will go to the competitor who does, if for no other reason than the unwillingness of the buyer to deal with numerous salesmen, accounts, and company billing procedures. The suspicion of nonrationality arises, however, because there is little or no evidence that the doctrine is put to experimental test.

A second doctrine justifying continued product unprofitability is that of customer responsibility. This usually involves a product of long standing which the company may have pioneered, and now feels in some sense obliged to continue even though its competitive position would dictate abandonment to competitors. A small company grown large may cling to its original field of operation out of almost unadulterated nostalgic sentiment. And although customer loyalty and distinct company clienteles must be reckoned with, the reckoning may be blithe assumption rather than inquiry or experiment.

Incidentally, giant corporations often seem not to understand that there are many markets for which they are too large, because of overhead costs if nothing else, and will continue to produce goods once appropriate but no longer profitable. Producers of chemicals, which have highly unstable and even volatile product mixes, seem to be best able to get into and out of markets. Manufacturers of "hard goods" and especially machine tools and other capital equipment seem to have an extremely limited capacity to understand the penalties of bigness. They tend to continue producing machines for a limited market and show a "paper profit" by carefully avoiding the allocation of the true overhead or administrative costs that only a mass market can support. Or they pursue a more forthright, because less self-deluding, decision to support the effort as a worthwhile charity for loyal customers.

A third doctrine is an optimistic one. It runs that the present is bleak but that the future will be brighter for various vague and often unspecified reasons. One consequence of this belief requires special notice. This is the fixing of blame for loss on current operating management. Once such a diagnosis is made, the obvious therapy is to bring in a new manager, preferably one with an outstanding profit record in another division. If the diagnosis is in fact incorrect, a whole succession of managers may have promising careers ruined while the company continues to lose money and the division develops the reputation of an East Siberian labor camp for political prisoners. For the others in the product division, this policy provides protection against the cruel consequences of competitive failure.

The significant point is that these doctrines may be believed even though they lack objective justification. It must also be borne in mind that a decision to drop a product or product line is likely to require costs in executive time that may motivationally offset the possible saving of other people's money. Executives face so many problems, they cannot take every rational action that might reasonably be expected. Some things must be permitted to drift along. Add the genuine human concern for displaced personnel at all levels, and the sufferance of loss becomes more understandable. It seems, indeed, justifiable to conclude that the policies add up to an internal welfare system, whereby the rich (that is, profitable undertakings) support the poor (that is, unprofitable ones).

Benevolent Taxation

We turn now to a second aspect of the corporation as a welfare state, "benevolent taxation." Some features of corporate organization and conduct need to be noted in order to comprehend this concept. In a large multi-product company many divisions and their managers have "profit responsibility," that is, they have costs of operation but they also are expected to produce income. Other divisions and their managers, including a great variety of "public" (that is, company-wide) services, have only expenses. They must be supported, and this is accomplished by assessments on the income-producing units, with consideration of ability to pay. In other words, part of the flow of funds within the corporation operates on principles of taxation and appropriation rather than on market principles. Just as the citizen does not buy governmental services, however much he may pay for them through taxes, the divisional product manager does not normally buy public relations or marketing advice. He may not even want the services or advice his division's profits help to support.

Goods normally move between divisions of a corporation according to market principles, and indeed divisional managers often have the option of buying from other producers. The same is not generally true of services. Even advertising costs are likely to be partially borne by internal taxation rather than by direct outlays by product divisions. This is particularly probable if the advertising contains a considerable quotient of "institutional" messages, that is, on behalf of the company as such.

I once asked a considerable group of corporate managers, all of them identified with real products and therefore with profits, what proportion of the company staff services would survive if these functions were forced to rely on an internal market demand for their wares. The estimates split between 10 per cent and 20 per cent. These figures should not be taken seriously, as I was willfully appealing to the anti-intellectual sentiments of the "real producers" and thus once more confirming the predictability of human behavior. Yet the exaggeration was not a contradiction of the essential point, which is that these services are provided by the governors on behalf of the governed. But the latter do not always welcome the beneficence, which, they feel, they pay for. They pay, of course, out of the divisional pocket and not out of their own. But since a good profit record is taken as a mark of excellence, and good profits tend to give a division a measure of autonomy as well as more prestige, uncontrolled costs can be as worrisome to the division as taxes are to the private individual. Under these circumstances, taxes or assessments *after* profits are computed are more tolerable than those which appear as assigned costs of operation over which the manager has no control. Over the former the divisional manager will raise perfunctory questions about budgetary priorities and possible waste. Over the latter, the costs that reduce the paper profits, he will fight bitterly, if usually vainly.

The rapid expansion of staff services, a contemporary phenomenon in the large corporation, has resulted from decisions at executive level rather than from any internal market demand. This expansion is commonly resented by managers with profit responsibility. Whether this expansion is economically justifiable from the point of view of the corporation as a unit in its relations with outside interests is extremely difficult to determine. The very absence of profit accountability means that demonstration of contribution to the corporation's goals is difficult or impossible. The point of present interest is that from the standpoint of internal operations the corporation here once more resembles the welfare state.

Conflict and Collectivism

I suggest that corporate conduct also provides analogies to nationalism and patriotism and even to some of the milder forms of collectivism. Although the pressure for conformity of belief and behavior within the corporation has been exaggerated by recent critics, such as Whyte in *The Organization Man*, there is ample evidence of deliberate cultivation of fairly pure collectivism. This becomes not only understandable but also loses some of its nasty overtones if we recall some of the organizational problems in large corporations.

Corporate citizens comprise a myriad of specific jobs and occupations. They are often widely scattered and only in indirect and formal contact and communication. Personal competition for placement and advancement is an established norm for many jobholders. Loyalties to functional units, to common status, and to particular occupations unite groups and divide the whole. Status and occupational loyalties commonly transcend corporate boundaries and extend to brethren in various enemy camps. Representatives of the corporation in its dealings with its significant "publics" must also perforce represent those publics within corporate councils, giving rise to conflict of expert testimony and suspicions of disloyalty. Diverse claims upon the collective resources require strategy, tactics, and ultimate adjudication. Budget hearings are scarcely occasions for comaraderie or altrustic sacrifice. Engineers, manufacturers, and marketers vie for identification as being of superordinate importance to the company's position in the market. Jurisdictional disputes abound at the frontiers of satrapies and small empires. In short, the organization is rife with divisive forces.

What holds the organization together besides the bribery of employment? Perhaps, for many, no other answer is needed, but corporate behavior indicates the felt need for collective goals and collective identification. This is promoted in many ways, ranging from the sublimity of uplifting messages to the ridiculousness of tribal festivals.

The rhetoric of corporate collectivism is instructive. The two human groups most commonly used as representative of the ideal of corporate behavior are the team and the family, neither one of which the corporation strongly resembles. Both, however, represent standards of interpersonal loyalty and even affection and an identification with the welfare of the group as a whole. Both require a considerable subordination of the individual to group interests. And both imply considerable equality within a framework of able and benevolent leadership. The mandatory use of first names among strangers, not to mention enemies, represents a degree of informal togetherness that not even ideologists of collectivist states have yet seen fit to emulate. It is perhaps the equivalent of "citizen" in Revolutionary France, or "comrade" in Revolutionary Russia.

Most corporations have not proceeded as far in cultivating collective group-think as Orwell portrays in his critical novel 1984. But some have come pretty close. I have in my possession an "I.B.M. Song Book," and, copyright laws being what they are, I can only report that the lyrics are downright revolting. They are designed not only to "build the group spirit" but to laud the wisdom of IBM's version of Big Brother, the founder, Thomas J.

Watson. Now that's a name difficult to work into a verse, and the recognized technical genius of IBM's engineers was not quite equal to the lyrical task. But the spirit is there.

Corporations do not rely on rhetoric alone to instill loyalty and collective identification. The discipline of "thought control" on matters of political and social policy is difficult to appraise but no doubt operates with some effectiveness, perhaps more in public (that is, with outsiders) than in private (that is, in the "family"). The goal of minimizing differences in rank and function is also abetted by company "management" courses with a clientele drawn cross-sectionally from the far-flung empire of management as well as by various recreational "mixers" ranging from Christmas parties through picnics to summer camps.

At a recent Princeton University Conference on "The Individual in a Corporate Society," Crawford Greenwalt, President of the DuPont company, was a principal speaker. He took pointed exception to the original published version of this chapter on grounds that universities, too, indulge in collective madness. In my reply I readily agreed but pointed out that a charge of insanity is not quite defeated by the response, "You're another." If the response is correct, it only makes the original allegation of odd conduct faintly less exceptional. I must also note that most of the wilder tribal rituals in universities are indulged in by the undergraduates, not by grown men. In the corporation, men are encouraged to be boys far beyond their time.

The corporation is not a state, but it sometimes behaves like one, both because it has some powers of autonomous action, and because its leaders take their responsibilities seriously. Its welfare activities for its citizens of all conditions are of course more extensive than those I have noted here. Many of these activities come under the heading of "personnel policies," from the physical amenities at the work place to the provision of "public" recreational facilities and private psychotherapy. The same immunity from precise economic accountability that permits concern for corporate welfare also permits some solicitude for the individual and his family.

It is of course easy to be cynical. The scorner's seat is the most comfortable resting place ever invented. My intentions, however, have been moderately honorable. By adopting a somewhat unorthodox approach I have attempted to explore some distinctly unorthodox behavior.

Part Four

CHARACTERS

X I

THE ORGANIZED INDIVIDUAL

*WHEREIN the inconsistency between
individual and corporate goals is related to questions
of why people work, and evil persons and practices are
regarded with mixed fear and hope.*

THE denizens of the large corporation have been widely portrayed as in a quite pathological state. They are, in fact, depicted as nearly comatose. Yet they appear to stir from their lethargy and display a fatal fascination with their own dissection. The picture, of course, is overdrawn to the point of caricature. The gray-flannel mind can indeed be found, and its owner's quest for conformity will keep the solitary crease in good order. They are a dull lot, the organization men, but not totally without interest or without their small hopes and fears, their tiny successes and failures. And it is easy enough to demonstrate that their organized apathy is quite unequal, and that they exist in an environment providing remarkable variety in the human fauna. The flora, too, are exotic, but those are mostly artificial status symbols and with those we are not, at the moment, concerned.

Bribed Cooperation

The relation between any individual and any group is at least a little uncertain. This is true even of the infant as he begins to develop a personality with "membership" in only one group, his family. Infants do not come with absolutely standard emotional and mental equipment, and in the complex interaction between infants and adults and older children, some friction, dissidence, and unpredictable outcomes must be expected. The situation is greatly complicated where the individual has multiple and often competing memberships and must exercise some effort if he is to preserve any integral identity, any cohesive life organization in the face of the pull-hauling of claims on his time, his energy, his basic loyalties.

The basic nexus between the member of a business concern and the corporate entity itself is the fact of employment. This relationship precedes all others, and all others are conditional on it for as long as the membership endures. Whatever else the member is doing there, he is basically earning a living or at least gaining an income. He normally achieves this desirable objective by performing tasks, by doing his duty. Whether he likes or dislikes his job may affect his performance, or it may not. Whether he likes or dislikes his associates, superiors, or the company as a whole is similarly of dubious relevance. Whether he cares about the organization, except that it survive and provide him with employment, may have no consequence at all.

If the organization were perfectly planned, perfectly secure in a benign environment, and perfectly staffed in terms of competent performers, the only link necessary between the individual and the organization would be whatever bribes the employer has to offer that are adequate to elicit the necessary performance. Cooperation would then be purely "structural," not motivational, a by-product of self-interest, not a shared and collective goal. For some workers at virtually all organizational levels this minimum affiliation is very nearly a true representation of the extent of their involvement. The proportions of persons whose cooperation is "bribed" is certainly higher than the proportions whose efforts are wholly selfless, dedicated to the common interest without thought of reward.

The bribes that corporations have to offer are numerous, but they invariably include money. The wage or salary is the way in which the specialized producer is permitted to become a generalized consumer. Workers generally constitute a small part of the consumers for goods they themselves produce; in capital goods production they have no use for the stuff at all. In an industrial society, there is no effective substitute for money as the link between production and consumption.

It is true that man does not live by bread alone; it is also true that money does not buy bread alone but a growing range of goods and services that "move through the market." The adult in our society who is not interested in money is probably certifiably insane.

Now it is equally true that employers offer and employees expect a great variety of "non-financial incentives." Some of these are simply deferred payments, like insurance and pension schemes, and others, such as security of employment, are simply assurance that the financial incentives will persist. Still others, such as safety measures or the comforts and amenities at the work place, have a price tag for the employer but not for the employee.

I do not mean to degrade the numerous studies that indicate that workers (including managers) are also interested in prestige and esteem, the approval of their peers and pleasant working relations with them, reasonable standards and fair treatment, a community fit to bring up their children in, and indeed a great variety of interests associated with the work place or the fact of employment. I do mean that these other interests and incentives are not substitutes for "adequate" financial rewards. Within narrow limits, the employee may accept less money for a pleasanter job. He is either independently wealthy or plainly mad if he accepts no money for a pleasant job. If the non-financial characteristics of the job are viewed negatively by the employee or prospective worker, then financial rewards may overcome his distaste. This substitution too has its limits.

I think that it is this last point, the cost but limited effectiveness of purely financial incentives, that has led to the substantial distortion of the true situation in the thinking of many managers when the motives of hourly rated workers are up for consideration. The notion that workers can be bought off by kind words and attention to their irrationalities may be comforting to both the budget and the ego of managers, but the comfort is likely to be short-lived as experience demonstrates that the notion is false.

The true situation is complex but understandable. Below some "minimum" level, which of course varies by occupational level and tends to increase through time, the employee is likely to hold financial rewards as paramount and nearly exclusive. He cannot afford to be interested in, and indeed is likely to feel exploited by, "human relations" tricks. "Psychic income" buys no groceries at the supermarket. Beyond a minimum level of expectations, other, non-financial interests may loom larger in the worker's scheme of things. If forced to choose from among alternative job opportunities, he may even choose one paying a little less but offering other advantages. But the idea that this behavior represents a lack of interest in money is either stupid or willfully perverse. The worker would also clearly like to have more money.

Several years ago a leading commercial polling organization reported to its business clients on a study of production workers' attitudes. Of the various possible interests that workers valued in jobs, the pollsters reported, wages were seventh in importance. This "scientific" evidence, comforting to managerial wage negotiators dealing with unions, represented a deception that may have been deliberate. The question asked the sample of workers was, "What do you like best about your present job?" As a fair proportion of the workers were apparently dissatisfied with their wages, these did not do well in the popularity poll.

Managers who accept the notion that workers are not "primarily" interested in money are not notably self-sacrificing in appraising their own monetary value to the enterprise. Yet if one had to guess about the relative importance of financial incentives among workers and various categories of managers, one would guess that they are of greater importance to those who get less, the workers. And since the ordinary conditions of work also favor managers, non-managerial employees may show an especially sharp interest in the absolute size of the paycheck.

I am not here commenting on the equity of pay scales, but only on the nature of the individual employee's incentives for doing his job. All employees are bribed, at least with money, and some are also lured by additional homely pleasures. There is no reason to suppose that any category of workers, at least in industrial employment, is exceptionally irrational or benevolent in offering their services for pay. If several motives run in the same direction the individual avoids awkward choices among them, and the chance that the bribes are effective is greatly increased.

Commitment and Identification

My emphasis on bribes represents a deliberate attempt at bluntness about money matters and other motives. Yet bluntness may also distort and exaggerate, as when a spade is no longer a spade but a "bloody shovel." Most corporate employees exhibit more than a narrow self-interest in their jobs and their employer, an identification with persons and programs outside themselves, a sense of collective cooperation beyond their individual duties. The ways whereby contrived cooperation becomes conscientious reveal some further aspects of the relations between individuals and organizations.

Psychologists and sociologists interested in the way in which infants as untutored savages become more or less civilized adults refer to this transformation as the "socialization process." Socialization here has no reference to socialism or the confiscation of private property but rather to the formation of personality. The socialized individual learns a vast array of things from manual skills to expectations of others. He also "internalizes" values and codes of conduct and behaves in accordance with conscience and not solely in terms of external rewards and penalties. He knows and believes, perceives and feels, thinks and emotes. All of this happens in the context of interacting with others, complying with expectations of those who matter but finally including oneself as one who matters.

Most of the attention given to the socialization process has centered on infants and children, the progress from infancy to adulthood. Yet in the modern world the significance of adulthood is neither simple nor steady. The various adult roles cannot be entirely preconditioned in childhood. Some roles, such as rearing a family or earning a living, involve movement and progress. They do not remain stationary. If the individual is to behave properly in these roles, without continuous supervision and admonition, he must be socialized. The greater his mobility in roles or the greater the dynamic element in nominally "the same" position, the greater is the learning and character change required of him.

It is this process of adult socialization that figures largely in the work experience of the corporate employee or, for that matter, most breadwinners. He must learn the gross and subtle information and skills necessary to do his job and, to a degree, the attitudes appropriate to his function and position. The worker who passes both tests may be said to be *committed*. Bribed he may continue to be, but not exclusively so. He also will have performance standards and expectations, binding on himself and attributed to others in similar positions.

Expectations are important, however. When they are mutually shared by persons in comparable positions, the individual's own standards are externally reinforced. The workman's morale is likely to be eroded if the external reinforcement is only in the form of bribes and discipline but not the approval of significant others. Significant others may include superiors as well as peers, but only if our man "identifies" with them or seeks to emulate their success. Otherwise, all he will seek from superiors is fulfillment of his objective expectations, his terms and conditions of work, but not his subjective ones, the codes of behavior and standards of competence that can only be judged by those who share them.

The committed employee is also likely to be convinced of the importance of his own job for the accomplishment of the mission of his unit or of the whole concern. If this conviction gets no external confirmation at the work place—"no one appreciates me down there"—the individual's identification with the employer will certainly not persist. A feeling of futility pushes the participant back to a pure form of accepting bribes and wanting them to be high enough to offset his general dissatisfaction with his job. There is no guarantee of course that the individual's sense of his own importance is not neurotic, that is, out of touch with objective reality. One function of seeking out other jobs is, if successful, to restore the individual's self-confidence and incidentally to improve his bargaining position in extracting recognition from his employer if he remains.

There is very extensive evidence, from all sorts and circumstances of social life, that participation in decisions that affect the individual's life increases his involvement with the system as such. The man who helps make things happen rather than simply has them happen to him is better prepared to accept even some of the negative consequences. Some would argue that this is too little understood by those ultimately responsible for organizational policies, with the result that employees remain aloof and uninvolved. Others would argue that it is understood far too well, with the result that employees become captives of the employer, trapped by their participation in small matters and unable to question large issues.

For those concerned with large issues, on whom major responsibility rests for organizational success, the entrapment may be fairly complete even if self-imposed. If one can believe the testimony of biographers and the writers of magazine "profiles," the company becomes a sort of alter ego of the executive, with a corresponding reduction or distortion of other elements of normal human existence. Unable to divest himself of his official role, he "lives with" his job constantly. This is the ultimate in commitment and identification, the submersion of the individual in the organization sea. There is some doubt that this ultimate stage of organization is necessary. There is no doubt at all that it is abnormal in the statistical sense and probably in the psychological sense as well.

Conditional Love

Organizations and individuals initially face one another in a situaction that reeks with uncertainty. Each may establish and mantain the relationship on a very tenuous basis, enduring it only so long as it meets the convenience of both parties. Or they may actually join in close, if chaste, embrace. Critics would even question the chastity of some relationships, for they feel that the individual loses his virtue without equivalent moral recompense.

Whyte's concern in *The Organization Man* is that the managerial employee is being smothered with kindness, to the destruction of both his individuality at work and his independence off the job. With income, amenities, and security, Whyte argues, the corporation encourages a kind of group conformity and a state of dependency.

I find it extremely doubtful that the quest for either security or conformity is any more prevalent now than in the past. It may, however, be more extensively realized in the large corporation. If the individual cannot gain either a sense of identity or a satisfactory sense of emotional security with individual components of the "faceless mass," he may lose himself in the mass itself and gain a sense of belonging by simply being common. There is no doubt that a number of pressures run in this direction, and particularly for the junior manager whose hopes and aspirations may be closely linked with the employer rather than with his colleagues or friends.

The man who "loves that company" or "loves that man" (his superior or someone above him) may find himself in the situation of the swain who goes a-courting and finds, despite his ardent pleas, that his love is unrequited. Security is likely to set in objectively only after several years of service and may never set in emotionally.

Uncertainty and anxiety are widely used as incentives. They may be generally effective in inducing a constrained conformity. In fact, for the immature they may induce a kind of pathetic dependence where the exceptional kind word or friendly gesture is given an exaggerated importance. ("He spoke to me today." "What did he say?" "He said, 'Get on with it Jones,' but his tone was friendly.") The evidence from psychology indicates that the child or man who has no emotional security and therefore slight basis for knowing where he stands on things is a poor risk in an uncertain situation or in one that provides moral dilemmas. He may be eager to please but end up doing the wrong thing or pleasing the wrong people.

Conditional love is generally what the corporation provides. Evidences of affection are tendered by the organization, not for the person as such, but for his obedient and compliant action. The source of excessive conformity, I am saying, is not a mutual relationship of stultifying affection, but a one-sided one. It is only in foolish novels that a marriage based on love by one party and convenience for the other ends up in deep mutual affection. The more probable outcome is a growing bitterness on the part of the "dependent" partner, and contempt on the part of the other. I do not doubt that "organization men" exist, but I do doubt that they can endure their futile search for affection, or *that the corporation can endure their unwanted, or rather, their welcome-but-excessive expressions of fealty.* Unstinting adulation palls and can only lead to increased coolness in the treatment of the craven captive, which may in turn increase his efforts to please. In the long term, the unacceptable admirer is a damned bore.

Endemic Pathologies

All administrative organizations are beset with various human frailties that cause chronic disorders in the ideal organizational structures. Some of these disorders are in fact common to most organizations, as they arise from the lack of an exact correspondence between collective and individual interests, the uncertain commitment of members to cooperative endeavors. Other pathological states are either peculiar to complex work organizations or flourish there to an unusually marked degree. This is why I have called them "endemic," like fungus infections in tropical areas.

FAVORITISM: "He's well meaning, and besides he's the boss's first cousin once removed." Nepotic practices in selection and promotion are probably less common in large corporations than in small ones, where the issue of competence may get intermixed with strong family financial control. But if kinship ties lose their strength in large organizations, perhaps because of explicit negative rules, other forms of social bonds do not. To reward one's friends and punish one's enemies is a common enough rule of conduct to persist even though it conflicts with the rule of competence. Naturally, favoritism flourishes most vigorously in filling positions that are fairly unexposed, that is, where neither personal qualifications nor the value of the performance can be specified easily. For example, "assistant managers" may be line officers and heirs apparent to higher office, but "assistants *to* the manager" have more ambiguous duties. Such positions indeed may represent part of the rather modest patronage that newcomers to the seats of power are accorded.

LETHARGY, SABOTAGE: "Don't sweat it." This crude advice from the vernacular is part of the arsenal of informal control devices used to discourage taking the demands of the job too seriously. Lethargic performance by the individual may arise from his own sense of futility and lack of recognition or from a properly sensitive response to the dampening pressure of his colleagues. Since every position is likely to entail a range of acceptable performance, "getting by" may be more common than pressing the upper limits. Sabotage, in its strict and original meaning of treading with wooden shoes or, in Veblen's language, the "conscientious withdrawal of efficiency," may actually take more effort than conscientious performance. Yet to the disgruntled employee anxious to fight the system, the trouble may be worthwhile. The tactics of delay and evasion may be as effectively disruptive as the flurry of apparently well-meaning errors. The handbook for organizational saboteurs has yet to be written, but one chapter would surely be devoted to the techniques of appearing to be very busy while actually doing nothing constructive at all.

CORRUPTION: "What's in it for me?" The substitution of individual for organizational interests is an omnipresent possibility in view of the "bribed" character of much organizational cooperation. Embezzlement is a crime available only to those entrusted with other people's money, but the requirements shade off into padded expense accounts, the conduct of personal business on company time, "liberating" office supplies or shop tools and materials, the use of company cars for week-end travel. Persons with the highest standards of personal honesty in their dealings with real people may have no hesitation in converting the property of that legal person, the corporation, to their own use. Notions of proprietorship through customary use may supersede the strictly legal rights of ownership. The man who would not dream of stealing a garden tool from a stranger may simply appropriate an office typewriter for his wife's personal correspondence. The attitude toward corporate property appears to have much in common with that toward public property. Belonging to "everyone," it may in effect be appropriated by those to whose custody it is assigned.

TECHNICISM: "There's no reason; it's just policy." The principal fault that gives "bureaucracy" a bad name is the ritualistic compliance with rules and procedures without realistic reference to the goals to be accomplished or problems to be solved. "Red tape," once thought peculiar to governmental agencies, is in fact common to all very large organizations and many small ones. Rules are made to fit "type cases" but cases of the pure type may rarely arise. Safety for the officeholder lies with applying some rule not in rational disposal of the issues. Penalties, for the most part, are prescribed not for failure to achieve organizational ends or even for failing to believe in them but for violation of the procedural rules presumably designed to stipulate the means to be pursued. Those rules may have long since lost their original sense, or may be encumbered with so many modifications and exceptions as to encourage a petti-fogging legalism in interpretation. The "bureaucratic personality" takes comfort in his knowledge of the rules, and indeed this may be his only claim to excellence. If chaos ensues from the rules of law, that is not his problem. He didn't make the rules, but he is intent on seeing that they are followed.

SAINTLINESS: "Now if we all worked a little harder. . . ." Although not commonly understood, saints are more dangerous in organizations than sinners. Rules are made to control evil-doers, and penalties are prescribed for their misbehavior. But how can one punish exceptional virtue? Someone has expressed the view that the historic organizational strength of the Roman Catholic Church is best exemplified not by its adaptability to different times and places and not for its retention of the allegiance of half-hearted members but by its capacity for retaining and generally immunizing its devout extremists. The dedicated man is dangerous, partly because he sets standards that others cannot or will not follow. The saintly conservative who says, "I think we're tending to get a little sloppy," may attempt to achieve progress by going backward and restoring an ideal never officially abandoned but long since disregarded. The "saintly imperialist" who says, "I'll be glad to take on some additional responsibility," not only threatens the comfort of less avid performers but may threaten the security of those who thought they were already discharging the duties in question. The preacher of true virtue may of course only be attempting to get the official ideal modified to conform with practices, but unless that purpose is absolutely clear, his efforts are likely to be viewed with alarm and disruptive hostility.

SURVIVALISM: "Don't break up a good team." Organizations do die, of course, and others are born. Yet keeping an organization going after its original mission has been accomplished or even after clear failure is a common kind of affliction in both public and private affairs. The National Foundation for Infantile Paralysis stayed in business after the discovery of the Salk vaccine, not only to help in rehabilitating polio victims but also to combat a considerable list of other human afflictions. Universities accept funds for setting up research organizations for particular projects. Part of the time and funds available will then be spent on developing proposals for other projects. Corporations set up temporary inter-divisional committees which then aspire to permanent divisional status in their own right. Occasionally survival may be assured by just being inconspicuous. Once a unit has a regular annual budget, it may be able to keep it almost in perpetuity as long as it is willing to curb its ambitions for larger resources. The agency may be dead, but no one may notice if it does not lie down.

Useful Troublemakers

Just as affliction may be good for character in some religious beliefs, so certain nuisances and discordant elements may be good for organizations, if one will just take a broad view of them. What is disadvantageous to individuals or other parts of the organizations may have positive benefits for the encompassing structure.

Several such troublemakers are sufficiently standard to be characterized as types. I shall comment on certain of these.

MEMORY AND CONSCIENCE KEEPERS: Despite my acerb comments at one or two earlier junctures about the preservers of rule and tradition, the problem is clearly one of balance. Standardization of many procedures is clearly more efficient than making them up anew on every occasion requiring action. But the standardized procedure must be known before it can be used. Although "universal" knowledge may be officially presumed, in fact some employees will be more expert than others. The neophyte in particular needs a source of advice, an expert in the law and lore. The degree of expertness is likely to have a high but not perfect correlation with length of service. Some men may, by this test, be old before their time, while others never grow up. The keepers of traditions and custodians of the corporate conscience are likely to be regarded as dusty pedants, and indeed they often are. "Technicism" is their most common ailment, and if they reign unchallenged, "correct" behavior may lead to gradual decay. But continuity is also consequential, particularly in situations where substantial turnover prevails. The newcomer may eventually and in exasperation find ways of circumventing rules and precedents, but he is unlikely to be able to do so unless someone is around who knows what they are.

CONSCIENTIOUS OBJECTORS: It is rather easier for a powerful executive to attract sycophantic subordinates than to discourage them. The "yes man" has become symbolic of the entourage of the mighty. Yet omniscience is accorded to few mortals, even among the successful men in corporate careers. The evidence and points of view appropriate for reasonably sound judgment are unlikely to appear unless doubt and disagreement are permitted and even moderately encouraged. The role of the objector is likely to be a dangerous one precisely because criticism may be asked for more earnestly than it is wanted or accepted when given. A recent magazine cartoon shows a man as a conspicuous minority of one in a raised-hand vote in the executive committee, and subsequently waiting his turn for interview in an employment agency. The "disagreeable fellow" may have a personality to fit the part, which can only add to the annoyance he may provoke. If some of his kind are not installed, no one may dare to say that the king, though majestic, is naked.

COURT JESTERS: "Many a true word is spoken in jest," the adage goes, and this was precisely the function of the jester in the medieval royal courts. Humor, too, is a dangerous weapon, as the point may be as sharp as if it were hurled in anger by a "no man." Humor is commonly distateful to serious-minded men, for it smacks of impiety. Yet I have seen some monstrously foolish corporate programs, which might have been scuttled very early after a little serious attention to objections, end in the disaster they deserved from the rolls of laughter that followed the first impious joke.

CREATORS: The most effective counterbalance to the weighty hand of traditionalists is the innovator. The memory keepers are only troublesome because they impede progress by being virtuous. The creators are troublesome because they attempt to upset habit and custom, to defeat lethargic conformity. It has become increasingly popular for corporations to harbor "idea men," but that says nothing about their popularity in the organization. Intelligence, like humor, is not universally admired, and "bright" can be spoken as a curse as well as an accolade.

SINNERS: Finally, I believe it is useful to note that evil has its place in the grand scheme of things and, paradoxically, may even do good. Laws are not made to be broken but to be kept. But without an occasional lawbreaker to evoke and renew the moral fervor of righteous men, the moral foundations of rules are likely to undergo steady decay. "Punishment," said the French sociologist Emile Durkheim, "is not meant for criminals but for honest men." By this he did not mean the deterrent effect of punishment that instills fear in the hearts of potential miscreants. Rather, he noted that wrongful acts provoke moral indignation on the part of those who obey and support the law. Without the occasion for righteous anger, the rules may lose their moral basis.

I do not mean to advocate mischief, because I do not think it necessary. All I am suggesting is that the occasional act of "disorganization" can have a salutary effect on the collective conscience. Like most other useful troublemakers, the wrong-doers are potentially beneficial only if they are kept in a strict minority. They represent the extreme rejection of the suffocating weight of conformity and as such may be accorded a nod of subdued respect.

X I I

CLIMBERS, RIDERS, TREADERS

WHEREIN *the notion that all good
management men aim for the top, dooming most
to frustration, is defeated, and the discussion of corporate
careers distinguishes between those who run
breathlessly and those who sit quietly,
mostly knitting.*

To some of its employees the corporation provides jobs; to
others it provides a succession of jobs constituting a "career." The
notion of a career carries the connotation of success, of growth in
wisdom and power, in rewards and respect. The hourly rated workman rarely has a career in that sense. He may change jobs and employers and improve his position with each change, but not much.
He may be the exception who becomes a foreman, but his further
advance is likely to be rather limited. He may fulfill the old wage-
earner's dream and start his own small business. Whether that
business succeeds, barely survives, or fails, this form of "mobility"
involves too sharp a break to qualify for the usual meaning of
career. Managerial employees and specialists of one sort or another
may have careers that involve the slight progression from A to B, or
they may travel both far and fast.

Far more is known about the social background and occupational histories of leading corporate executives than about their

subordinates or the men who started but did not finish with them. In any statistical sense it is simply not true that there is always room at the top. If everyone in the corporation is aiming for the top, most are doomed to disappointment. Yet enough is known of the corporate environment to dispel some fables and to fill in the outlines of various kinds of careers.

The idea that managers can reasonably expect an orderly progression to higher responsibilities and rewards is clearly correct only for part of them. And for most of those, it is true only within the intersecting limits of personal capacities (or influence or luck) and objective opportunities. There is no reason to suppose that the coincidence of capacities and opportunities is always neat and orderly, that chance plays no part in the outcome, or that mismatches do not occur.

Between the extremes of outstanding success and miserable failure lie many middle courses. In some of these the race is to the swift. In others, the prize is awarded for endurance or for mere persistence in the safe and steady pace. "He also serves, who only stands and waits."

Ladders and Escalators

The graded career consisting of a sequence of promotions through successive stages in the hierarchy of managerial authority is often called a ladder. For many persons in corporations the figure of speech is apt, as promotions do not come about automatically and for all aspirants. The triangular or pyramidal shape of the organization insures some selectivity, and the ideal of selection on the basis of performance normally requires effort. Thus climbing the ladder requires skill but also energy, a destination and a course of action.

Career ladders vary in length, the steps may be unevenly spaced, and the rate of ascent even for the same person may be uneven. Thus the language provides us with a variety of phrases descriptive of career differences. Certain career lines, which are potentially the longer ones, are called the "main line" or the "main stream." Others promise early arrival at a "dead end" or maroon people in some "backwater." The man who has reached a critical juncture in his career may be "bouncing his head against the ceiling," and his head may be less durable than the ceiling. Some individuals by some combination of merit and opportunity may have a "meteoric rise." By a kind of standing high-jump, an occasional contestant may skip several rungs of the ladder altogether. Others, after years of slight progress, may turn out to be "late bloomers." Still others, the "plodders," advance inch by painful inch, until age overtakes them at a fairly low level.

The ladder may be so short that the simile is questionable. First-line supervisors, normally recruited from the ranks of hourly-rated workers, are assured by higher management that they are on the bottom rung of the managerial ladder. This is normally deceitful, for the situation is that the ladder has at most one or two more steps, and often none at all. The foreman has mounted a platform rather than started a long climb.

Several large corporations have made much in their "institutional" advertising of the humble beginnings of their current top executives. Such advertising though certainly not false is certainly misleading. Current top executives started their careers and in fact completed much of their ascent prior to the extreme emphasis on higher education, general and technical, as a virtual prerequisite for a successful managerial career. If the presidents of large corporations started work as lathe operators, stock boys, or shipping clerks, it is quite unlikely that their successors will have started at ground level and virtually certain that their next-but-one successors will not have done so. Most current executives in fact had college educations, and the first company job was a brief "authenticating" apprenticeship.

The educational barrier in fact introduces a sharp discontinuity in types of careers. It is the principal reason for the low ceiling for supervisors. In the absence of precise data my guess is that the realistic horizon for a foreman in a large company stops at the level of assistant plant superintendent in a small plant or "general foreman" in a large one—in other words, two additional steps. Other managerial careers start with college diplomas and company training courses, perhaps followed by further apprenticeship in definitely non-supervisory positions. The man's first strictly managerial assignment, such as sales manager for a small and distant district or assisant production manager for a small unit in a manufacturing plant, is really the bottom step of his ladder. But he got on that ladder somewhere around the third or fourth rung.

This discontinuity in career opportunities is often criticized as signifying a sharp decline in opportunities for "upward mobility." That seems to me a gross distortion. Certainly the number of "managerial" positions has increased faster than the growth of the population or labor force. The "demand" for managers has increased rather than diminished. The supply comes from a different source, but it can scarcely be argued that this represents a radical reduction in social opportunity. The possibility of higher education is still not free, at least in terms of the foregone earnings of youths from poor families if they continue their education. But the whole course of public educational policy has been to increase the opportunities for higher education, not to contract them.

What this means is that mobility between generations is greatly affected by the educational attainments of the young. It also means that a considerable part of "career" mobility actually takes place prior to the individual's entry into the labor force. The sifting and selective process begins in the school and goes on in the office or factory.

It is not even clear that the opportunities for wage workers have decreased in absolute terms. They were never high. Most of the "captains of industry" in the last century came from rather favorable family backgrounds rather than from the laboring poor. The workmen may have had greater opportunity to move into "higher" management in small companies, but the absolute distance traveled may have been no greater than the possible rise in a large company now. It is the length of the ladder that has changed, perhaps more than the probable level that can be reached if one starts at the very bottom.

The competitive effort to fashion a career, each step won with a struggle, is clearly one form of career orientation. The men who are ambitious, who seek success in the new fashion of the administrative career rather than the old fashion of commerce or the individual enterprise, are the *strainers.* These are the men who keep alert, look smart, avoid missteps, and attempt to show up well on assignments or in group policy discussion. They have ideas if requested and otherwise find cogent reasons for supporting the wisdom of the boss's ideas. They learn golf, join the right clubs, think the right thoughts. Their wives are attractive but not brazen, entertain the right people, and suggest that John is brilliant as well as hard-working, a dedicated corporate servant but also a wonderful husband and father.

These strainers are widely depicted as typical of managerial folk. To their competitive aspirations, their "status seeking," are attributed the competitiveness of their children, their conspicuous consumption, their political conservatism, their superficial religious conformity, and their latest struggles with crab grass.

I do not doubt the existence of strainers. Some of them are my neighbors and some of them are my friends. I do think their typicality is questionable. I question it because it seems to me that for many corporate careers the analogy of the ladder is scarcely appropriate. Some moderately successful people in corporations appear to be on escalators. Once they successfully mount the bottom step, it would take positive effort to avoid going to the next level.

To contrast with the strainers I offer the category of *secure mobiles.* Their lines of ascent may not reach to the dizzy heights attainable by some who struggle all the way. They do, however, provide assurance of modest progress not by doing nothing but also not by doing anything exceptional. Many staff positions have low ceilings from where the man starts, but that may be fairly high in the organization. The ceiling constitutes the level beyond which the man ceases to be a technician or professional, an information supplier, and becomes an administrator. That transition may be neither easy nor, to the occupationally committed employee, desirable. Short of that transition, the man may grow in value and rewards and possibly in autonomy of action by doing what he presumably likes to do—his job.

The secure mobiles are not lazy, but neither do they exhibit the anxious insecurity of the strainers. They may be ambitious but generally not for the power and position offered in a line career. They do not spurn money, but as payment for doing what they are doing and not for something else.

Some escalator riders, it is true, aspire to higher positions than can be achieved in their line of ascent. Thus to "upward" (and occasionally "downward") we must add the concept of "diagonal" mobility. The staff man who enters a managerial position has not just moved up but also across. He has entered a functionally different occupation and a different prospective career.

Over the relatively recent past the most common "diagonal" shift has been the transfer from engineering into administration. Many current engineering graduates are frank in their aspirations to start at their profession (generally at a higher initial salary then the liberal arts college graduate can command) but with no intention of making drawings and computing formulas all their lives. Their aim is to enter administration by the side door. My guess is that they are off-phase.

Such scattered evidence as I have been able to get leads me to a kind of "stage theory" of the primary talents sought in the executives of large corporations. Prior to the turn of the century, financial skills were paramount in assembling and organizing the capitalization of giant concerns. Public reaction and particularly "trust-busting" led to a brief ascendancy of lawyers. Financial operations and legal limits became more stablized than technology, and with corporate success heavily dependent on technical change, the engineers had their day—that is just about to end. Their successors appear to be in high degree men concerned with organization as such, although this was a common minimum qualification for the others too. My guess is that the near future belongs to "relations experts," men concerned with the corporation's external environment, as that now seems to present the critical problems.

This kind of evolutionary pattern or any other pronounced shift in the demand for talents may not affect the majority of careers. For some, the changing structure of opportunities may be absolutely crucial. Some engineers may end up being engineers and some feeler of the public pulse may end up being president.

The Rat Race and the Treadmill

Some corporate strainers refer to their work situations as the "rat race," some threaten to get some less demanding job and "live a little," and some in fact do. To the true believers in fighting the good fight, the drop-outs are battle casualties who couldn't stand the gaff and the company is better off without them. (Of course the elimination of competitors does not hurt the career chances of those who remain.) The man who drops out of the rat race may be treated with patronizing sympathy or open contempt. Yet of those who stay, only a few will run the complete maze and reach the cheese. The others are either doomed to frustration or they must find some rationale or rationalization for their positions.

The interplay between aspiration and achievement is an extremely complex one. It is symptomatic of a basic part of American ideology that this problem is nearly always discussed in terms of the handling of frustration. It is assumed that everyone aims for the top of whatever career he enters, and then, if his mental health remains in moderately good repair, he goes through a succession of reality adjustments as objective results fail to match subjective expectations. As a consequence of this ideological bias, almost no attention has been given to the man who has relatively limited expectations (leaving aside his Walter Mitty daydreams) and then succeeds well beyond those expectations (though perhaps still short of those wilder dreams).

For the man who is ambitious but somewhat realistic, expectations and achievements are periodically compared, and the expectations are inflated or deflated accordingly. Since every readjustment involves also an estimate of the future, there are ample opportunities for honest error as well as for neurotic failures in making a reasonable judgment of present reality or future prospects. The man who is "way off the pace" must, as time passes, invent bigger and bigger miracles. The line between this and insanity may become increasingly thin.

There is certainly some unknown incidence of acute frustration among the aspiring men in corporate employment. I think it would be easy to exaggerate the problem by starting from incorrect assumptions. The disparity between aspiration and achievement does not always carry a negative sign, as I just noted. Career choices radically delimit both the nature of the competition and the number of competitors, as the struggle for success is not "a war of each against all." Even the limits of rewards in money, power, or prestige are strongly conditioned by occupational characteristics.

It is particularly the strainers in the main stream, those on the long ladders that lead ultimately to positions carrying very high financial rewards, that raise the issue of frustration. The man who does not aspire to reach the top is unlikely to admit the fact, because he is "expected" to be ambitious. But surely the withdrawal from reality is not so general that most men expect to reach the uppermost ranks. As aspirations approach the quality of being realistic, the disparity between hopes and achievements becomes tolerably narrow.

One major element in limiting aspirations is that the rewards of success are not "free." Particularly in administrative careers, power carries responsibility, unless the organization is grossly unstable. The severity of the burden of responsibility naturally tends to increase with position and power. The time-and-energy demands are likely to grow, and accountability for the actions of others will certainly grow.

In talking with college students aiming for business careers I find them disbelieving that a man might choose to stop his career well short of the highest levels. With the confidence of the young they assume their future willingness to carry any responsibility and instead fix their eyes on the rewards. I think this attitude is partly ideological as well as simply inexperienced. In the American ideological baggage, the man who professes to be satisfied has "given up." He has left the rat race and entered the treadmill, where progress is foredoomed. Contentment is not a permissible goal; in fact, it is downright immoral. The notion that a man likes his job but would not like to replace his superior raises questions as to whether he is suitable for the job he has. I know a successful manager who succeeded too well. He actively dislikes his job, which he got because of his excellent record at the next lower level in a more technical assignment. He was afraid to refuse the appointment because he did not believe he would be permitted to keep the job he liked. He would, he believed, be put out of harm's way in a job even less to his liking than the one he accepted and hates.

Many men are protected against revealing their weakness of character, their dislike for devoting their lives exclusively to their job and for living dangerously. Others apparently enjoy the challenge and the rewards. Out of common human decency, one can hope that these men of a strong will are not far more numerous than the positions that need them.

Tenure and Pasture Lots

Business organizations engage employees under short-term or at most annual contracts. Yet many managers enjoy what amounts to employment security, to what would be called "permanent tenure" in the public civil service and many colleges. After a man has served and progressed in managerial positions for five to seven years, he is quite unlikely to be fired except "for cause." That is, if the "tenured" employee is not guilty of "gross neglect of duty" or "moral turpitude," his employment will remain secure. In business such permanency is not officially recognized, although its factual consequences are. Tenure in the corporation is a kind of common-law marriage, not a ceremonial union.

The two major ways an experienced manager may lose his job, other than for gross misconduct, is by company reorganization that abolishes the position or by being "promoted out of the area of security." Even with company reorganization long-service employees may well be transferred to other operations, so that not many experienced men actually lose their employment. The other case is more interesting. In few organizations do the very top officers have security in their positions. The reason for this is that such officials must take responsibility for failure as well as credit for success. Even though the failure may not be the official's fault in any just sense, a conspicous dismissal may have to be made to satisfy the scalp-hunters.

Where security of employment prevails, the problem of insuring performance arises. The man who is "bucking for a raise" will behave very much like the committed worker. The question is, will he relax to the absolute minimum performance if he is given security? The tests to determine the difference are not wholly reliable, as various snags of "dead wood" in organizations bear witness. Generally, however, sacrificial behavior in crisis situations is a fairly good indicator of personal commitment.

Mistakes are made in any system, providing employment security. Often the problem is an error of omission. The organization may provide no juncture at which permanence is decided. The individual may then "drift into tenure," acquiring security by mere length of service. Corporations, by refusing to recognize that they do in fact give employment security, are more subject to this failing than are organizations that make it official. The lack of official tenure might provide an excuse for dismissal of the long-service but distinctly mediocre employee. Few employers and very few large corporations are so harsh. The large company is especially able to absorb its errors. This is partly a question of financial resources but more a question of organizational resources. Large organizations afford a considerable number of positions with titles more impressive than the functions, of harmless sine-cures, or what I have called "pasture lots." Sometimes the incompetent performer in an important position may keep the title but not the functions, either by quiet reorganization of duties or by the installation of an able "assistant" who really does the work. At times it may be necessary to build new pastures, to invent impressive but meaningless titles that will protect the individual's ego and protect the organization from his service.

The Old Love and the New

It is not uncommon for a man's business career to be confined to a single employer. The largest companies in particular generally have a policy of "promotion from within" so that most administrators will in fact have started work with the company they finish with. This kind of durable union though common is not absolutely standard. Many young managerial prospects, say the recruits for a training course, do not stay with the company. The general experience seems to indicate the loss of about one-half of an entering "class" by the end of five years. Few are lost thereafter.

I have little evidence on the reasons for staying or leaving among young managerial recruits. Some simply fail "to make the grade," and others see more rapid advancement opportunities in other, usually smaller, companies. There are many intermediate shades, however. The "graduate" of a training course may not get an assignment he wants or want the one he gets. Did he fail to make the grade or did the company fail to hold him? Both possibly, but which side gets the demerits may be very uncertain.

Some undeterminable number of eager young men secure employment with large corporations with no intention of staying there. They count on the training course and perhaps a few years of experience to increase their market value to a small company, where they expect to put their ambition and talent to more rapid and effective use. Perhaps because this kind of exploitation might be encouraged by publicity, the "public relations" advertising of large corporations never mentions their substantial contribution to training the managers of small companies.

For managers, strictly speaking, there seems to be little movement between employers after the first few years of employment and before the limited and highly specialized market for top executives is reached. Movement is discouraged not only by such objective circumstances as non-transferable pensions but also by subjective loyalty and commitment to the employer. Loyalty in fact is so strongly emphasized in corporate personnel policies that one wonders what happened to the morality of a competitive labor market. The suspicion that the belief in it is not strong is enhanced by the term "piracy" applied to job offers from other employers.

Many managers have few alternative opportunities at equivalent income levels because much of their value is based on experience in a particular company and is not marketable. The spread of "professional" standards in management may serve to provide common *occupational* criteria of excellence, and the growth of managerial associations may serve as the market mechanism for bringing buyer and seller into contact. But the establishment of a truly professional reputation for the inconspicuous junior or middle manager is still very difficult.

The staff employee, with his primarily occupational identification, is likely to be more movable in subjective terms, and in fact more likely to move than the line employee. Since the staff man's information is what he has to sell, some nice ethical questions are raised when he changes employers. Who owns the particular knowledge developed during his previous employment? This problem clearly arises from transfers of research personnel who may be on the verge of a patentable product or process. Some employment contracts provide that patents must continue to be assigned to the original employer for several years after the man leaves. Because of the intricacies of patent law and the usual possibility of several paths to the goal, it is doubtful that this policy is very effective.

There are all sorts of reasons to expect the probability of changes of employers to decrease with length of service. In many walks of life home and community ties provide a strong deterrent, but large corporations have loosened that grasp on many people by the policy of frequent transfers and the residential mobility of the American population in general seems to be increasing. I do not expect any great upsurge in employer changes among "middle management" unless brought about by radical shifts in defense policy. I do, however, expect some growth in occupational loyalty as compared with loyalty to particular employers, which, in terms of performance, is implied by occupational identification. The best protection of any employee against either objective exploitation or subjective suffocation is the existence of alternative opportunities. A competitive labor market may not have made America great, but it has certainly kept it moving.

XIII

TWO-FACED EXPERTS

WHEREIN *the men who represent the corporation to outside interests are shown to be the spokesmen for those interests in corporate councils, not always happily.*

IF BUSINESS concerns were self-sufficient, little states with autarchical economies, their problems would not be fewer but they would be different. The provision of all the economic necessities, public services, and social amenities would pose on a small scale the problems faced by totalitarian states on a grand scale. Company towns occasionally approach this condition, and the company finds itself in a multitude of businesses and activities scarcely related to its principal reason for existence. The relations among these various functions are administrative rather than economic (through the market) or political (through the state). It is significant that true company towns and their owners are almost invariably small, permitting an informality of procedure and decision-makers who "wear several hats" simultaneously. Large organizations invariably become internally specialized, and administrative problems, the problems of balance and coordination, multiply with size and with diversity of operations. It is also significant that true company towns are steadily disappearing. One suspects that companies find diversity distracting; besides, community self-sufficiency is increasingly hard to maintain in the modern world, and the inhabitants will not remain the company's captives.

The organizational alternative to "doing everything," which is finally impossible, is to maintain some kind of relationship with essential functions and their human agents that lie outside the organization. The counterparts of the men (or executive man-hours) in town-owning companies devoted to running stores, laying streets, or repairing houses are the men in ordinary companies who maintain essential contacts with important elements in the community, the economy, the state, and society.

The Rise of "Relations"

Time was when even in the ordinary company the maintenance of necessary contacts with the external world was primarily a managerial and even executive responsibility. The increase, seemingly at an exponential rate, of contact men, or, more honorifically, of relations experts can be attributed to two somewhat independent causes. The first and simpler source of specialization is sheer organizational size. The executive may be able to wear two or even three hats simultaneously or seriatim, but he looks silly if he tries to wear ten or fifteen. Although the executives cannot escape ultimate responsibility for company policy, they are less than omniscient and omnipotent. They require expert advice on matters beyond their ken and expert performance on matters beyond their competence.

The second reason for the increase of relations experts has to do with the evolution in the concept and control of the corporation. Business or market relations with suppliers and customers have been there all along. So have, to some degree, relations with public authorities. But the Board of Directors no longer serves as the exclusive agency of contact with stockholders, nor does the ordinary managerial structure serve as the exclusive mode of contact with employees. The notion of the public responsibilities of business, and particularly big business, have multiplied the identifiable interests whose welfare or good will become objects of corporate attention.

My favorite corporate title appears on the business card of an officer of an oil company operating in a Near Eastern country. His title is Relations Director, which invites speculation about what relations he directs. His primary function actually is the maintenance of political relations with the royal court, a task difficult and probably impolitic to convey in a title. The circumstances are, however, exceptional. In most instances, titles are rather explicit, and their owners' relations to other services clarified on office letter heads if not on business cards. The man who is Director, College Scholarships, will be located in the Educational Services Department of the Public Relations Division. The man who is Head, Employee Counseling, will be located in the Personnel Services Department of the Employee Relations Division. The language of titles and relative rank of units—for example, divisions as parts of departments or vice versa—will vary from company to company but the principles of specialization and partial coordination will not. Naturally the degree of specialization will depend upon the size of the operation and its relative importance in the company's policies. A small company may buy its public relations services, if any, from an independent consulting firm; a medium-sized company may have one or two "wholly owned" advisors; and the large company may have a technical staff of ten or fifteen specialists plus secretarial and clerical employees in addition to an outside consulting firm.

It is not difficult to construct a kind of minimum list of contacts that are likely to require specialized talents and duties. Securing raw materials and components is the duty of the purchasing agent. He may need to be backed up by assistants who know particular kinds of markets and others who can determine the necessary technical specifications and qualities.

The sales or marketing manager is concerned with the other

end of the supply chain, the securing of orders and delivery of the product. His assistants may include advertising men, market researchers, and experts on transportation.

The personnel or industrial relations manager may provide essentially "internal" services to employees, but he must be especially concerned with negotiations with unions as partially external organizations. His staff may well include an expert on "employee communications" to bypass or supplement the union as a channel of contact with workers, a labor-market economist, and a labor lawyer.

Relations with suppliers of capital are of at least two sorts. Communications with stockholders are likely not to be confined to annual meetings and certainly not to their representatives on the Board. Stockholders are increasingly treated as an especially significant part of the corporation's "public," with appropriate techniques of maintaining interest through carefully tailored reports and other mailings. However, new stock flotations, bonds, or bank loans are likely to be the responsibility of the financial vice-president and his staff, including security analysts and men with appropriate contacts in financial circles.

Relations with the government are extremely complex, but some of them fall into a specialized province of sales. Since the law is pervasive, the corporation's relations with any external interest-group are likely to have legal aspects. The office of the general counsel may thus have specialists or consult with outside specialists on matters ranging from patents to stream pollution, from taxes to tariffs, from accident liability to fraud.

With competitors, corporations ideally should have no direct contacts because of the many possibilities of illegal or unethical collusion. This is a difficult position to maintain, as there may be common and legitimate interests for the industry as a whole. These interests may be represented by "trade associations," providing another staff function for the company in maintaining its representation. And even if there is no contact with competitors, their behavior is clearly of keen interest to the company. My impression is that this interest is usually represented in marketing and sales, since that is where the competitor is "met," but people in research and development, in manufacturing, and indeed in almost any company function are likely to spend some time looking at their counterparts in other companies.

The contacts so far enumerated still omit one major corporate concern, its relations with the public "not elsewhere classified." But the public may be and often is sub-classified—for example, the voting public, the press and other mass media, organized community and charitable services, and educational institutions. Each of these interests will in turn call for expert knowledge and modes of favorable contact.

All of this proliferation of specialists, when added to such primarily "internal" operations as manufacturing and accounting, necessarily compounds the problems of coordination. The basic reason is that there is absolutely no assurance that the specialized activities always complement and never conflict with each other or that the relative weight to be assigned to one activity or another can be determined by neat formulas. With so many voices raised, it would be miraculous if they shouted in unison or in neat harmony. Only in the imagination of the philosopher Dr. Pangloss in Voltaire's *Candide* do "all things work out for the best in the best of all possible worlds."

The difficulty of integration of specialists arises from still another source. Experts tend to be dedicated as well as merely self-interested men. Self-interest alone would lead them to exaggerate their importance to the enterprise as a whole. Dedication leads them to plead their cause with deep moral fervor and to take their responsibilities so seriously that a balanced judgment, a proper consideration of other views and other functions, becomes quite unlikely.

Let me illustrate this problem by comments directed at two types of contact men, the lawyers and the public relations men. There is probably some malice in my selection, but I shall stand by my comments anyway.

Because the law is ubiquitous, a pervasive feature of social life, the lawyer tends to assert the importance of legal clearance on virtually every external relationship of the corporation and some internal ones as well. This gives to lawyers, in effect, a very wide range of negative responsibilities, not of performance but of preventing unlawful or questionable performance. They hold extensive "veto powers." Now this problem would not be so serious were it not for some characteristics of the law and lawyers. The popular and relatively desirable belief in the certainty of the law is not shared by its experts. In many instances the legislation is unclear, the judicial cases and precedents either ambiguous or not clearly applicable to the questioned conduct. The lawyer commonly does not deal in certainties but in probabilities—that is, reasoned guesses as to how judges or juries would decide if the case went to trial.

If the probability of an adverse decision, of defeat, is significantly above zero, the lawyer turns cautious. He is among the most suspicious of men. Indeed, at least in corporate circles, the lawyer is a professional paranoid. His motto is, "If in doubt, say No," and he is often in doubt.

This is a different picture of the lawyer from that of the instrumentalist, the "slicker" who permits his client to keep within the law while doing something ethically wrong. The story is told of the original J. P. Morgan that his lawyer, commenting on a proposed business deal, remonstrated, "But you can't do that, Mr. Morgan." Mr. Morgan, the story goes, replied, "Your job is to tell me how to do what I want to do." Mr. Morgan's attorney may have done so, but I do not see the modern corporation lawyer so easily subdued. Within his own field, and it is a tremendous territory, his word is literally law. In my opinion this has a distinctly dampening effect on whatever spark of spirit the large corporation still permits.

My case concerning the exaggerations of the public relations man can be illustrated by a true story. Several years ago the public relations director of a very large company circulated a memorandum to all company officers expressing the view that big business had only seemingly won its case for public acceptance. The opposition, he claimed, had simply gone underground. Such opponents as William H. Whyte, author of *The Organization Man,* C. Wright Mills, author of *The Power Elite,* members of The Small Business Committee of the U. S. Senate and others had, he claimed, formed a secret conspiracy to carry on the battle against large corporations. The journalist who publicly commented on this nonsensical document attributed its preparation to cynical motives. Just think, he suggested, what department would get the axe first if there were serious budget cuts in the company. My view is more charitable but therefore more troubled. I credit the memo writer's sincerity, and I worry a little about how such a state of mind can be offset by seasoned sense in corporate policies.

My case against lawyers and public relations men could be extended, with suitable modifications, to other experts. The problem they pose is that, with the best will in the world, their counsel may be silly or downright dangerous to company welfare.

The Interests of Clients

The title of this chapter refers to "two-faced" experts. I do not mean this in any necessarily derogatory sense but only as a kind of shorthand for dual accountabilities. Any highly trained person, we have noted, tends to have a strong occupational identification as well as some feeling of responsibility to his employer. My interest here, however, is in the experts who deal with external interests and clienteles on behalf of their corporate employers.

The purchasing agent represents the company to suppliers, the lawyer to courts and governmental bodies, the marketing manager to customers, and so on. They may perform their functions well or ill by technical standards and, what is not the same thing, by standards of company welfare. The interesting point here is that they must perforce *represent their clients within the company*. The purchasing agent will fail in his duties to the company if he cannot present a fairly accurate picture of the markets in which he operates. The man charged with "investor relations" may well need to know the probable reaction to skipping a dividend or retaining a larger share of earnings for expansion. The lawyer may be a far more effective deterrent to antitrust violations than the Justice Department, which, in a sense, he represents. The marketing manager is the vehement spokesman for the customer. Even the labor relations director may be an eloquent, if reluctant, union representative in managerial circles. The two-faced expert, in other words, may not admire his "clients," but he cannot do his job unless he fairly presents their views and probable actions.

From time to time reformers of corporate organization earnestly suggest that representatives of labor, customers, and "the public" should be elected to boards of directors. Such changes appear to me to be harmless, possibly symbolically useful, but essentially insignificant. These and other interests are already represented within corporate management because they have to be. If the representation is not adequate or accurate, and the interests are important, then the company suffers too and may be expected to attempt some improvement. The marketing manager who persuades the company to sink millions of dollars into an unacceptable product or the industrial relations manager who predicts union acceptance of a company offer that precedes a six-month strike is likely to be taken less seriously the next time, if he is still around.

I have referred to the "clienteles" of external relations experts, and that is their essential position even if the relationship is guarded or hostile. The representatives of these clients thus constitute access points to the corporation other than through the chief executive. (The customer with an unsatisfied complaint may still be well advised to address the company president, because bosses are bosses and customers only customers, but this tactic is generally necessary only when the client does not know or have an established relationship with his spokesman.)

There are really two points here, but they intersect. The relations man essentially "votes his constituency" in corporate decision-making and may do so with reluctance or positive conviction. At the same time, this provides the constituent with a "friend in court" or, in some cases, a court assigned counsel who must still do his best to represent the client.

The dual responsibility of the external relations men undoubtedly is a source of strain, both for the individual and for the organization. It has, however, a very intriguing consequence. The large corporation has moved very far toward a "pluralistic government," representative of many constituencies, without ever really intending to. That government is not precisely democratic, but neither is it autocratic or monolithic. The experts are heard—and sometimes believed after suitable deflation.

Part Five

CHANGE

X I V

EVOLUTION, REVOLUTION, REACTION

WHEREIN *the forces that produce change
within corporations are identified, including periodic
and only partially successful attempts
to suppress sin.*

IF CHANGE is a law of life, its lawful characteristics, the orderly qualities of social transformation, are only slightly understood. Most "models" of corporate behavior or of other administrative organizations, are "static." That is, they deal with enduring features of corporate life, with relationships that, persisting through time, are nearly timeless. Tomorrow follows today as today followed yesterday with comforting or dismaying regularity. Yet corporations are no more exempt than individuals or families or nations from past history and present perils, from accumulation and erosion, from slow evolution and rapid mutation.

Change is a producer of tensions and uncertainty but also a reliever of them. Persistence, though possibly dull, has the great advantage of permitting predictability of human conduct, an assurance that the same people and the same groups will behave in much the same way from day to day and year to year. Without considerable persistence, social organization becomes impossible

and human life intolerable. Orderly change also permits predictability, the forecasting that tomorrow will be different in about the
direction and degree that today differed from yesterday. Even
orderly change, however, is tension-producing if for no other
reason than because of the continuous adjustment it requires. In
addition, in any complex organization it is impossible to find or
even to imagine a change that does not affect some interest adversely. Even an across-the-board increase in wages and salaries
will affect the relative or absolute differences in income to the
disadvantage of those at the top or those at the bottom.

The example of income increases illustrates how change may
alleviate tensions, however. The equity of a given income distribution is much less likely to be questioned if all are experiencing a
favorable change than if only some people get a raise or no one
does. Adversity, and especially adversity as compared with the past
or with "reasonable" expectations for the present, is more likely
to produce discontent than is the relative degree of prosperity.
"Equal sacrifices" are harder to implement and accept than possibly unequal benefits.

Complete certainty is almost as intolerable as complete uncertainty. The quest for a change of pace by people caught in routinized jobs, the introduction of elements of risk or uncertainty in
situations providing only a boring regularity, offer testimony to
the need for change as a way of alleviating strain as well as a
source of further tension. Points of tension or strain, possibly the
result of past changes, provide hospitable environments for further change. Order and regularity, though necessary, do not reign
unchallenged either in fact or in principle.

The Paths of Progress

Some organizational changes are essentially evolutionary in nature. That is, they represent the gradual transformation of the organization in response to its own characteristics and its adjustment

to relatively stable environments. Some persistent problems of organization, for example, though never finally "solved," provide the basis for the continuous quest for further approximations to perfection. The troubled question of the relations between individuals and organizations and the manifold ways in which competition and conflict plague a nominally cooperative system provide challenges that will normally lead to changes in both doctrine and practices.

On a visit to the River Rouge plant of the Ford Motor Company several years ago I casually observed the entrance to a suite of offices designated "Employee Relations." That was normal enough. But a hundred yards farther along in the seemingly endless building a somewhat more imposing group of offices was identified as "Management Relations." From the old days of "scientific management" concerned only with improving the productivity of manual workers, we have now progressed to a concern with the nature of organization itself including the manager's relations with it.

Organizations also tend to accumulate a body of customary law. Since the formal law is never complete and exact, preventing any latitude or uncertainty, decisions become doctrines and practices become precedents. Lore is added to law and eventually takes on the aura of law and perhaps even its reality, if a challenge is made and defeated by citing the long-established practice as the basis for affirming its binding quality. The rules may be silent on the right of appeal for an employee who is dismissed and has no union spokesman. If, however, a higher officer and an "unbroken" line of predecessors have insistently announced an "open door policy" with regard to subordinates, the practice of appeal may well become a genuine right.

Some corporate changes, though evolutionary in the sense of gradual change consistent with past trends, may have a high component of purpose, that is, of deliberate alteration. Corporate missions or objectives are often rather vague (for example, good corporate citizenship) or open-ended (for example, profit maximization). The sharpening of objectives and their translation into specific goals for specific future periods become a steady source of fairly orderly "progress." This process is enchanced by more or less constant emphasis on implementing the doctrines of efficiency and rationality. The injunction to "find a better way" may apply to almost any phase of operations from the muscular movements of the production worker to the cerebrations of the expert on organization.

We have then the paradox that organizational evolution may occur by the accumulation of precedents, which are essentially "conservative" in nature, and by the improvement of techniques, which are essentially "liberal" in character. The paradox often becomes an overt contradiction, as when the innovation challenges practice based on precedent and either interrupts one evolutionary trend by establishing another or fails through rejection by conservative opinion. The appeal to experience is always a strong enemy of the appeal to reason, for experience often wears the cloak of rationality to cover the irrational sentiment that attaches to tradition.

The paths of progress are not entirely smooth and may appear so only much later and in retrospect, when the difficulties that seemed to loom so large can be regarded as temporary, the outcome inevitable, and the struggles or delays downgraded or quietly forgotten. The great advantage of the historian is that he knows the outcome of the events that he seeks to interpret, but to the participant without the gift of superior foresight the outcome may be very much in doubt.

All continuing complex organizations tend to add to their original mission, to accumulate functions. Some of these additional functions may be thought of as instrumental, as aiding the principal purpose, but in ways not precisely demonstrated. Others may simply be viewed as good in their own right and, resources permitting, worthy of pursuit. Thus corporate aid to higher education may evolve from specific scholarships for students in technical fields represented by the company, through aid for continuing research in the colleges and universities to encourage the progress of useful knowledge, to general support for all branches of knowledge without precise expectations of company benefits. Personnel policies may evolve from those designed to increase the employee's productivity to those designed to encourage his general growth as a social being.

When the future causes the past, as it does in a sense when change is deliberately planned and implemented, conventional notions of causation are upset. When conservative restraint—the expression of alarm by asking "whither are we drifting?"—appeals to the future to inhibit the present, conventional causation is reversed by a "feed-back" from what has not yet happened to that which is now proposed.

One of the main pressures for organizational change is the deliberate cultivation of growth. This is commonly justified by an aphorism that is accepted as unqualified wisdom, another law of life. This admonition is "Grow or Die." Biological organisms are mortal and have in any event highly variable characteristics of growth (and decline), so the notion is not even a very good analogy. Corporations may survive by growth or despite it. They may survive by maintaining a stable size and, not rarely, by judicious contraction. Growth, as with human obesity, may very well shorten the corporation's life expectancy rather than build up its increasing strength for dealing with the hazards of the environment. Many a company has been tempted into expansion out of all reason by forecasting an endless growth of the market at an accelerating rate or by venturing into totally unfamiliar markets where the opportunities for profits appeared greater than in the intensive cultivation of what the company was already prepared to do.

The objective falsity or exaggeration of a human belief does not as such destroy its significance. Men act in accordance with their beliefs whether those be true, false, or incapable of objective judgment (such as the belief in life after death). Acting in accordance with their beliefs, corporation executives generally equate progress with growth and then attempt to fulfill their aspirations by expanding their enterprises. The company that does so, and the company officers that do so, may be accorded recognition for their success by other true believers. This is clearly one of the strongest forces for continuous change in the contemporary corporation. It affects participants at nearly every level and in nearly every functional position. Each year should be better than the last, and the phrase "bigger and better" tends to be redundant, because bigger equals better. The objective basis of this belief is, to repeat, extremely shaky and relatively dependent on a multitude of variable conditions in the corporation's external environment and internal structure.

The distortion of nostalgia, which leads to the notion that progress consists of going backward, of recapturing the simpler past, may be equaled by distortion of dreams of future greatness. Size may prevent excellence rather than achieve it. There are other ways to grow—for example in wisdom and virtue—besides just getting bigger.

Fashions and Fads

It appears to me that a great deal of organizational change in large corporations is imitative in character. That is, some one persuades Company A that it is important to have a special department to deal with the theory of organization and management itself. Company B, seeing this development, reasons that Company A must have made a thorough study and reached a decision only after mature consideration. Under this assumption there is no need for Company B to make its own study or linger long over the decision. It adds its own staff. Company C finds this reasoning even more persuasive, since two companies have added the new department. By the time Company E gets into line, there will be enough technical people in similar positions to form an association, hold meetings, and read learned papers to one another.

Meanwhile the organizational specialists in Company A or B will have studied enough and heard so much from their compatriots in other companies that they will want to spread the good word more widely in their own companies. After all, what is the use of having experts on management if they have no effect on those who are doing the managing? The next move then is a kind of staff and command school or an advanced management program, not for the young recruits from the campuses but for the men who need "retreading" to broaden their vision and skills. Soon no self-respecting company of substantial size can be without an advanced management training program.

The initial impulse to many organizational changes is less important than the quick way in which an innovation becomes a fashion. Some are more properly called fads, that is, they last a very short while and are replaced by something newer and even more stylish. A number of years ago training programs in "sound economic principles" were all the rage, although the principles were straight out of Nineteenth Century textbooks and had almost no bearing on the conduct of the corporation. Currently, decision-making games are in vogue, but I expect the novelty to wear off and the tired businessman can go back to playing "Monopoly" with his children instead of playing business strategies with his colleagues.

It is rather hard to find true business fads, as a matter of fact, because most organizational innovations have hardy survival qualities. Employee counseling, for example, which was an outgrowth of the cynical views of manipulation of workers' sentiments that the Western Electric researchers concluded was at the base of informal organization, still has its sponsors and staff in the Bell System, despite the subsequent progress in comprehending the motivations of workers and managers alike. Even when they pass from the center of the stage, the faddish schemes do not leave the theater. The ephemeral character of fashion and fad is thus applicable only to a part of the organizational changes in the corporate world. "Old agencies never die," and few in fact fade away. Their claims to provide cure-alls are likely to be down-graded, but some seeming virtue remains, and so do their supporters. There is enough uncertainty as to just what *is* worth-while not to take undue chances.

Drift and Reconstruction

The organization being prior to the man, the position more enduring than its incumbent, a succession of office-holders has little theoretical consequence for the on-going system. Each comes, plays his part, moves on to other roles, and is followed by another bit player to take his turn. Yet individuals do differ, despite valiant efforts to cast them into molds, and the molds do permit a little freedom to the man who is being shaped. A man never really leaves a position to his successor precisely as he received it from his predecessor. He will have added a little or subtracted a little from his duties, he will have changed directions at least slightly, and he may have actually set records difficult for anyone else to match, let alone improve upon.

Some consequences of turnover are fairly cyclical in character. "A new broom sweeps clean," goes the adage, and often the new appointee is expected to make a number of changes during a short time just after his appointment. This is his opportunity to make his weight felt, to establish expectations for himself and others. Reorganization is likely to be easier then, not only because it is expected but also because the reorganizer will not yet have had time to become personally involved with the people who will suffer from the change. The dull hand of sympathy often restrains the man who "knows all the circumstances," but the stranger can protect himself from sentiment by ignorance.

There is one particular cycle of growth and reorganization that operates in executive offices. The corporate executive is the residuary legatee of unsolved problems. Thus when new agencies are established or new functions added, they may not be neatly assignable to a part of the organization as it already exists. The alternative, and it is a frequent one, is to attach the new unit to the executive office. Thus for any given executive, his number of direct subordinates and the range of their functions is likely to increase during his tenure in office.

The time of succession in the chief executive office often becomes a time for tidying up the organization and reducing the direct responsibilities of the executive. Occasionally I have seen this reorganization substantially accomplished by the outgoing officer anticipating his retirement. He wants, he says, to leave a neat organizational structure for his successor. He doubts, he means, that the man who follows him is half the man that he is and had better be relieved of some of the responsibilities that the retiring man has capably carried. There is every reason to expect the new man to go through the same cycle, for he will acquire responsibilities by default if not by intent.

The new executive commonly attempts to refurbish the "old line" contacts with major divisions and other interests of central importance to the executive function. His time, interest, and accessibility almost inevitably decline as he discovers that new problems preoccupy him. The aura of good feeling gradually evaporates as some new palace crowd stands between the king and his traditional subjects. Even old-timers, forgetful of past cycles and disappointments, may be repeatedly trapped into believing that "this time it will be different." In detail it certainly will be, but in general it is likely to be the same old story with a slightly new cast of characters.

The Cycle of Sin and Penance

Corporations, like individuals, are unlikely to maintain a steady state of virtue. In some respects their conduct reminds one of the small-town sinner who gets "saved" annually at a rousing revival meeting but backslides and needs a new treatment the next year.

The commonest corporate example of backsliding and salvation is in the abuse of "indulgences." A ten-minute coffee-break gradually extends to three-quarters of an hour, at which juncture some one in authority decides things have got out of hand. A new and firm edict is issued that, let us say, a fifteen-minute break is the maximum tolerable limit, with the threat that the privilege will be withdrawn altogether if further abused. Generally, this is an idle threat, as the next repetition of the cycle will demonstrate.

Psychologists sometimes use the term "perseveration" to refer to actions carried to ridiculous extremes. The one-martini, hour-and-a-half lunch may be extended to the three-martini, three-hour lunch before a man's colleagues or boss exercise, respectively, informal or formal control. Competitive systems occasionally become perseverative to the point where the defeat of the enemy takes precedence over the object of the game.

Because the removal of privileges is always more resented than failing to accord them in the first place, it might appear that preventive action should be taken when a clearly sinful drift begins. The problem is where to draw the line. The manager scarcely wants to appear stuffy and ridiculous, and he probably keeps hoping for corrective self-discipline. This is not a wholly impossible dream, for self-discipline or "group controls" may occur. Often, however, no one quite knows where virtue ends and sin begins until, by any standard, the line has been passed some distance back. The progress toward general slackness may be very gradual, with each day's behavior looking very much like that of the day before (but not the month or year before). Where does one draw the line between the box of cigars to the purchasing agent and the air-conditioned Cadillac? At what point does arriving late and leaving early constitute perfunctory performance? What is the precise difference between the easy good fellowship at an office Christmas party and a drunken orgy? Commonly an extreme instance of misconduct is required to trigger a conservative retreat, a new set of rules, or even prohibition of the privilege altogether.

Extreme misconduct, particularly if it is accompanied by adverse publicity—attempts to "hush it up" having failed—are likely to lead to righteous moralizing on the part of officials and the conspicuous imposition of penance.

A few years ago a sales division of a large electrical company was caught supplying call girls to customers at conventions. The divisional manager and several subordinates were disciplined, and top company officials declared themselves forthrightly against sin. More recently the president of one of the "big three" automobile companies was fired for awarding supply contracts to companies in which he had a substantial interest. In this case other company officials were opposed to "conflict of interest."

Virtually every company has its nurtured memories of "Black Thursdays" when heads rolled, houses were cleaned, and moral austerity imposed. Such memories of course rarely lose content as the story is retold, but they may lose a firm coincidence with fact.

The heads that roll may not be those of the "real" culprits but of those "responsible." This is one of the costs of power. For the external public, the punitive actions must be made to appear "appropriate." For the members of the corporation, somewhat less cynical standards are needed, as punishment should be reasonably just to have its effect in maintaining the morals of other potential sinners. Thus public and private justice may not coincide, but a conspicuous dismissal and inconspicuous reemployment may satisfy the demands of both.

Conservative revolutions may be about as temporary as the moral fervor of the backsliding convert. Yet at least in the corporate case there is likely to be a residue of restraint. As long as personal capacities for mischief and various organizational pathologies persist, conspicuous instances of misconduct may occur again but commonly not the same ones or of the same degree that caused the last blood-letting. The corporation's capacity to change includes the capacity to create or harbor new ways of misbehaving, leading to new reactions, and so on and on down the vistas of the future. The thought is not entirely comforting, but not entirely dismaying either.

X V

INNOVATION AND INHIBITION

*W HEREIN creative innovators meet
conservative opposition, and the thesis is expounded
that business careers provide too little security,
not too much.*

> Ah Love! could thou and I with Fate conspire
> To grasp this sorry Scheme of Things entire,
> Would we not shatter it to bits—and then
> Re-mould it nearer to the Heart's Desire!

The charming quatrain by Omar Khayyam nearly a thousand years ago indicates, if we needed any indication, that "social improvement" is not a new notion. Biblical doctrine for the most part encouraged individual reform not social transformation directly. The Greeks, especially Plato and Aristotle, developed the idea of legal and constitutional planning, but it did not catch on very widely. In fact, the widespread acceptance and purposive implementation of deliberate alteration of the Scheme of Things is only a few hundred years old. Concerted action to meet crises, to extend power, or to resist tyranny is very old in human history. Concerted action to create crises, to institute change as a regular feature of social life, is rather new. In most societies through most of human history, the predominant human effort has been directed toward holding things steady or restoring a steady state if it is disrupted by some natural or man-made crisis. The phenomenal thing about modern industrial societies and others attempting to follow the same path is the great energy devoted to deliberate disruption of existing conditions and the creation of new ones. A rather remarkable proportion of the legitimately employed labor force is devoted to "messing up the system" rather than holding things steady. These honored disturbers of the peace include scientists and engineers, scholars and many teachers, lawmakers and many judges, and myriads of experts in public and private employment whose mission in life is to improve everything from the farmer's seed to the techniques of estimating consumer demand for products not yet invented.

The chaotic state of the world and especially its extreme state of political disorganization make general predictions of the future difficult if not impossible. Yet we can know much of the future with considerable reliability and not simply by extrapolating past trends or by well-established scientific laws of social change. We can predict some things with confidence, because "that's the way we're planning it."

Planning as such is not a doctrinal or ideological problem. The essentially secular view of nature, including social nature, as capable of understanding and control is pretty generally accepted. Centralized planning by the state, particularly if rather extensive, is valiantly opposed by believers in free enterprise and indeed generally by upholders of private liberties. But those who oppose centralized planning and control do not generally espouse the alternative of "letting nature take its course." They are, on the contrary, often among the most avid seekers after both prediction and control of the future environment.

Corporations are among the principal perpetrators of change. The most highly advertised changes involve the technology of physics and chemistry in the development of new processes and products. Yet corporations also attempt to develop the social technology of organization, of markets and distribution, of public influence and private negotiation. If they do not quite succeed in grasping this sorry scheme of things entirely, they make a noble attempt.

The Organization of Change

Technical innovations are probably about as old as human history, for one distinguishing feature of *homo sapiens* is that he is a tool-using animal. As far as one can determine, however, it is only in industrialized societies or newly developing ones, that technical change is *organized and institutionalized*. Concretely this means that substantial funds and human resources are devoted to deliberate change. This has involved an intellectual as well as a structural revolution, and its consequences are not yet completely in evidence anywhere. The intellectual revolution might with some poetic license be called the "rise of the rational spirit." Essentially it views the world or at least the non-human world as capable of being understood, reduced to principle, and eventually controlled and altered to meet human goals.

In industry, "research and development," commonly abbreviated to R & D, is normally established as a distinct, organized activity, complete with budget, equipment, and creators of ideas and compounds and hardware. The problem-solving mentality is more generally sought and encouraged, however, and the cumulative effect of small innovations by unofficial creators may be almost as great as the sponsored inventiveness in laboratories and on the blackboards of bright young thinkers.

The amount of money spent by corporations for R & D is rather spectacular. A National Science Foundation survey indicated that the sum reached $6.5 billion in 1956 and it may have reached $9 billion by 1960. The rapid rise in expenditures is partly accounted for by governmental support for national defense. This is further confirmed by the fact that the aircraft and

electrical industries account for about half of the R & D total. The
chemical industry accounts for only around 8 per cent of the national research budget but supplies a high proportion of the funds
from private rather than public sources. The proportions of corporate budgets spent on R & D range rather widely, but the
three hundred seventy-five largest corporations accounted for 70
per cent of the national total. These expenditures include most of
the vast research sums spent by the federal government, although
the accounting is not always easy because of the high component
of R & D expenses in defense contracts awarded to private corporations. Colleges and universities contribute additional large sums
toward altering the world, although they still support some scholars who only seek to preserve it. Again the allocations are not
easy, as between teaching and research for example, but the number of dollars is not so important as the fact that the outlays are
tremendous. Many universities in fact are so deeply into the "research business" that their budgets for "project" or sponsored research far exceed allotments for the old-fashioned academic pursuits of teaching and individual inquiry.

Research in short has itself become big business, with some
companies exclusively engaged in inventing things or solving technical problems for other companies. Understandably the organization of research has come under scrutiny. Research units, it is
commonly conceded, cannot be organized like stenographic pools
or even like assembly lines, although there are types of experi-
ments that can be sufficiently routinized to permit farily standard
organizational forms. Research productivity consists of doing
something different, and preferably useful to someone willing to
buy it. Patents represent one measure of useful novelty, but no
one would pretend that all are equally significant. And there is
very little evidence as to what selection, working conditions, and
rewards are effective in assuring that the "geniuses at work" will
indeed produce results befitting their dignity, to say nothing of
results proportional to the investment.

Although it is quite easy to demonstrate by national comparisons that investments in technology are correlated with rates of

economic growth, it is scarcely possible to do this on a smaller scale. I have the impression that in chemistry, which is primarily an experimental rather than a theoretical field, useful innovations may be closely related to the man-hours of chemists' time in the laboratories. The relation of money or time to results in, say, various aspects of physics is much more tenuous. The plain fact is that investments in research are more often a "vote for virtue" than they are a carefully calculated bit of economic rationality. Yet the subsidies for scientific and technical research, both in institutions of higher education and in business enterprise itself, make possible and indeed probable a more or less steady flow of suggested innovations. My concern here is with the consequences of such suggestions both for the distribution of productive labor and for the managerial modes of adjusting to the constant flow of creative novelties.

Technical innovations come in all shapes and sizes, and derive from the physical sciences (especially physics and chemistry) and the life sciences (various branches of biology). I am going to leave aside many otherwise important distinctions, and especially the important applications of social science. One distinction must be made, however, and that is the difference between *process* and *product* as the form of technical innovation or, more precisely, between changes in producers' goods and in consumers' goods. Of the two, the process changes have the greater immediate impact on productive organization, particularly in their implications for employment, job specifications, skill distributions, and the like. Product innovation commonly, but not always, involves new processes, but a radical displacement of existing products is rare. Most products have a remarkable longevity. Even within the single "enterprise," new products commonly add to rather than displace previous ones. Thus the effects on individuals are likely to be relatively subtle over considerable time spans. The relative power and prestige of occupational groups, including career opportunities and expectations, may be affected by consumer product innovation (and relative downgrading of other products), but these consequences may be difficult to diagnose and predict.

A man may find himself identified with a product that has a declining market, like hand carpet sweepers, rather than an expanding market, like motor-driven floor scrubbers. But some carpet sweepers are still made and sold. One might not advise a young man to go into the business, but the older man may only have to face more limited opportunities than his counterpart in an expanding market.

But new industrial products and especially new machine tools have an immediate and visible impact on work organizations and on matters associated with "occupation" in the broad sense. Some workers are simply displaced, while others find new opportunities accompanying the changing methods of production.

I am going to assume, for the moment, a position that is fundamentally untenable, namely, a view of industrial technology as a kind of original and sovereign cause, a prime mover, and the attendant changes as results. Technologists have long since warmly welcomed this doctrine, which is a kind of vulgar or poor man's Marxism—namely, that technology leads, social institutions adjust tardily, and the intervening interval represents a "culture lag." This is of course flattering to technologists—after all, they lead—but the doctrine is wrong in all sorts of ways and all sorts of instances. Often the technology lags behind the recognized needs for improvement. I had this illustrated a few years ago when in a large corporation there developed a small contest for precedence between vice-presidents. The marketing vice-president decided that the salesmen had been too long subservient to the inventors, being expected to find a market for whatever R & D people turned up. This man accordingly asked a group of social scientists to assemble a list of needed physical inventions for the guidance of the technologists—where, in other words, they were lagging. This bit of gamesmanship was not very successful, but I admired the idea.

Machines and products are designed by men, for human goals. The whole business is highly purposive and for the most part highly organized. If we attribute good or evil to physical things or their consequences, we are indulging in a kind of fantasy. The *thing* is only an inanimate connection between people. Once this is recognized, the myth of "technological determinism" is relatively harmless and rather convenient.

The important point is that organized, deliberate change has additional consequences or side-effects, and it is virtually impossible to imagine, much less to find, a situation in which a change will benefit everyone.

Technological Impact on Workers

The consequences of technological change for production workers have been debated for over a century. A kind of anthropomorphic view of the machine, attributing to soulless metal various satanic powers, has been a favorite literary device. Even without this kind of conventional madness, the interpretation of the ill effects of the industrial revolution has commonly featured the notion of "Paradise Lost," once-noble spirits steadily degraded by mechanical monsters or their human masters. A more sober and dispassionate view, coupled with superior historical hindsight, permits us to make a somewhat more balanced appraisal of the long-term trends.

The presumed initial "downgrading" of industrial recruits is debatable. No doubt some craftsmen had their skills downgraded in specialized but relatively unskilled factory employments, and some craftsmen and agricultural workers may have been "expropriated" from ownership of the tools of production. This fine, ringing Marxist phrase is in fact generally true in industrial societies and most particularly so in the communist variety. As to status, however, the transition to industrial work involved a radically different type of productive organization with little legitimate basis for comparision of skill or status on a common scale. The historical experience, contemporaneously repeated in newly developing countries, involved new man-machine relations, new time disciplines, new jobs and work relations, and new systems of authority. Specialization was not necessarily more minute in absolute terms, as certain kinds of farm or handicraft production can get fairly routinized on short cycle—weeding vegetables or sanding furniture, for example. The industrial worker, however, does tend to be part of a more complex productive process and thus encounters a more attenuated relation between individual effort and total product. These differences were not and are not unimportant, but their importance does not rest on the loss of an idyllic situation of creativity and self-mastery by workers.

Changes in productive technology, particularly "process" changes, have generally involved the substitution of "capital" for "labor." Whether the aim has been direct labor cost-saving or improved quality control or both, the long-term occupational consequence has been an upgrading of minimum and average levels of skills. Unskilled workers have steadily declined as a proportion of the total labor force, for the tasks assigned to them are those often readily transferable to machines. The "ditch digger," once the common representation of the type of job demanding a strong back and a weak mind, is now commonly the operator of a rather complex earth-moving machine, and he is highly skilled. It is especially but not exclusively the unskilled workers who inhabit the category of the "hard core" of unemployed workers. Their lack of skills gives them wide maneuverability in the type of industry or specific "occupation" where they can seek employment—a dishwasher today, a janitor tomorrow—but virtually no basis for preferential selection over any other "casual" laborer.

Over the short term, process changes have often resulted in the subdivision of jobs, the *division* of labor in the strict sense or, somewhat more precisely, the *dilution* of skills. When coupled with short-cycle routinization, as on the assembly line, the worker becomes in effect a somewhat unreliable machine. As far as I can determine, this was an organizational innovation partially independent of the conveyor system as a mechanical matter. Since the machine-like worker can eventually be displaced by a true machine, it appears that social and physical technology have alternated as instigators of change in the organization of work. Clearly, the principal impact of automation in physical production has been the displacement of the routinized work assignment.

Particular skills thus have been subject to dilution or outright obsolescence. Most of the economic and personal costs of such obsolescence have been borne by the worker and his dependents. A strong case can be made for the view that this situation is unfair, that this particular cost of technical "progress" should be added to other costs borne by the employer, as part of the economic decision to change his technology. Retraining at the employer's expense, preferential rehiring of displaced workers, and severance pay for those who cannot be rehired represent partial shifts in cost-bearing. I am convinced, however, that public intervention is also necessary, because the single company or even the whole industry may not be able to bear the financial costs of loss of earnings by workers. If coal is to keep any substantial part of the fuel market, for example, it must not only continue to mechanize but also it must avoid some of the cost of retraining displaced miners for jobs in completely different industries.

Since the adoption of technical change is primarily a managerial decision, it can be used as a threat or weapon against strategically placed workers as an offset to their individual or combined bargaining power. Technical changes also are occasionally introduced to facilitate rather than impede creativity and identification with work as well as to foster "informal" relations among workers. Some, although very little, attention has been given to the social isolation of workers whose sole visual or audible environment may be inanimate.

High degrees of mechanization, including automation, radically change the man-machine relation, with the machine (tool) once more under the "mastery" of the worker. At the same time, the increase of planners, designers, and maintenance workers may not represent a net "labor saving" as such but rather a substitution of occupational types. In some instances, this may mean a substitution of "management" for "labor."

Several years ago I participated in a two-week "tour" of a large corporation, a program sponsored by the company's public relations department to improve educators' understanding of corporate organization and problems. The program generally served its purpose, but I recall one incident with relish. At a particular plant the local managers reported enthusiastically on their success with "methods study" (also called "scientific management," time-and-motion study, efficiency engineering, etc.). By their calculations a rather substantial saving had been made in direct labor costs as a result of the program. In the question period I assumed the most innocent voice I could muster and asked whether their cost-accounting system permitted them to compare their payroll savings with the salaries and other costs of the methods study. After some consultation among the managers it turned out that the comparison had not been made. I then proceeded to rub salt into the wounds by suggesting that even if the program was in fact losing money, as I thought likely, they might still want to continue because of their preference for the kind of people who make methods studies over the kind of people who handle materials. It did seem to me, however, that the financial dimensions of policies should be known. I have not been invited back to the plant.

Incidentally, "productivity" measures relate units or value of output to man-hours of labor input by workers only. A company that steadily substitutes one or more clerical, technical, or managerial employees for every displaced production worker can ride to the bankruptcy court on a wave of productivity increases. Elementary arithmetic indicates that a reduction of direct production workers will increase the proportions of other occupational groups, but I get the distinct impression that productivity gains also result in some fairly extensive overstaffing, especially in various technical and advisory capacities—adding the luxury of service and advice to the luxury of custom-made office furniture.

Some other changes in the total occupational structure of the enterprise may be justified by physical technology, at least in part. The technology of mass production interacts with a mass market to facilitate large-scale organizations. The consequences of size, in turn, include a *disproportionate* growth of communicators, coordinators, and record-keepers—in short, of managers and clerical workers. Although the number of white-collar workers has expanded more rapidly than the general rate of increase in industrial employment, some of these workers are now "under the gun" of electronic business machines. The expanding market necessary for mass production also calls for a *disproportionate* increase in salesmen, market analysts, and advertising specialists. Other changes in the "managerial" occupational structure—such as the rapid growth of internal and external "relations" experts— are less readily traceable to physical technology than to the growing social complexity in industrial societies as a whole.

Innovators and Coordinators

In the public polemics over the "trusts" in an earlier generation, a principal complaint against giant concerns was that they stultified initiative. That they often managed to keep or drive small competitors out of the market seems clear, but the record with regard to technical change is more mixed. Although the evidence is extremely flimsy, such scattered indicators as can be found comfortingly confirm what should be expected in theory, namely that "process" innovations are disproportionately introduced by large concerns. In a competitive economy such concerns can take a longer view of cost-saving, and they have larger absolute resources for underwriting technical obsolescence and new capitalization. They are also likely to have maximum bargaining power with resistant workers.

It is also probably true that both absolute amounts and proportions of current budgets spent on R & D are correlated with size of enterprise. Yet actual product innovations reaching production and the market may be disproportionately the means *small* enterprisers have for getting a foothold in the market. The large company may be especially prone to withhold a patented improvement that would lengthen a product's useful life and thus reduce the market for replacements.

The principal reason for the supposed minimal product innovation by large enterprises, however, is to be found in the administrative structure of the industrial corporation. The number of internal "veto powers" multiplies with the size of the organization, and in a bureaucracy "no" is always easier than "yes." The former opts for the status quo, while the latter requires implementation by responsible officials.

This line of reasoning brings us to the detailed organizational source of technical innovation. The steadily increasing complexity of physical technology insures that innovation will be initially a staff function. Although many economists follow the late, eminent Joseph Schumpeter in viewing innovation as the critical function of the business entrepreneur, in no modern enterprise, public or private, can the entrepreneur in that sense be equated with policy-forming executives. The latter agree (and implement) or disagree, but they do not invent. In these circumstances the likelihood is great that a veto will be exercised, especially in view of the executives' other accountabilities—the rest of the organization, suppliers, investors, dealers and distributors, possibly even customers. Thus risk-taking is likely to be minimal where its "economic" possibilities are greatest, because those possibilities are offset by internal structural constraints and the reality of multiple external interest groups.

We are now in a better position to appraise the intra-organizational impact of deliberate technical change. Managers and executives "above" the innovators in the formal structure of authority either implement or veto (the latter often on grounds that the technician will not quite accept). Indeed, the organization becomes pervaded with inexpert managers of expert subordinates, that is, with coordinators of activities beyond their personal competence. The most outstanding example of this organizational problem is in research organizations themselves. The research directors, whatever their scientific background, must steadily lose current competence as researchers. Their administrative duties will preclude their keeping up with, to say nothing of adding to, the store of knowledge. Although the term may not be used, out of gentle forbearance or nervous apprehension, the scientific administrator will be regarded by his own staff as one who has "sold out" to the enemy, the unlettered administration.

If suggested innovations are accepted by superiors they are not thereby assured a smooth course. Middle and lower managers and production workers may have no legitimate voice in the innovating decision. If affected adversely their only recourse is non-cooperation or, strictly speaking, sabotage. If unions or similar organizations have gained the right to bargain over the speed and impact of technical change, production workers may be better protected than junior management. It follows that junior managers should exhibit the maximum hostility to staff officials and this indeed squares with experience.

The example of "line-staff" conflict just indicated is given added point by a more general problem. The technician, along with many other professional and quasi-professional types, is likely to identify with his occupational peers in the first instance and his employer only secondarily. Managerial distrust of his organizational "loyalty" is likely to be well founded and thus to heighten the resistance of coordinators to the "irresponsible" suggestions of innovators who do not "take the company point of view."

The Supply and Use of Creativity

Creativity is a virtue. Like many virtues (democracy, progress, motherhood), creativity as a goal and standard of conduct may not survive with unanimous support once it is defined. Risking that hazard, I shall use creativity as almost synonymous with "individual initiative," with the proviso that the initiative be constructively innovative. This begs many questions (for example, who is to judge?) but will serve well enough for present purposes. Our problem is the supply and use of individual, constructive innovation in a multi-individual and indeed highly organized setting. The solution to this problem is neither singular nor finite, but some places where partial answers may be found will be suggested.

We may assume that educational requirements for employment, perhaps supplemented by selective procedures that particularly emphasize evidence of rational problem-solving, will result in a positive selection of talents in the business firm. Within the select universe of the educated, however, there are some hints of a negative correlation between evidences of talent and initiative on the one hand and the size of the recruiting corporation on the other. Ambitious young men may regard small companies as providing more immediate opportunities to use their talents than do the very large corporations. I am impressed with the frequency that bright college seniors comment adversely on their impressions of the bureaucracy of large companies, their assumption that seven years of servitude can be expected before one is given an interesting job, and especially their view of long corporate training programs as a further extension of infancy rather than the start of responsible adulthood. Even if the large corporations' uses of talent were above reproach, negative attitudes such as I have just stated would reduce the qualitative supply of talent by systematic negative selection.

Now if constructive innovation is regarded as a universal human potential, differences being a matter of degree and quality, the supply in a business organization is potentially pervasive even if individually not large. The organizational problem is not only the selection, identification, and use of highly unusual talents, although it is that too, but also the general problem of capturing, containing, and mobilizing individual initiative to meet the requirements of large business enterprises.

The matching of individual talents with organizational necessities would be pathological if complete, a product of an abnormal personality. That is, a specialized organizational role, however enriched and personally rewarding, cannot occupy the individual's total life-space if he is to fulfill other responsibilities and aspirations. "Total" commitment of the individual would be abnormal for him, inimical to other groups and organizations to which he owes responsibilities, and probably dangerous to the corporate object of his affections, since exceptional saintliness is disruptive to organizations in manifold ways. Although a measure of individual loyalty is often convenient and actively sought in corporate policy, the totally dedicated man is to be approached with exquisite caution if at all.

The opposite extreme, however, is little if any better. The individual whose commitment to the job is minimal and bribed, having nothing to do with either organizational objectives or intrinsic personal satisfactions, is unlikely to be very creative even in the techniques of subversion. The totally indifferent man, though less dangerous than the saint, is also somewhat less challenging. Although commonly part of the solid backbone of the organization, one does not get ideas and unusual action from him. He can be approached with absolute safety, but why approach him at all?

The middle course, as usual, is to be favored: creative individual participation consistent with organizational conditions and objectives and without gross distortions and imbalances in life patterns. We seek the interested and creative man who is not married to the corporation.

I think too much has been made of the contrast between the individual and the group. The isolated individual is as pathological as the company captive. *Purely* individual initiative is both unlikely and unlikely to be judged as constructive. The questions, rather, are, Which *other* individuals or groups does our potential creator take as the objects of his loyalty, the sources of approval, and the legitimate sources of restraint on his manic enthusiasms and his depressive tendencies to lethargy? Do these "significant others" encourage and reward initiative? Large business enterprises are not likely to be accorded such trust as organized entities but may well permit personal identification with functional units, with aggregates of occupational peers, and with administrative superiors who are accorded legitimacy as well as mere power. If these significant others give deference and esteem to creative individuals, such exemplary activity is likely to spread. Otherwise the talent is likely to dry up at its source.

It would be improper to leave the question of the general supply of creativity without mentioning one additional aspect of
motivation. Creativity, although rarely self-rewarding without external confirmation, is self-regenerating. We know clinically that
nothing fails like failure, and there is strong evidence to support
the aphorism that nothing succeeds like success. The implication
of this "spiral" effect may be seen in two contexts. First, the individual who is frustrated at work is quite unlikely, despite home-
spun psychological theory, to use his talents elsewhere. Second,
the individual accorded recognition for creative achievement at
work is likely both to participate more actively in his other roles
and activities and, more to the present point, to undertake to
build upon his recognized record in his work. Success, I am suggesting, is as habit-forming as failure.

We return then to one of the critical problems of creative innovation in the large enterprise, and that is that companies that
have the economic capacity to support research may lack the
bureaucratic capacity to take risks and implement change. Large
organizations may very well have superior capacity to foster ideas
and even to harbor distinctly odd personalities but a rather severely
limited capacity to translate ideas into action because of the many
hurdles on the paths of progress. Producers of ideas dismissed as
impractical may be more frustrated than those not encouraged to
think in the first place. And frustration, I have argued, is more
likely to lead to apathy than to renewed efforts to sell an idea,
perfect it, or come up with a new and better one.

No simple formula will determine when initiative and creativity
are "constructive" and when tangential or irrelevant or definitely
destructive. A purely static (and wholly unrealistic) model of an
organization in a benign environment ideally planned and ideally
staffed with participants perfectly motivated has no need for constructive change. Such a situation also has no need for managers,
since there are no new goals to be determined, no hostile forces to
be counteracted, no plans to be made, no personnel to be recruited, no incentives to be invented, and no discipline to be imposed.

The appropriate occasions for creativity thus can be identified: (1) the relationship between the organization and its setting— for example, the strategies of competition, techniques of negotiation, procedures for assuring a favorable public image; (2) the sharpening and modifying of organizational objectives—for example, determining the balance between economic objectives and all those functions that fall under the head of "good corporate citizenship"; (3) improvement of the means for achieving these objectives—for example, technical efficiency, organizational effectiveness, and personal motivation. In effect, these occasions for creativity unlock many doors, if they do not precisely open them.

If, within limits, the virtue of creativity is to be encouraged in the setting of the complex organization, it can consistently occur only as a result of favorable policies and procedures.

In the first instance, what is required is a modified theory of administrative organization. The "received doctrine" of administrative organization in corporations represents relatively slight modifications in the models provided by public civil and military structures. (These, too, however, do and must change.) Essentially, this doctrine places not only final legitimate authority for policy at the apex of a pyramid of power but also the determination of procedures in increasing order of particularity through a "chain of command." In each instance, the manager or supervisor applies policies and determines procedures for his subordinates—guiding, training, and correcting them when necessary. Each executive, manager, or supervisor is assumed to be more capable than any subordinate. At the extreme, to which this view is rarely pushed, the chief executive should then be able to "lick any man in the outfit."

The "modified theory" would not change the final authority for policy but would change the way of determining relevant information and action. Stated in positive terms, operational decisions and the knowledge required for them would be assembled where the problems arise or where the talent, formal training, and practical experience exist in the organization. In other words, wisdom is where you find it, not necessarily correlated with position in the administrative hierarchy. When the problems and the talent needed for their solutions occur in the same unit, decentralized management has a chance for success.

Now I am not arguing here against a "bad old theory" and for a "good new theory" of administration. Rather, I am arguing for a relativistic theory of administration, the principal variable being the supply of trained talent. The earlier "chain of command" theory was probably approximately consistent with the distribution of talent in organizations recruited from a pyramidal social order with a wide base and thin top. If one were concerned with organizing a large factory in an undeveloped area, recruiting a reluctant labor force that was unskilled and innocent of industrial traditions, one surely would not contemplate much managerial decentralization, nor using discussion groups to settle production procedures. The "chain of command" principle, I am arguing, is not consistent with a distribution of talent where the minimum base is very high in historical or comparative terms, and the sheer diversification of talent is extreme. At the very least this view argues for great flexibility in organization, consistent with the variable but generally increasing supplies of talent. If a certain level of education is necessary to get a job but not to do a job, then talent is being wasted.

The organizational counterparts of this view of the supply of creativity are reasonably clear. Supervisors and managers become coordinators of specialized performers, each of whom may be superior to the coordinator, each in his own field. There is no theoretical limit to this principle of organization at any rank or function. I do not doubt that in many instances implementing this principle will require some changes in attitudes by managers and in some instances a change of those managers who find themselves incapable of education. The principle is not after all so esoteric. In our society every father of a normal son must sooner or later face the awkward fact that the boy genuinely knows more about something than does his father, and this unalterably changes his father's supervisory role.

Coordination then becomes itself a specialized function capable of professionalization in terms of both skill levels and performance standards. This is part of what is meant by "professional management." The coordinative function demands of the managers the capacity to acquire at least amateur standing in the appropriate specialities, a standing adequate to understand their significance, balance their functions, and deflate their exaggerated claims. Paradoxically, generalization becomes a form of specialization. We are used to that in scientific disciplines, however, as that is the specialized role of the theorist.

Since a business enterprise cannot be a wholly self-governed entity, operated solely on behalf of its employed constituents, coordinators must also exercise delegated powers that derive from the company's external interests and accountabilities. This principle, incidentally, is not materially affected by the pretense that the workers are the owners in a socialist economy.

Such a theory of administrative organization, if put into effect, does not automatically resolve all conflicts of views and interests. Indeed, some of them that are latent may thereby become overt, such as the possible contrast between approval by professional peers and disapproval by a non-professional superior. The organizational principle, however, does stand a chance of tapping talents not otherwise accessible.

One structural by-product of this view should be noted. "Decentralization" of decision-making permits a substantial broadening of the coordinator's span of control (number of direct subordinates), since he is to be discouraged from "close supervision." The geometric consequence of this change is a "flattening" of the power pyramid.

A functional by-product may well be a loss of tight accountabilities and some "waste" motion in the allocation of time to rational decision as opposed to rule of thumb or rule of the mindless intuition of superiors. But the knowledge relevant to decision, the meaningful supply of information, the exercise of rational thought are likely to be greatly enhanced.

The encouragement of initiative is not simple, and since conditions for innovation may be genuinely adverse and reasonable men may reasonably differ, some "frustration" is inevitable. I am going to suggest some ways for avoiding acute frustration and its consequences in drying up initiative.

Policy is the balanced outcome of weighted advice and the assessment of uncontrolled conditions. The advice may not run in uniform directions, and conditions may be unsuitable for following one or another or any recommended direction. But the technical excellence of contributions, even though these are not "practical," may still be recognized and rewarded. This is best accomplished by the technical judgment of occupational peers, for such recognition is both a means of identification and validation of excellence on the one hand, and an intrinsic reward on the other.

The employer of a professional is still a client less knowledgeable than the practitioner and not in a position to dictate procedure. And the professional attends to the judgment of his competent colleagues and only reluctantly to his patrons. Employers and their delegated representatives would be well advised to adopt the habit of overt humility in dealings with specialists, for the latter will in the nature of the case accord them power when necessary but never competent technical authority. A "professional manager" may accord deference to the *competence* of his administrative superior, but only if he is always heard and sometimes believed.

There are all sorts of ways in which universities should be more businesslike. There are also some ways in which businesses should be more universitylike. Business organizations might well reconsider how essential anxiety as an incentive is for the maintenance of performance. On the record, anxiety is generally inconsistent with both morale and creativity, and the threat of dismissal is likely to yield only passable performance. Security of position coupled with positive rewards for excellence stand as the demonstrably superior set of conditions for linking morale and productivity.

Most large business enterprises do in fact provide relative security of employment (though not necessarily of precise position)

for those in the middle and upper-middle ranges of rank and income. Why not make tenure official? The inevitable mistakes may
be much less costly than the loss of initiative created by fear.

I do not mean to exaggerate the contrast in policies, for I have
sat in solemn departmental conclave where the chairman has been
instructed to warn Assistant Professor X that unless his scholarly
productivity improves he is not long for this University. And you
can imagine the spurt of creativity that this probably unnecessary
warning fosters. Nor do I argue that the reward of security should
be made for poor performance, although even that exceptional
risk may be occasionally sensible. What I do maintain is that
security should be offered as quickly as possible for creative effort
as an effective means for its continued encouragement.

The plain fact is that the history and theory of human motivation are consistently and persistently misread by the business
community and most of its intellectual interpreters. *Security and
initiative are positively not negatively correlated.* The current risk
in business enterprise is not that office holders have "gone soft"
by seeking security but that they avoid risks including the risky
business of creative thought because they have not been accorded
enough security. The freedom to disagree, to suggest improvements, to question time-honored but irrational formulas requires
for most men in most times a relatively stable place to stand.
Saints and heroes are neither needed nor desirable in complex
organizations. Secure and positive thinkers and doers are.

I shall state a position more extremely than I am willing to
defend, for purposes of establishing a point by exaggeration. The
power of corporate executives is generally exercised with restraint
and even beneficence in the external world. Internally, what
passes for stern justice in maintaining disciplined performance is
mostly a misuse of unconscionable power that reduces the capacity of the organization and of its members to act constructively.
The carefully cultivated reputation for being "tough" may help a
Marine officer to extract unusual performance by his troops in
battle, but it does not follow that this is the way to win the battle for men's minds for peaceful pursuits.

Part Six

CIRCUMSCRIPTION

X V I

SUPPLIERS: SHARP AND SUPPLICANT

WHEREIN *the corporation is shown not to be self-sufficient, and the securing of capital and raw materials raises questions once more of corporate power and responsibility.*

THE business enterprise has "relations," mostly chaste, with a variety of external groups and agencies. Prominent among these are suppliers of what economists call the "factors of production," that is, capital, materials, and labor. No private business is self-sufficient for its supplies, and the socialist state still finds it necessary to divide up various functions into separate organizational units and then arrange for transfers among them. This is the beginning of the circumscription of corporate automony and power, for the company and its managers do not in fact entirely control the means for fulfilling their collective objectives.

In their quest for autonomy, corporations may attempt to own, control, dominate, or effectively neutralize suppliers. Sooner or later there are intrinsic limits to such policies, for no single organization is really equipped to produce all money and materials and certainly not to produce the human populations that will constitute the labor supply. Moreover, the captor becomes the captive, for he is then dependent on the very strategies he has used to achieve control.

Capital

In principle, the capital of corporations comes from investors who own equity shares in the company's assets and expect to receive a share of profits in the form of dividends. These are the company's "owners." In fact, where stocks are widely dispersed and the corporation has achieved independence from stockholder control, the "owners" are treated like another interest group, an important part of the public. Older organization charts, showing the flow of power and control, started at the top with stockholders, then the Board of Directors, then the actual executive officers of the company. Some companies maintain this as a pleasant fiction, but no one acts as though it were a fact. In many large corporations a close inspection of organizational charts will show a staff agency somewhere near executive territory that is labeled something like "stockholder relations." This is the tip-off. The preparation of annual reports, distribution of proxies to be voted for management policies and personnel, and the distribution of encouraging or reassuring circulars tend to be handled by people with "public relations skills." The occasional obsequious bow or respectful salute to "our real bosses" must fool very few. The stockholder has been sequestered.

The first problem in relations with investors is that of "retained earnings." A growing company needs new capital for expansion of facilities. It has, essentially, three courses of action, which are not mutually exclusive. It may go into debt by getting straight commercial loans or selling bonds, in the expectation that its profits on new production will more than offset the interest on its debt and can be used to pay the principal as well. It may "float" a new stock issue, bringing more "risk capital" into the business. Or it may achieve its expansion by a "bootstrap" operation, that is, finance expansion out of past earnings that it retains instead of distributing them as dividends to stockholders.

From the point of view of corporate autmony, these three alternatives are in an ascending order of desirability. Commercial credit tends to come from a single source, normally a large commercial bank. Even bonds are normally sold through large investment houses and end up in the hands of fairly wealthy investors. These creditors are likely to take a keen, and indeed a rather insistent, interest in company policies and may well interfere in certain aspects of management.

Floating a new stock issue may have desirable features of further dispersion of shareholdings and thus further domination of investors by division, but it must be nicely timed to avoid depressing the market value of the stock.

Retained earnings place the capital entirely at management's disposal without any promises or guarantees. In principle, retained earnings become "forced savings" for the stockholder, presumably enhancing the market value of the stock. There is no guarantee that the new investments will in fact yield higher returns in the future, but the dissatisfied stockholder normally has only the option of selling his equities for others that may yield higher current dividends.

By retaining earnings the corporation may become self-sustaining. If no dividends are paid at all but the stock continues to grow in market value, the "capital gains" investor will be satisfied, and persons seeking to supplement current income from dividends will simply seek other investments. Unless holders of a majority of shares protest, a corporation would never need to declare a dividend. (The opportunities for plunder by management are obvious; however, even a minority stockholder has access to the courts to require management to account for grossly improbable uses of corporate funds.)

Since corporations as "legal persons" can themselves own stock, an interesting speculation presents itself. Suppose the corporation simply uses its retained earnings to purchase its own stock, finally achieving complete independence from capital suppliers. I have been unable to find any *legal* impediment to such a course, and the lawyers I have asked confirm this but shrug it off with the opinion that "it wouldn't work." I am not so sure, and rather expect some corporation to try. That would finally present in sharp focus the question as to the accountabilities of corporations.

The advantages of self-capitalization are so great that they may occasionally obscure the alternatives. Several years ago the New Jersey Bell Telephone Company petitioned the State Public Utility Commission for an increase in basic rates. The Company argument did not rest on rising costs and the need for higher income to protect a "fair" return on investment. Rather, it argued that the rise in demand for service exceeded its financial capacity to install lines and equipment rapidly enough. The rate rise was intended to supply new capital. As a telephone subscriber I was happy to see the Company sent away empty-handed. As a contemplator of corporations I was amused by the curious blindness to the alternative of selling new stock in an enterprise that combines security with growth.

New stock flotations for an established company may in fact offer advantages almost equal to self-capitalization, and may be the best course available for rapid expansion. This is given added point by the current character of capital markets. A prominent feature of those markets is the "institutional investor," particularly insurance companies, endowment funds of non-profit organizations such as universities, pension and welfare trusts, and mutual funds designed to offer diversification to the small investor. Now many of these institutional investors may need to emphasize security and current income, but this does not mean that they will object to rising market values and the benefits of "capital gains." The identification of "growth stocks" may be self-confirming, since regular purchases will tend to raise the market value. Stock-market values have no necessary relation to gross earnings and declared dividends. Therefore the rate of return on investments may steadily deteriorate unless some of the capital gains are "realized" through sale.

The significance of this process for the corporation seeking new capital is clear. If it can float a new stock issue without seriously depressing the market price of its stocks, it can get new money at very low cost. An extreme instance of this was recently provided by International Business Machines, a "growth" stock. At the market value of the stock, the current rate of return was under 2 per cent. The Company offered new stock, representing about a 10 per cent increase in the total shares outstanding. Although in a sense the previous shares were "watered" at least temporarily, the market value was not depressed at all, and the Company continued to pay the same dividends—thus getting new money at a price far below bank or bond rates.

The cost of capital to large and established corporations and to small and new or unknown ones is showing an increasing divergence. One effect of this may be new pressures toward concentration, that is, the suppression of small companies by the unequal advantage of large companies in money markets. The antitrust regulations were aimed at keeping *goods* markets open to small competitors, and this new form of inequality has largely escaped public notice.

Because of the advantages of large companies in money markets, they may be increasingly placed in the position of "investment bankers." In fact, that is already a principal role of the central financial structure of large and diversified manufacturers, for the officers of the corporation must decide on the internal allocations of its disposable funds, that is, retained earnings or new capital. However, the company may find that it can make a higher rate of return on its funds by external investment. There is growing evidence that such investments, often in the form of loans rather than stock purchases to avoid awkward questions of control, are directed to the company's suppliers. The reasons will appear presently.

Corporations may thus be both recipients and suppliers of capital. With their own investors, that is, the final beneficial owners of equities, the company may adopt a rather cavalier attitude. With intermediaries, the institutional investors, the corporation must tread somewhat more cautiously, for these organizations are both more powerful in the old-fashioned sense of voting their stock and more knowledgeable about financial matters. Because of the concentration of some stocks in relatively few institutional hands, and the wide dispersion of the other holdings, the institutional investor may directly affect company policies. At the very least, a loss of confidence, a decision that the company does not promise growth, can be as self-confirming as an optimistic view. Widespread sale of stocks in a company by institutional investors is not a happy omen for the dreamier prospects for expansion that the managers may have permitted themselves to indulge in.

Energy, Materials, and Components

Several decades ago there was considerable enthusiasm in corporate circles for "vertical integration," that is, for controlling the entire productive process from raw materials to finished products. The Ford Motor Company was a leading exponent of this policy. Ford acquired its own iron mines in Minnesota, ore ships for Great Lakes transportation, and a steel mill at the River Rouge plant in Michigan. Rubber plantations were established in Brazil and soy bean farms acquired to provide raw materials for plastics. Ford also made glass and tires. The company went fairly far toward "wholly-owned" employees by establishing part-time farming plots for workers in Dearborn to carry them through shut-downs and by setting up a wondrously titled "Sociology Department" to provide workers with welfare services and protect them from such dangerous thoughts as sympathy for unions.

Although some of these wholly-owned supply mechanisms persist at Ford—notably steel fabrication—the effort at self-sufficiency was doomed to failure. The basic reason for this is that the number and variety of materials are finally beyond the capacity of a single company, however large, to manufacture. The *reductio ad absurdum* of vertical integration is the single-company economy, and not even socialist states have that at the operating level.

Knowing the background at Ford, when I had the opportunity to tour the River Rouge plant I began noticing things that the Company did not manufacture, and thinking of many more. In the shops, most of the workman's hand tools and the machines or at least many of their components were certainly purchased. So were articles as diverse as electrical supplies and factory hand-trucks. In the offices, furniture, files, typewriters, paper, pencils and paper clips were certainly not made by vertically-integrated subsidiaries. The point is surely clear. Vertical integration has very early limits.

The obvious problem in vertical integration is that for many of its supplies the company represents an extremely small portion of the total market. If it attempts to manufacture them it must either make an uneconomically small amount or enter essentially alien markets to sell its surpluses.

The subtle problem is that with vertical integration the company becomes "married" to a particular set of materials and technology. If its investment is to be protected, it has lost its flexibility in changing materials or taking advantage of cost-saving improvements introduced by other suppliers. Even for materials or components for which the company is a major consumer, these disadvantages are likely to outweigh the possible advantages of greater reliability of supplies or greater protection against unfavorable price bargains with independent producers.

In dealing with independent suppliers, companies must attempt to avoid the same kind of trap as vertical integration provides. A large customer for small producers may have a major impact on their competitive situation. If one supplier has some kind of advantage owing to its technology or relative size, it may be able to offer the lowest price to the corporate buyer. The large order, however, may add even further to the producer's competitive advantage and eventually force other producers out of business. The bargaining advantage then shifts to the surviving supplier, for the company has no other place to turn. The enthusiasm of corporations for competition in their own product markets may be very small, but they do mean it when they favor a competitive market among suppliers. It is by no means uncommon for large corporations to divide their purchases among various suppliers, even though some purchases are made at higher unit prices. This is a kind of self-interested charity, keeping alive the small businessman to avoid becoming the captive of a middle-sized one.

The large corporation with substantial disposable resources is not likely to be victimized for long by "extortionate" prices from suppliers. It may either buy the supplier's business outright or set up its own "integrated" production. The threat to do the latter may be sufficient to keep the supplier in line. As an alternative, technologists may be assigned the task of finding another way to get the same results. These defensive moves, however, imply that the supplier has a measure of influence and limitation on corporate autonomy. Suppliers taken one by one may feel that they have little influence, and any attempt to combine with others would be viewed with considerable lack of enthusiasm by the Antitrust Division. Nevertheless, from the point of view, say, of the corporation's purchasing agent or that of the external observer, the total power of suppliers is rather restrictive of corporate autonomy.

The "make or buy" decision may even involve materials or components that the company already produces. In a diversified but partially vertically integrated company, one division may become the captive of another even more readily than it becomes subject to the independent but exclusive supplier. It is common for divisional managers to assert and maintain the right to buy from outside suppliers if components are thus obtainable at a lower price than offered by the company. This has a somewhat chastening effect on the supplying division if it cannot count on a captive market. It also gives the company as such a kind of love-hate relationship with some suppliers, although the conflicting emotions are likely to be entertained by different corporate units. With suppliers, the threat is, "We can do it better and cheaper." With a unit of the company, the threat is, "We can get it better and cheaper." Either threat may be real or a bluff. Game strategy may have been invented either by politicians or poker players, but many businessmen have learned its lessons well.

X V I I

LABOR: THE SPURIOUS DIALECTIC

*W HEREIN all corporate employees are shown
to be proletarians under their skins and other
superficial differences like income and power, and the
question is posed as to why
managers are Marxists.*

SINCE people in orderly relationships comprise the units of that
social entity known as the corporation, it seems a bit peculiar to
speak of those units as "suppliers" of labor. The peculiarity increases with recognition that workers at all levels including executives are suppliers, and the recipient of those supplies, the
employer or purchaser, then becomes a kind of inhuman, disembodied being called the corporation.

Employers, being simultaneously employees, may be selecting
subordinates as part of the duties of their positions at the very
time they are personally "contemplating a change" or courting
offers from other firms. It is precisely this fact of transferability,
of participation in the "labor market," that warrants consider-
ing labor as a supply factor. Employer-employee or superior-
subordinate relations within the organization are inevitably col-
ored by considerations of abundance or scarcity of particular
skills and talents. Although many corporate personnel policies

are designed to minimize the movement of workers between employers, to "capture loyalties" and thus reduce the will of the worker to extract the best possible bargain, any worker's welfare is at least partially determined by his market value.

The Market for Labor

Whenever managers are playing the role of purchasers of labor supplies rather than sellers of their own services, they have a much higher regard for competition among suppliers than for competition among purchasers. Epithets like "raiding" and "piracy" are attributed to highly moral conduct, that of competitive bidding for employees. As an employee the manager may happily contemplate the prospect of being the booty in a raid.

Labor markets, however, are among the most complex transactional systems. There is not a single market for "labor" but a multitude of fractional markets comprised of those with similar skills—a combination of talent, education, and experience. Any one of these fractional markets may be relatively open or fairly "sticky," that is, permitting considerable mobility or very little. Supply and demand situations are affected by all sorts of chance factors, such as variations in the prosperity of different industries and the way in which individuals choose or drift into different occupations. They are also affected by technological changes, which may simultaneously make some skills virtually obsolete while creating substantial demand for new ones. Thus technological changes, particularly in productive processes, are often made for the explicit purpose of substituting machines for men or for avoiding the exceptional bargaining power of skilled workers in short supply by making them unnecessary through substitution of less skilled workers. The company then "makes" rather than "buys," or it "buys" in a cheaper market.

Unions serve as suppliers of labor, even as labor markets. Essentially they attempt to substitute collective for individual bargaining (that is, market transactions), either on behalf of a single occupation (the craft union) or on behalf of "all" employees (the industrial union). In the nature of the case, unions attempt to monopolize the supply of labor to the employer for the workers they represent. If their bargaining strength is adequate and they are legally permitted to do so, unions will attempt to make union membership a condition of employment (closed shop) or a condition of continuing employment after free selection by the employer (union shop).

I have suggested in the chapter on "Conflict" that the assumed solidarity of management and of labor in dealing with each other is spurious on both sides. There is no very good way to tell the difference between the two groups, since all parties are employees and no fundamental way of designating why their interests should be in conflict. Yet the fact remains that representatives of corporations do deal with unions, and the bargaining is "collective" on both sides.

Management-Union Relations

Corporate policies with regard to unions are marked by a history of opposition and conflict and a present situation of reluctant acceptance. In both the past and present, government has been a not always silent third party to the relationship. The explicit legalization of the rights of union organization and collective bargaining derives on the national scene mainly from New Deal days of the 1930's, although some craft unions had been able to operate effectively much earlier.

Although the economic bargain, the supply-price of organized labor, remains a key basis for management-union bargaining, the bitterest industrial disputes commonly involve issues of "rights" and power.

The economic relation between the purchasers and suppliers of labor is in a sense "contaminated" by the inclusion of negotiations on any other subjects—which may range from "working conditions" as a minimum to company location decisions or price policies at the other extreme. The claim of unions to bargain on matters additional to wages and hours is based in large part on the fact that union members are also members of business organizations, and thus also have interests in safety, discipline, employment security, and so on.

Business leaders first opposed unions as such on the grounds that any form of joint decision was an interference with "managerial prerogatives." Having lost that point, chiefly at the hands of Congress, state legislatures, and the courts, businessmen have countered the successive attempts of unions to extend the scope of bargaining by the same "principled" resistance.

"Managerial prerogatives," however, rest on extremely shaky foundations. Once corporate managements abandon the bald claims of the power of property, claims that will not stand the most casual scrutiny in the corporation with dispersed stockholders, the moral justification of unilateral power by management is shattered. The argument must then shift to more prosaic claims, those of "function" and efficiency. Managers may claim with some justice that they represent a diversity of interests beyond those of workers, but this is scarcely a basis for denying representation to labor interests. In fact, some unions claim to be more representative of consumers than corporations who "represent" consumers by vying for their patronage.

The resistance to union "encroachment," if based on the claim that efficiency demands cohesive and therefore unshared power, neglects all of the divisive forces within management itself and would require demonstration that "co-determination" through negotiation is in fact less efficient than unilateral and possibly uninformed decision.

The net effect of what I have been saying is that most of the moralistic arguments against the "interference" of unions in the determination of company policies strike me as spurious.

Neither the moral nor the intellectual basis of corporate leadership is manifestly superior to that of union leadership. One can find cases to prove the superiority of either group. The United Automobile Workers, for example, are embarrassing to automobile manufacturers not only because of the policy issues they present for negotiation but also because the union leaders are at least the intellectual and technical equals of the people who make corporate decisions for the industry.

The reluctance to share power through negotiation is understandable in psychological terms, particularly as it implies that the benevolence of power has not been accepted. But the moral tone of managerial rationalizations concerning union policies is also understandable as a further manifestation of a neurotic incapacity to face facts rationally—or else as a cynical attempt at willful deception. My own view is tolerant but patronizing. I think the managers have deceived themselves.

What they resist in the behavior of unions they accept with equanimity in the behavior of professional groups. Managers, being incompetent to judge their professional superiors, must perforce accept the judgment of a job candidate's peers. If corporate executives feel the need of a person in a particular professional field, they will either inquire of the professional society and its clearinghouse agency, or they will start inquiring among professionals in the field concerned. In either case, the managers have only nominally retained control of selective processes. In effect, they have turned over that "prerogative" to those whom they must trust, because they have no reasonable alternative.

I do not mean to imply that union organizations are uniformly happy havens of democratic processes, that union leaders uniformly and accurately represent both the desires and the "interests" of their constituents, or that the constraining powers that unions exert on business concerns are uniformly beneficial. My central concern here is with the fact that to get part of the labor supply they need, corporations must negotiate with combinations of workers, and the conduct of these negotiations necessarily circumscribes the autonomy of management on yet another frontier.

Union Effects on Corporate Organization

The existence and legal protection of independent unions, that is, labor organizations free from managerial control, affects the internal structure as well as external relations of corporations. The wider is the scope of bargaining on behalf of workers *as subordinates and company members rather than simply as suppliers*, the greater is the effect on the organization. Hiring and firing, promotion and discipline, become matters of negotiation rather than simply company rule. Grievance procedures through successive steps, with matching stages of company and union administration, provide union members with a kind of judicial system. If impartial arbitration is set up as the last stage of the procedure, then the similarity to the judicial system is nearly complete, for decisions are likely to become precedents and a body of case law develops.

The extension of union power over "internal" management is not necessarily an unmixed blessing for the unions. Nor is the attempt to have a voice in purchasing policies, such as insistence on raw materials and components produced by union labor, or on price policies, such as insistence that wage demands be met by reducing waste or profits rather than raising consumer prices. Power without responsibility is difficult to maintain. The wider the extension of union influence on corporate policies, the less effective is the union's capacity for protesting those same policies. The union becomes "entrapped" by the very negotiating system that it uses to increase its influence and power.

If management-union relations represented simply a market transaction, then failure to reach an agreement would simply be an incomplete transaction. But actually neither side is quite in a position to "take their business elsewhere." They are, in short, stuck with each other. It is for this reason that a strike, like a war, is punishing to both sides, and the question then becomes one of the capacity of each to take as well as to give punishment.

The strategies of these contending parties, caught in a situation of mutual dependence, are too numerous and too subject to variable legal circumstances to permit generalization. A few points, however, are of special interest because they bear on the containment of corporate autonomy. Success in bargaining depends upon both strength and strategy, and both of these are quite subject to changing conditions. A few years ago the International Union of Electrical Workers conducted a long strike at Westinghouse plants. At the time both the labor market and the market for goods were "tight" or "good," depending on the point of view. Workers, though on strike, were commonly able to find temporary jobs with other companies. The Company, meanwhile, not only lost sales to competitors during the strike, but also suffered substantial long-term losses because its former distributors and customers continued to buy the brands they had shifted to. The Westinghouse management finally settled for the union's demands.

More recently, the same union called a strike at General Electric plants at a time when unemployment was increasing and the Company had vast unsold inventories of consumer goods. This strike soon ended with the union failing completely to win its objectives. The Company has taken, and received, credit for its announced policy of stating its terms and sticking to them. The experience in fact proves nothing about Company policy under conditions like those facing Westinghouse. The union (or rather, local units that simply failed to follow the policies of national officers) at least recognized the error in timing more quickly than did the managers in the Westinghouse dispute.

I commented earlier, again in the chapter on "Conflict," that I do not regard the future of industrial unions as bright (from their point of view) or awesome (from the point of view of employers). Rather, the diversity of occupational interests and the strength of common interests within occupations seem to me to point to a proliferation of occupational organization. This will, in my opinion, give corporate bargainers little comfort, for the bargaining simply becomes more complex and the criss-crossing of lineups on successive issues more unstable.

There is one notion circulating through company corridors that I find particularly unpersuasive. This is the notion that unions were at one time a necessary evil and have now outlived their usefulness. That is, the unions called attention to company failures and abuses. By their pressures they forced rectification of evils either by making them bargaining issues or by influencing managerial strategy in competing with unions for the loyalty of workers. In other words, unions had a historic mission now accomplished. Why don't they just go away?

A minor but vocal opinion in corporate circles goes beyond reluctant acceptance. Where unions are no longer battling for survival, where a kind of *modus vivendi* has been established with management, their positive use as agencies of communication and as agencies of industrial government may be recognized. I have heard some industrial executives—not many, but some—say, "I don't know how we did without them." The union, enforcing standards of conduct by the pressure of peers rather than the imposed discipline of superiors, concerned with working out satisfactory rules rather than defeating the enemy, may become a more intimate part of corporate government than the stockholders became or could have.

The key to industrial peace is not golden and does not open all doors. It is, however, essential that all interests in industrial disputes recognize the survival qualities of the parties. E. Wright Bakke expresses this point in a small book entitled *Mutual Survival*, and its message is clear: Any kind of continuing arrangement between corporations and unions on a more or less orderly basis depends on acceptance of the necessity of each to survive. The *ultra* position, a war to the death, is likely to lead to a murder-and-suicide situation that cannot reflect very favorably on the mental health of the participants. I deliberately refrain from Cold War analogies but they are very inviting.

It is not at all self-evident that "if the company had done thirty years ago what we are doing now, the union would never have gained a foothold." The argument is, of course, academic as are all retrospective reconstructions. The problem, however, is more basic. Collective interests are intrinsic in the structure of large-scale enterprise. They are not simply the result of easily rectified failures or abuses. I think "collective bargaining" in one form or another will grow, not decline. Nor is it self-evident that "management" would have either the will or the capacity to "represent" all labor-supply interests and all other member-of-the-organization interests in place of spokesmen for those interests with real power.

It is essential to underline the diversity of "labor" interests including those of various "managerial" categories. The dialectic, that is, the polarization into two warring camps, is fostered by some managerial policies as well as by unions seeking to represent "all" workers. It is nevertheless spurious.

Given full employment and the retraining of displaced workers, market forces might provide a fairly adequate protection for the price of labor. Only a clear-cut corporate constitution including a "bill of rights" and an independent judiciary could provide an adequate protection of "member" interests. I see no real prospect for such developments within the private domains of business, but there are signs that the public lawmakers and courts may take an increasingly active part in the government of both unions and business enterprises. If this has scant resemblance to the notion of business leaders as benevolent despots, their despotism resting on the sacred rights of property, neither does the corporate world resemble the business climate of the last century. There are those who will assert with alacrity or admit with reluctance that the picture, on the whole, has improved.

XVIII

THE ADVICE MARKET

*WHEREIN some light-hearted notes are
recorded concerning the purchasing of information
and advice, and the business of being an expert is shown
to be as risky as any other.*

THE "make, lease, or buy" decision applies to many services that
corporations need or want as well as to raw materials and components. Such services range from transportation and construction
to pure advice. It is the market for advice that I wish to discuss
here. The term "egghead" or its alternate form, "double dome,"
has been applied derisively to intellectuals and to experts of all
sorts, particularly when they venture into the political arena. Yet
often the very people who distrust talents greater than their own
find themselves seeking counsel from just such experts.

With the possible exception of electronics, the fastest-growing
businesses in the United States are those engaged in research
and consulting. Occasional bits of hardware may issue from commercial research laboratories, but the principal products of these
businesses have either the tangible form of paper or else cannot
be seen at all but only heard in conversation.

Consulting services represent in fact a major opportunity for small business to get access to the market. The capital required is very small. Aside from the cost of acquiring expert knowledge, which is then carried in the consultant's head, the business needs the price of a few month's office rent and secretary's salary, some stationery, a typewriter, and contacts. If the contacts produce contracts, the business prospers and may be able to expand. If there is no business, the monetary cost of failure has not been large.

In Princeton, the number of one- or two-room research and consulting firms is very large, sharing with physicians and lawyers most of the converted residences in the center of town. Every month seems to yield a few additions to the inventory of commercialized brains. Now this seems odd because Princeton has no industry. It is near New York, however, and it does have a University, with which commercial consultants often hint they are somehow connected. Together with the polling agencies that do attitude surveys and market research, the consulting businesses represent a professed range of expert knowledge that few universities could match.

Although engineering consulting firms have been around for some time, most of the new firms—I think this is generally true across the country—offer applications of psychology and the social sciences. They attempt to portray, for a fee, the inner workings of men's "minds" (possibly as affected by their glandular systems) or else the characteristics of groups, organizations, or the "public." They offer personality tests for the selection of managers; charts for reorganizing managerial functions; advice on the "language that sells" for communications to the customer, stockholder, or the public; estimates of the degree of acceptability of a new store or new product; temperature readings on attitudes toward big business; identification of the kinds of people that others will imitate; analyses of the labor and tax situation in a town that is being considered as the site of a new plant; anthropological description of exotic customs in a foreign area where manufacturing or sales efforts may be attempted. The commercial consultants are willing to forecast the future as well as to portray the present, and the one may be about as accurate as the other.

The Uses of Social Knowledge

I think that this proliferation of commercial information and advice arises from a combination of several trends. One is the genuine and growing recognition of the complexity of psychological and social phenomena and the desirability of getting expert knowledge if it exists. Another, and this especially accounts for the independent firms, is that a small or medium-sized business can scarcely afford a full-time "wholly owned" staff of consultants in all the fields where knowledge is thought to be important. I believe these two sources of demand for expert advice are greatly increased by managerial uncertainty of where they stand or how they should act, particularly in the "soft" areas of attitude and opinion, motivation and values. Compared with something firm like machine design or cost accounting, these more subjective or ephemeral features of human conduct constitute mysteries, and mysteries that threaten.

When there is a great demand for answers, answers are likely to be provided even if they are not right. The technical and ethical standards of commercial consultants are highly variable. In many instances the basic theory and fundamental research that would form the groundwork for practical application simply do not exist. This situation invites the appearance of the charlatan who persuasively offers the simplifying "gimmick," the dandy little problem solver for all occasions. Even the conscientious expert may be tempted, because he is flattered to be asked (and paid), to offer advice far beyond the boundaries of reliable knowledge, his or that of anyone else.

Psychologists are just beginning to develop explicit technical and ethical standards for practitioners outside the college situation. Other social science fields regard themselves only as academic disciplines and have scarcely recognized the problem. Meanwhile, advice based on theories never tested or long since discarded, information based on sample surveys that violate many of the technical rules of research design, mathematical formulas based on assumptions that could never exist—these are part of the stock in trade of at least some of the purveyors of advice.

Unreliable information, I noted in a previous chapter, is protected by its "confidential" character, by the secrecy that protects the buyer's investment but also protects the seller from detection in his errors of fact or judgment. Where advice is followed and its consequences can be appraised, a kind of test is afforded. That may be too late, as the consultant is secretly selling his services elsewhere.

I do not by any means intend to say that commercial consultants on psychological and social matters are uniformly knaves or fools. I do think that there are considerable numbers of such consultants without any professional standards and that the consumer may not be able to tell the difference. Where basic knowledge is uncertain the honest man can only say so, but the dishonest one is the more attractive because he exudes confidence and promises answers.

The Roles of the Consultant

The reasons for using outside consultants and for the existence of this market for advice are somewhat more numerous than may at first appear. I offer here a list of the distinctive roles I have detected, either as participant or as observer, in the consulting relationship. There are no doubt others, as well as combinations of these.

THE IMPORTER: This is the simple and straightforward situation where the consultant supplies information and activity not otherwise at hand. If the company is large enough and the demand for information fairly steady, the role is likely to be temporary, for the company will generally prefer the additional control and convenience provided by having a regular employee. Like other consultants the importer is likely to have a rather uneven demand for his services, even if he has a number of regular customers. By building up his own store of background information usable for a variety of particular situations, he may be able partially to fill orders out of "inventory." Generally, however, time is required, and that cannot be effectively stored.

THE CATALYST: The consultant may add little or nothing to the supply of information and opinion already available to the company, but by his mere presence the necessary combination of ingredients to reach a conclusion may occur. The pure role is rare, but close approximations are fairly common. An innocent question or casual remark may change perspectives and provide an "obvious" solution to a problem long and ineffectively discussed.

THE TROUBADOR: Like the catalyst, the troubador may not add information but simply be effective in getting it used. Going from office to office and even division to division, the troubador can carry tales. He may provide an avenue of communication among persons who do not speak to one another for emotional or organizational reasons. He may in the process be a translator of alien languages. The information appropriate to a decision or problem solution may simply be inaccessible by ordinary procedures, or its existence may be unknown where it is needed. The consultant, not being restricted by the boundaries imposed by separate fiefs or feudal domains, becomes an agent of communication and therefore of possible coordination.

THE ORACLE: A consultant may have such a talent for ambiguity that whatever decision is reached as a result of his advice, he has no chance of being categorically wrong. This is an extremely difficult part to play, for the advice must seem to be clear while actually leaving ample room for varying interpretations, for condoning contradictory courses of action, leaving the situation at least as obscure as before. The talent is best exemplified by the majestic but meaningless opinion, the art of "doubletalk." Professional jargon often serves oracular purposes. The consultant may address the small group of company people who have sought his opinion something like this: "Gentlemen, the situation you present is almost a clinical case of the backward-sloping demand curve. Now the only course of action in such cases is to increase the gradient of the curve by greater inputs of energy at the strategic places, which are clear to all of you. I do not mean to make this sound trivial, because the situation has probably not previously occurred in your company. I run into the problem frequently in my work." He withdraws, grandly but courteously and unscathed. It is the brave buyer who will reveal his ignorance or dull understanding by asking for clarification (the true oracle will deepen the mystery in his patient and condescending explanation) or act the "poor boy" by asking, "What did he say?"

THE MAGICIAN: An even more difficult role to play, particularly more than once, is the miracle worker. Finding a situation intolerable or a problem that seems incapable of solution, the advice buyer asks only that the consultant do the impossible. The magician is safest when any course of action is better than none, and he simply selects one at random and thereby succeeds. The true magician, however, must seem to do something spectacular that rests on misdirection, on diverting attention from what is really going on. He may, if he is fortunate, see a simple solution that would be embarrassing to his petitioners if suggested quickly and bluntly, that would not offer much grounds for a fat fee. He must, therefore, create enough pointless activity so that the simple operation is accomplished and the problem solved without his clients quite knowing how.

THE ORNAMENT: Quite frequently, the last thing a client wants from an advisor is advice. Particularly if the consultant has an outstanding reputation or occupies a prestigeful position say in a ma-

jor university, his name and title may be all the company really
seeks. He can then be listed on the divisional roster or named in
brochures, to the credit of his part-time employer. He becomes a
part of the company's conspicuous consumption, indicating the
purchaser's opulence in being able to afford an embellishment so
expensive.

THE LORD PRIVY SEAL: Like the ornament, the Lord Privy
Seal does not give advice or solve problems. That has already been
taken care of. However, the "in-house" problem solvers may not
have a very exalted professional position. It may therefore be
thought worthwhile, particularly if line officers suspect the lowly
status of their captive consultants, to have a leading figure confirm
the solution. The consultant then gives a kind of majestic authentication to a decision already reached and "lends his name" to the
results.

THE UNWITTING PARTISAN: Several years ago the head of
a consulting firm told me that when he was approached with a
proposal from a *small* company, the initial assumption was that
the inquiry was fairly normal and straightforward, as the company would not have its own staff for the job. When a representative of a *large* company called, however, the consultant had
learned to try to find the answer to a question he could not ask
overtly: "Who's he trying to get?" The consultant tried to avoid
the role that I have called the unwitting partisan. The unwary
consultant may find that it is not his advice as such that is sought,
but his "impartial" support for one faction in an internal dispute.
Since each side may seek out its own "outside expert," such situations may increase the employment opportunities for consultants
without net effect on the outcome, but playing the part has its
dangers.

THE SCAPE-GOAT: In some company situations, dissatisfaction
and tension may reach dimensions requiring visible action. When
distrust is widespread, it may be impossible to dissociate any ac-

tion sponsored from the partisan position of the sponsor. This is the ideal situation for the sacrificial lamb or, in the vernacular, the "patsy." Bringing in an outsider not only demonstrates that action is being taken. If the solution proves unsatisfactory (as it certainly will to some), it is the expert who carries away the collective tribal guilt and permits the enemies to restore peace once more.

THE LORD HIGH EXECUTIONER: This role is a grander and more majestic variant of the scape-goat. The management of a company, having decided on a controversial course of action, does not want bloody hands to remain as reminders that jobs and whole divisions were wiped out. They therefore "reluctantly" accept the findings of "Axe Consulting Associates, Inc." and let the head of that firm wear the black mask of the headsman. The difficulty with this role is that the strategy works only if the executioner is named, and his mere presence in another company, however innocent, may cause a small panic if word has got around about his hatchet job at the first company.

The influence of consultants on companies can be easily exaggerated. As a general rule advisors have much less effect on company autonomy than do other suppliers. And yet where managers are caught in recurrent crises of uncertainty and indecision, the firm, clear voice may provide bad advice, which prevails over doing nothing at all. Not that it should, but it does.

X I X

COMPETITORS: CRITICAL AND COMFORTABLE

W H E R E I N *large companies are shown to be capable of vigorous competition as well as immoral collusion against customers, and small concerns find that not all giants are bullies.*

C O R P O R A T E executives become distinctly restive or downright irritated when they read or hear learned discussion of "the end of competition." The notion that corporations are not competing vigorously, that something mysteriously called "monopsony" or "oligopoly" characterizes their market behavior, appears to executives as silly or mischievous. For every example of illegal collusion for price-fixing or indication that prices are "administered" rather than determined in a competitive market, company spokesmen can cite several contrary examples pointing to competition in price, in product quality and style, in service, and in every other phase of the market.

The critics and the defenders are both right, but they tend to talk past one another. Many markets in which giant corporations operate have virtually no resemblance to old-fashioned "atomistic" competition among many producers. This does not necessarily mean that such markets are cozily divided or otherwise "rigged," but the modes of competition and the ways of gaining an advantage are radically different from, say, competition among small retailers in a large city.

On the other hand, the economists and others who have emphasized the significance of giant size and concentration have tended not to hear the defenders' contrary arguments to the effect that the corporation operates in many markets with different competitive situations, some of which are rigorous enough to satisfy all the tests for living dangerously.

I am not going to attempt to rewrite economic theory so that it bears some resemblance to the facts of corporate life, although that is a task that is seriously needed. I shall, rather, note the ways in which the autonomy of single corporations is restricted by different competitive situations.

Competition among the Few

In the so-called "basic" industries in the United States, "oligopoly," that is, domination of the productive facilities and markets by a very few companies, is the rule and many-sided competition the exception. In steel, United States Steel is the giant, Bethlehem a very poor second and other producers trail well behind. Automobiles in the U.S. are produced by five companies: General Motors, Ford, Chrysler, American Motors, and Studebaker-Packard. In electrical generating equipment, General Electric, Westinghouse, and Allis-Chalmers have virtually no other domestic competition.

In all these situations, there is likely to develop some form of "market sharing," even if not by such illegal collusion as that uncovered in the electrical industry. If costs and efficiencies are nearly identical from one company to another, nearly identical prices do not necessarily indicate a "conspiracy" or a "combination in restraint of trade." But exactly identical bids, which some electrical manufacturers persist in submitting even after they have been convicted of illegal conduct, at the very least raise the reasonable suspicion that they were not arrived at independently.

By attempting to prevent increased concentration or outright monopoly in an industry, the Antitrust Division may encourage market sharing. Whether or not there is such a rule of thumb, it is commonly supposed in industrial circles that 40 per cent of the market is pretty much the upper limit of concentration by a single corporation. Above that limit, the corporation may be threatened with dismemberment. Now let us take a situation that apparently prevailed in the automobile industry a few years ago. General Motors had very close to one-half of the total market. It is claimed that their relative efficiency was such that they could have reduced prices substantially and still made an acceptable profit on each car, and perhaps an increased gross profit because of increased volume. They were, it is argued, "stuck" with high unit profits because they did not dare capture any larger share of the market. Indeed, some commentators claimed that GM deliberately introduced an ugly model of the Buick, which had overtaken Chrysler's Plymouth in popularity, in order to keep Chrysler afloat. GM officials denied that there was any defensive benevolence intended, but in effect the "big three" did persist and did not become the big two or big one.

The concept of "administered prices" has aroused considerable controversy, through which it is very difficult to thread one's way dispassionately. Essentially, the notion is simply that large corporations tend to set prices with little reference to day-to-day competitive factors or variations in demand. Price determination is an "administrative" decision, deriving more from direct costs, calculation of overhead charges, and desirable level of unit profit than from market conditions.

Administered prices may thus simply derive from the way corporations are organized—the greater ease of setting prices in advance from information largely known, than responding on short notice to market situations. The concept, however, is usually used with a negative or critical connotation, implying that the prices have been set by illegal agreement, or at least that they provide a kind of shelter against vigorous competition and keep membership in the "club" about constant.

I think it is fair to say that where a few corporations dominate a market, price competition is not very prominent. Though this may mean that the companies have established a kind of "shared monopoly" or only that their costs and pricing conventions are fairly uniform, I think that there is considerable and reasonable reluctance to enter a price war. Price-cutting is likely to be countered by the competitors, but no company can be certain of its power to win an unqualified victory (even if it were permitted to do so by the government). Price-cutting thus impairs short-run profits without assuring the long-term advantage of capturing a greater share of the market.

Avoidance of price competition does not mean avoidance of all competition. Companies will attempt to claim quality differences in products, to capture and hold distinctive clienteles, to find effective advertising appeals, or to develop efficiencies in distribution. It appears, in fact, that large corporations are more interested in improving their "position" in the market than they are in maximizing profits, either in the short or long run. Price-cutting might therefore have short-term advantages, were it not for the ease with which the strategy can be countered. Other forms of competition may give a longer advantage because they are less easily met.

Competition among the few does not in any event always assume the same form. At the very time that leading electrical manufacturers had decided on market shares for some of their capital goods and agreed to take turns bidding in order to allocate the shares, they were engaged in vigorous competition in various consumer-goods markets such as household appliances. Those markets had turned fairly "soft," but even when there was a generally increasing demand there is little evidence that each producer was content simply to accept the same share of a larger pie.

The few giants in some fields—steel, automobiles, electrical goods—are easy to identify, and their competitive policies are fairly conspicuous. However, the matching of companies and "industries" (or markets) is increasingly difficult. This difficulty comes about through the growth of product diversification in large companies. The result, for any one company, may be that in each of several product markets they may have few competitors, but the cast of characters changes when the scene shifts. Even when the same companies face one another in various markets, the actual people involved will represent different product divisions. Detecting a common company policy in these circumstances may be difficult or impossible. It may not in fact exist.

The situation becomes even more complex. Competitors may also be suppliers or customers, and different units of the same company may offer different but functionally equivalent products and vie for the same trade. At least one large corporation maintains a senior staff of *company* representatives, known as "commercial vice presidents" who attempt to keep each form of business transaction somehow consistent with other relations between the same corporate participants. I suspect that their success has been rather limited.

I noted that "industry" classifications of companies are increasingly tending to break down. It is probable, for example, that General Electric meets General Motors in nearly as many markets as it meets Westinghouse, and in some, such as home appliances, all three are present. This means, among other things, that giant corporations may not compete with other giants *as single entities*, but rather they have a large variety of inter-company relations including competitive ones. Product diversification thus adds to the problems of coordination not only for reasons of purely internal organization but also because market operations tend to fracture corporate solidarity. The restrictive effect of these centrifugal tendencies on corporate autonomy is more subtle than if competitive relationships were singular. In other words, I suggest that the maintenance of corporate identity is much more difficult precisely because the "enemies" keep changing and sometimes turn out to be friends.

Protective Custody

The degree of domination of American business by large corporations does not appear to be increasing much if at all. What economists call the "index of concentration" has changed very little in the last fifty years. Small business has shown hardy survival powers even in manufacturing. The mortality rate of small enterprises is certainly high, but so is the birth rate. In fact, although there has been no "population explosion," the number of small producers has grown.

Antitrust legislation and administration have certainly had some effect on preventing the "gobbling up" of weak companies by strong ones, but I think other more strictly economic considerations have been equally important. I noted in a previous chapter that the fad of vertical integration backward to sources of supply had run its course, with some companies actually "spinning off" wholly-owned suppliers. I also noted that corporations no more want to be prisoners of other suppliers than of themselves and tend to favor maintaining a number of small businesses for reasons of simple self-interest.

Small businesses have some distinct competitive advantages that may offset the "monopoly powers" of large ones. The economies of scale gained by large size are pointless if the scale is not in fact appropriate to the size of the market. Where the market itself is small, the giant company with its administrative and other overhead costs is likely to be priced out of the market, unless it maintains production as a kind of company charity, as I suggested in the discussion of "private socialism." An insecticide sprayer is more likely to kill a mosquito than is a 75 millimeter shell, to say nothing of costing substantially less.

This frivolous illustration implies another point as well. The small company is likely to counter massive power with maneuverability. In volatile markets such as electronic components, some small companies are likely to fail, but large ones are not likely to be able to act at all. Just getting company approval for a price change may turn out to be a "federal case" in the large enterprise.

This maneuverability of small companies is not limited to competitive strategies in existing markets. Product innovation is often more easily accomplished by small concerns than by big ones, again because the very size of some corporations gets in their way. True, the risks are greater for small firms, but risk-taking remains one of the principal ways of getting a foothold in markets seemingly dominated by giants. If large concerns eventually buy out the most successful innovators this scarcely indicates the competitive failure of small businesses as such, but rather it gives testimony to the failure of large corporations to use their own innovations as competitive strategies.

I am not suggesting that large corporations never force small competitors out of markets. From time to time they do. But the reverse situation is also true, and perhaps about as frequent. Generally, I think the situation that has developed indicates more interdependence than it does frontal competition among large and small firms. The phrase "protective custody" is clearly poetic license for the situation in some markets, but it does seem rather apt in others.

Jungle Warfare

In some product markets, competition is not just vigorous; it is positively dirty. Large companies may lack high maneuverability, the capacity to "wheel and deal," but small firms may find that the law of the jungle is the most prominent feature of their relations with competitors. In such markets, price-cutting may be the cleanest tactic used. Down-grading the competitor's product, suggesting that the company is in difficulties and will not be able to fill the order, or just plain strong-arm methods to discourage rivals can all be illustrated by battle-scarred salesmen. The fundamental principle here is that manysided and keen competition always places pressure on the rules of "fair play" and is likely to produce both ingenious new strategies and clear violations of existing rules.

Large corporations are not "above" engaging in various sharp practices, but they are likely to be more sensitive to their "image" and enduring reputation and therefore not be too blatantly aggressive in the presence of customers. The customer, in effect, may be protected from knowing what is happening.

A few years ago one of the three companies producing lamp bulbs held basic patents that it had acquired by a kind of "cartel" arrangement with the Phillips Company of the Netherlands. The American company used a domestic licensing arrangement to allocate shares of the market to the two competitors, until ordered by a Federal Court to stop the practice. However, it still had the basic production facilities for the manufacture of the proper glass, which it supplied for all the producers. The company proceeded to increase the price of glass to the point where one of the competitors decided to install its own productive facilities at considerable expense. Once the second company had done so, the originator of the strategy played his high trump by promptly lowering his price, leaving the competitor with an uneconomical installation and a radically reduced profit. This was a kind of "reverse coup" on the old Standard Oil formula of cutting prices below costs until competitors were eliminated then recovering the losses by charging monopoly prices.

With prices showing scant flexibility as a factor in competition among giants, other strategies are fostered. Advertising and sales appeals may emphasize quality and service for particular products or attempt to build a "corporate image" that will extend to all products bearing the company's seal, brand name, or other form of identification. Market research may be directed toward identifying any special characteristics of customers of different companies. If special "clienteles" exist, other persons with the same characteristics become targets for specific sales appeals rather than

shot-gun or mass sales campaigns. But since the attention of potential customers has finite limits and since the number of channels for gaining attention have even narrower limits, saturation of
information channels may suggest itself as a way of shutting out
competing messages.

The saturation technique has other uses too. Where there is
no differentiation of products or prices among different producers,
the distributor or retailer may stock only one brand, because he
does not want to deal with different salesmen, set up different
displays, or pay several different accounts. For example, at a given
wattage, it is pretty much true that a lamp bulb is a lamp bulb is a
lamp bulb. The manufacturer who first reaches the distributor is
likely to get and keep the business, for the saturation is in a sense
automatic. The more outlets he reaches first, the closer he comes
to achieving total saturation. Competitors must then seek out still
other outlets, or attempt some kind of product differentiation
that will once more open up the market.

Still another saturation technique is that of multiplication of
brand names for products otherwise alike, as is the current practice of soap and cigarette manufacturers. The theory here is that
there is some kind of upper limit for any one brand and that several seemingly competitive brands will increase the producer's total share of the market. Marketing specialists have quite different
views on this strategy, and the argument can continue with considerable vigor because neither the proponents nor opponents of
brand diversification have any reliable factual evidence to get in
the way of their speculative convictions.

Some competitive strategies like saturation techniques may have
considerable durability until a way around the blockade is found.
Others may be matched or outmatched very quickly, and this encourages innovation in strategies if not in the products themselves.
Current high-level thinking among marketing strategists in the
consumer goods fields points to a kind of anticipatory strategy.
That is, the company attempts not only to forecast such things as
population growth and the level of economic activity and distribution of income but also trends in consumer preferences and un-

filled consumer "wants" that the consumer may not know yet. This strategy is essentially sound, but is likely to sound better than it works. The marketing strategist then becomes a "consumer representative" in the councils of management, but he faces the veto powers of his colleagues and the rather limited capacity of large companies to reach decisions to alter their course.

The restrictions placed on corporate freedom by competitors may arise from markets that are as challenging as those implied by the phrase "jungle warfare," as lenient as some of the relations between giants, or as comfortable as the division of function among large and small producers. Competition as such is more a condition of life than a goal of corporations, but the condition is real enough in its inhibiting consequences.

X X

CUSTOMERS: CAPRICIOUS AND CAPTIVE

WHEREIN *businesses and non-profit
organizations as well as private households are
depicted as capable of irrational decisions, and ways are
noted whereby the consumer may survive a surfeit
of goodies.*

ON SOME occasions corporation executives assure stockholders that the company is being run for their benefit. On other occasions similar disarming assurances are addressed to the company's customers. Neither assertion is wholly true, and neither is wholly false. Neither group precisely controls the corporation, but both have substantial reserve powers of limitation or veto. Stockholders naturally tend to be most contented when a steady volume of sales at a profit keeps the company in eminently sound financial condition. Ironically, that is when the suppliers of capital tend to be treated with the most condescension if not contempt, for new capital can simply be withdrawn from earnings. If potential customers do not appear in sufficient numbers and with sufficient money, however, both managers and investors quite naturally grow uneasy or downright alarmed.

A "free enterprise" system is usually defined in terms of the freedom of the productive system from governmental direction, the capacity of the businessman to make essential decisions concerning products and prices within a framework of laws but without political dictation. An equally important component is the freedom of the buyer to choose among various suppliers, or, for products and services not literally necessary to life, to choose none. Economists sometimes call this freedom "consumer sovereignty." Both of these freedoms are somewhat less than total, but each is sufficiently general to make the customer a highly important element in the environment of business. Corporations may attempt to develop captive clienteles such as customers with a blind loyalty to a brand. Except for the regulated public utilities, major success in such endeavors is fairly rare. On the other hand, corporations will themselves attempt to avoid capture by a customer, as when a single but independent distributor negotiates for the company's entire output. Both buyer and seller, in other words, normally attempt to maintain some independence of action in dealing with the other party.

Institutional Buyers

Many large manufacturing corporations have remarkably few direct dealings with the ultimate household consumer. Much of their production may in fact never reach the householder's door, because it may consist of products for other manufacturers or for various "institutional consumers" such as state governments, schools, and hospitals. For products destined for the individual family, the manufacturer's own customers may still be other businesses—distributors, wholesalers, and retailers. The customer at the end of the supply line must still be dealt with through intermediaries, whose own purchasing decisions may or may not actually reflect consumer demand as that is determined by individual purchases.

It may be supposed that having dealings predominantly with other businessmen would be distinctly advantageous to the corporation's purveyors of products. Businessmen, on the one hand, might be supposed to act "rationally," making purchases primarily in terms of genuine need for business purposes, quality specifications, and price. Household consumers on the other hand, may act on whim, motivated by subconscious insecurities or suppressed libidinal drives.

There is some faint basis for the supposition of rationality by the business buyer, but it must not be accepted as axiomatic. The businessman, too, may be whimsical, and motivated by considerations of prestige, if not by nasty Freudian disorder.

Machine tools and other "capital goods," the foundation of industrial mass production, are themselves rarely mass-produced. There is rarely a "mass" market for a complex machine, and routinization of a production schedule scarcely makes sense for one-of-a-kind product. Yet even for some fairly standard equipment, such as generators of electricity, production is still largely on a "job shop" basis. This leads to the anomaly that capital goods require large inputs of skilled labor.

There are two reasons, or excuses, for job shop production of machines intended for fairly standard purposes: peculiar adaptations needed by the customer or the incorporation of latest technical improvements. I am convinced that these are often rationalizations. A large generator, for example, is in production around two years, and during all that time the machine bears the name of the customer. The customer (a local utility company) has a representative who can drop around and note progress on his machine, like the man who visits his new house daily while it is being built. The customer's man may even yield to the temptation to give the impressive monster a loving and encouraging pat from time to time. I do not know what proportion of sentiment there may be in this insistence on "custom-made" machinery, but I strongly suspect that the financial costs far outweigh the slight benefits in incorporating special features. Certainly the manufacturing time is greatly lengthened by the lack of standardization.

For the corporate buyer, and for most other "institutional" buyers, the costs are of course not personal. Purchases are made with "other people's money." Aside from ordinary principles of honesty, which we must assume the businessman shares with the public at large, the principal restraint on the businessman customer is that he, too, is under some pressure to behave according to rational cost-accounting and profitable operation. Utility companies, being rate-regulated natural monopolies, feel this constraint rather less than most. The example I have chosen, therefore, may not be representative of other customers for capital goods.

The increasing diversification of large manufacturing corporations, particularly the producers of capital equipment, reduces the probability that these giants will sell much to one another. Giant corporations tend to be the customers of small companies, and vendors to small companies. The special capacities of large producers are likely to be found in research and development investments, and in their ability to design and install entire manufacturing systems. The small-company customer, although seeming to buy hardware, is actually also purchasing "embodied services"— the design and development services that the large company's greater resources have made possible.

Armament production, particularly in the "cold war" situation since World War II, has also become increasingly labor-intensive and custom-made. The reason here seems genuine enough: the extremely rapid technical developments that discourage "freezing" of designs for large-scale production. As with capital goods, the customer and supplier collaborate and negotiate over specifications as well as such mundane items as delivery dates and price. There is, however, an important difference which leads to many others, namely, that the Defense Department is not a "small business" and has a considerably larger voice in determining technical design than does the small manufacturer who wants a drill press or even a whole new factory.

The character of the Defense Department as an industrial customer calls for certain comments. In this case the customer will insist on having a monopoly on consumption while seeking to maintain competition among suppliers. The buccaneering days of the "war-provoking munitions makers," who fomented strife within and between small countries in order to create markets for their wares, are clearly over if indeed they ever existed in the ways portrayed. The corporation that dislikes the bargain offered by the customer is not permitted to peddle its products elsewhere. It does not even have a reasonable option of picking up its marbles and refusing to play.

A few years ago, under a Republican Administration, the transplanted businessmen in the Pentagon behaved in such a businesslike way in contract negotiation that their political sympathizers in large manufacturing corporations developed a distinct distaste for the whole affair. I heard, within one large corporation, fairly serious talk about simply refusing to bid or negotiate on defense contracts at all. The company's accountants had convinced the officers that the "cost-plus" contracts were actually yielding a net loss because of indirect costs they were not allowed to recover. I volunteered the opinion that the discussion was insane. For some types of defense demands only two or three companies have the necessary equipment and staffs and for some orders *all* available facilities and more have to be used. Under such circumstances the freedom not to produce is simply non-existent. If negotiations were to come to an economic deadlock, the customer (the government) would simply use its political power to commandeer the company, letting the courts adjudicate the issue in due season. Failure to cooperate in the "defense effort" would also have had rather grim public-relations implications, which soon occurred to the outraged managers.

Incidentally, I am convinced that the cases of companies taking turns as low bidders on defense contracts are not, in the minds of the people entering such cozily collusive arrangements, sharing the wealth or combining to fleece the customer but rather sharing the loss on what they regard as necessary but unprofitable business.

As one looks at all sorts of business sales other than those leading eventually to the individual household, one is struck by the great disparity between these transactions and those of the traditional, open market. Where the customer holds in his hands a shopping list of items never before made, as in the case of many capital goods and weapons, his shopping ideally consists of getting bids, but actually it may be a case of finding the single company that has the facilities to produce the goods at all or to meet the time-schedule that the shopper demands. What then ensues, of course, may involve more real "bargaining" than when the housewife selects items with marked, and firm, prices. But if the number of purchasers and suppliers is in each case one or very few, influence and simple power may figure more in closing the bargain than any mere economic calculus.

Even the "institutional buyer" of mass-produced goods is likely to behave differently from his housewifely counterpart. "Consumption goods" do not always reach the household consumer. One need only think of light bulbs, lamps, office furniture, cleaning equipment, and paper products for toilets as examples of the large and growing number of products bought by businesses, schools, hospitals, and governmental agencies for the efficiency and comfort of employees, customers, and clients. Few of the ultimate beneficiaries of these products have any voice in purchasing decisions. The decisions are largely in the hands of purchasing agents who may operate under a great variety of rules laid down by the employer or formulated by the agent himself in selecting suppliers. In general, however, the agent has sufficient latitude of judgment to make his good will, and not just his good sense, worth cultivating.

This leads to a consideration of the range from the little gestures of good will and good fellowship to the outright financial bribes that figure conspicuously in contemporary commercial culture. It is fairly standard practice for the customer to be "entertained" by the salesman in a manner presumably proportional to the prospective value of the order. The salesman, or his employer, is not likely to have much choice about this practice, as he is trapped by the "principle of the least moral determinant." This principle, the phrasing of which I borrow from my colleague Melvin Tumin, is simply that in a great variety of contexts of social behavior, the actual standards of conduct will be set by the least moral participant. Competitive tactics, as long as limiting rules are absent, vague, or unenforced, provide rich ground for this principle to flourish. A new strategy, however "immoral," must be matched by other players if they are going to stay in the game. Of course, any such principle tends to be carried to intolerable extremes, followed by an attempt to set limits. Corporations have shown remarkably little interest in setting "entertainment" limits, and thus their sales and "negotiating" employees share the rich fare of the "expense account culture." The salesman, who is reimbursed, has scant incentive to desist, and the company, for whom this is a tax-deductible cost, may enter the discount and assume that its direct cost, even if avoidable, is only some "50 cents on the dollar."

It is interesting that services such as entertainment are commonly not regarded as bribes, although gifts usually are. The business "Christmas gift," representing even less Christian good-will than the mandatory exchanges among relatives, friends, and neighbors, is ubiquitous. Because of the same phenomenon of "perseveration"—carrying things to greater and greater extremes— that besets any competitive situation, many companies have forbidden their purchasing agents to accept any "commercial" gift. I asked one business supplier about this, and his response was direct and immediate: "The telephone directory always has the agent's home address."

There is simply no reliable way of knowing whether bribery as a way of doing business with national, state, and local officials is also common with private officials. One can hazard the guess that the constraint of a cost-limiting profit system may provide some greater checks in the strictly private sector of the economic system. I do not think this necessarily says much for the greater morality of businessmen when compared with politicians, as the bribe-givers are businessmen in either case. The possible element of extortion practiced by the bribe recipient in public office may be greater because of a monopoly position. There is, after all, only one Federal Communications Commission or Wyoming State Highway Department or West Greenleaf School Board.

An important development in corporate dealings with the "institutional" customer is the rising role of the intermediary. These are not individuals and businesses in the chain of distribution but in the chain of contact and influence. Some intermediaries simply become employees of corporations. Retired military officers are favorite company representatives for dealing with their active-duty counterparts in the Services, and one has to be naive to believe that their value to the employer lies exclusively in their military and technical skills. Other people act as free-lance agents, bringing together buyer and seller for a fee—the 5 per-centers or influence peddlers. One cannot say categorically that their activities are mischievous, but neither can one take a purely benign view of such tenuous relations between producer and consumer. Whatever, one might ask, happened to the impersonal competitive market?

Part of the reply to such a querulous query is of course that it still exists, especially in the distribution of household consumer goods. Mass-production manufacturers of consumer goods tend to compete vigorously for the customer's trade, although to a remarkable extent they deal with the customer directly only by advertising. Historically the economic functions of distributors, contractors, and retailers were to share with manufacturers part of the risk of product promotion and to serve as links in two-way communication with customers. To an increasing degree the retailer adds only "time and place utility" to the product. Distributors and contractors "bundle" orders to ease the inventory, purchasing, and shipping burdens of manufacturers.

With pre-packaging and brand advertising the manufacturer has tended to shorten the message lines to ultimate consumers. The grocer and clothing retailer, for example, have virtually lost all advisory functions. To these the customer goes with a prepared "list," although he may select other things also from displays. The one merchant that the ordinary customer presents with problems rather than specific demands is the hardware dealer. To the average car buyer the salesman's run-through of technical specifications is so much doubletalk. The man bases his preferences on price and "performance" (that is, fast acceleration) and the woman on color and style. Neither is immune to the automobile as a status symbol and as an adult toy.

It appears that increased automation of warehousing and shipping will further reduce the importance of middlemen as customers. Whether the large manufacturing corporation can "integrate" all the way to the customer is doubtful, however, because that would further imperil the "small" businessman, who has powerful political friends. The retailer also serves the function of supplying service on appliances and other consumer durables, but if his service is unsatisfactory, the manufacturer receives a major share of the blame. The manufacturer thus may be tempted to perform services directly or through a separate contract with a company that only furnishes parts and repairs, or he may try to maintain close control of service quality by retailers under threat of loss of franchise.

The franchise system, which appears as another taint on the purity of business markets, is defended by manufacturers chiefly in terms of reliability of supply and service. It is also a way of shifting to the distributor a considerable part of the sales effort and even of inventory costs, if the dealer must accept an assigned quota in order to keep his franchise. When products and service become very nearly alike, middlemen are likely to respond to customer demand for wider selection in a single establishment as against seeking out exclusive dealers for one brand or another. The "super-market" for appliances is already with us in the form of "discount houses," and the super-market for automobiles may appear very shortly. This tendency, which runs counter to the tendency of the manufacturer to control his own distribution, may not be very comforting to believers in truly *small* business, but may be comforting to those who fear further encroachments on the economy by truly *big* business.

When the business dealings between manufacturers and distributors depart from strict market purity, corporate misbehavior is more likely to be the exercise of unequal power than the corrupt persuasion of bribes and influence. When a distributor gains sufficient size and loyalty of clientele to have some bargaining power, his good will may also have some value. To accomplish this rare feat the distributor or retailer must be something more than the man who stands between the manufacturer and the pre-sold customer. Otherwise, the luring luxury of effortless sales may be offset by the middleman's rather poor position as a captive customer of the supplier.

Mass-Produced Individuality

The size of giant corporations depends in part on the diversity of products they manufacture or of services they render. Many of these products taken individually have rather limited annual production schedules and reach a very limited number of users. This is particularly true of many capital goods and of some other industrial products, such as machine tools or giant computers. Yet other products, and these especially include those destined for the household consumer, are produced in very large numbers. Mass production depends upon mass consumption. The sheer size of the American population and its relatively rapid growth have provided the numerical foundations for industrial bigness.

Effective demand for manufactured products depends of course not on numbers alone, but on numbers equipped with wants and needs that match the goods offered for sale and the financial resources for buying them. The growth of American mass production and mass consumption has depended then on rising minimum and average levels of real income, that is, effective purchasing power and not just inflated currency.

Corporations take credit for a major part of the exalted American standard of living while also taking profit from it. Yet neither the producer nor the consumer has been free from pointed social criticism, sometimes by the same author; Vance Packard followed his book on *The Status Seekers* (the social climbing consumers) with *The Waste Makers* (the manufacturers fostering and catering to consumer irrationality). Prosperity itself is sometimes viewed fearfully, as in John Kenneth Galbraith's *The Affluent Society*.

Throughout history, and indeed in most of the modern world, human poverty is the rule and prosperity the exception. Economic well-being has been commonly limited to small privileged classes, justified in their positions by ideologies ranging from allegations of "natural" superiority to assumptions of divine grace. Counterparts of such rationalizations have been platitudes for the poor. Poverty, or at least struggle and adversity, has a long association with virtue. Surfeit, it is argued, leads to softness, whereas adversity ennobles the character and may even be rewarded by hard-won material improvement. The dangers of wealth form a recurrent theme in the traditions of the Western World. The dangers are partly those of divine retribution for arrogant self-indulgence, partly those of overturn and defeat at the hands of the virtuous poor, domestic or foreign. The presumptively paralyzing effects of prosperity have long been used to explain the superiority of Sparta over Athens, the northern barbarians over decadent Rome, or more recently, the contemporary Soviet challenge to American world power.

One danger of a so-called "consumption phychology" is that Americans increasingly stress immediate as opposed to deferred gratification. This is part of what is meant by the decline of the "Protestant ethic." Although not strictly a doctrine of work as the way to salvation, evangelical Protestantism did encourage frugality, responsible trusteeship of money, avoidance of conspicuous consumption, and thus encouragement of savings and reinvestment. In a sense, Veblen's *Theory of the Leisure Class*, with its emphasis on the "conspicuous consumption" practiced by the wealthy, might be regarded as the watershed between the homely encouragement to frugality in Franklin's *Poor Richard's Almanac* and the common cultivation of snobbery depicted in Packard's *The Status Seekers*. The degradation of thrifty foresight, starting with the rich, finally contaminates all.

There is a considerable array of evidence, however, against the thesis that Americans show a decreased interest in and capacity for taking thought for the future. The two principal sources of economic decisions—business units and families—tend to lengthen rather than shorten their planning horizons. Life insurance, pensions, and long-term savings plans (including home mortgages) scarcely square with the notion of exclusive preoccupation with immediate indulgence. Nor do long-term investments by corporations indicate a tendency toward improvident plunder.

Rising minimum levels of living and some reduction of income inequalities have combined to broaden the base for private savings. The notion that the erstwhile poor cannot be trusted to handle their money wisely is somewhat analogous to the view that "culture" is automatically cheapened by becoming popular.

Savings and investment, gross or net, remain a remarkably constant proportion of the gross national product. The composition of such investments varies through time, and there may be legitimate worries concerning the maintenance of appropriate flexibility in the economy's capital equipment, and about whether suitable sacrifices are being made for survival and future growth, but it does not appear that we are collectively living up to or beyond our income.

Democratic governments depend upon popular consent as to which tax-supported expenditures are proper for either survival or future growth. For example, private educational investments for assured future returns in the professions are made somewhat more easily than expenditures for upgrading public education as a whole. It is also noted, with perhaps exaggerated cynicism, that both private and public funds can be more easily secured for the construction of monumental buildings than for the salaries of teachers. Yet citizens do constitute themselves into pressure groups for better schools, and the competition for teachers does eventually introduce market principles into the determination of their rewards.

In addition to being improvident, the American consumer is also charged with being imitative, with the effect that individual creativity and taste are buried under a mass of goodies, just like those of one's neighbor and the stranger across the continent. Again, however, the verdict must be "not guilty" or at least "not proved." Here we encounter another paradox, for one can find proponents of the view that consumer life-styles are becoming increasingly homogeneous and of the view that they are becoming increasingly diversified. The resolution of the paradox is fairly simple. The trends simply relate to different parts of the consumer's budget.

For most of life's necessities the minimum tolerable level tends to rise without correlative increases among more well-to-do consumers. In other words, in both standards of living and in actual levels of consumption of many conventional purchases, increasing homogeneity is to be expected in all sectors of the population. Regional, racial, rural-urban differences are steadily narrowing. Participation in various aspects of "popular culture" is steadily broadening. Symbols of rank are quickly "degraded" by copying. Since yesterday's luxuries are tomorrow's necessities, there is some tendency for the relatively "homogeneous" aspect of consumer behavior to expand through time.

Rising income levels, however, also add disproportionately to "discretionary" income, to money available for purchases other than necessities, for optional allocation for goods or services of any kind. Spending decisions put products in competition that are not ordinarily regarded as substitutable—luxury clothes, boats, and summer homes, for example. Many families may decide to buy experience, which needs no storage space, and others to fill the walls with advanced art. In these expenditures diversity and even individuality are made possible by the opportunity for choice.

A few words of gentle praise for money are in order. Money-mindedness is often equated with crude materialism. This equation, often accepted by Americans with defensive guilt, is partly spurious. It is an inherent characteristic of highly developed industrial economies that the number and proportion of goods and especially of services that move through the market steadily increase. If grandma baby-sits, that is a family matter. If the neighbor girl comes in, money changes hands and adds to the gross national product, the net national income, and the net cost of maintaining a family's way of life. Money is useful for whatever it will buy, which may be quite non-material and even philanthropic. The world's materialists are perforce the have-nots and not the haves. In a prosperous economy or household, money becomes increasingly essential for maintenance of the good life, true enough, and a decreasingly reliable predictor of exact consumption expenditures, of what the good life is to the family budgeters. Thus there are often sharp differences in the life styles at equivalent income levels.

Even for mass-produced goods, the quest for individuality is not hopeless. Products ranging from high-fidelity systems to entire houses can be produced in standard components that can be assembled in very different ways. It is technically quite feasible to produce "modular" housing units so that new rooms can be plugged in when children are born. Do-it-yourself furniture is growing in popularity, and a return to our ancestors' do-it-yourself architecture may be next in line.

We have been down at the ranch house. Meanwhile back at the corporations, what is their conduct toward the consumer? Well, mixed.

A long but by no means uniform or predominant record of businesses in defrauding the consumer has led to a substantial abandonment of the principle of *caveat emptor*, let the buyer beware. If the consumer cannot be protected against outright silliness, he can be protected from outright bodily harm (injurious foods and drugs, explosive sweaters, dangerous electrical equipment) and some of the grosser kinds of fraud (adulterated products, false and misleading advertising claims, failure to deliver goods paid for).

The gray areas of corporate tactics with consumers involve influence and manipulation, appeals to irrational or subconscious impulses, artificial stimulation of senseless "wants" by advertising appeals.

The line between information and influence in advertising is a thin one. The one assumes that the consumer knows what he wants and simply needs to know where to get it and what it costs. The mail-order catalogue is perhaps a good example. The other assumes that the consumer must be persuaded that he wants a product and persuaded of the superiority of a particular brand. The television commercial, with demonstration by a live model and the "hard sell," is an example. No doubt, for different consumers and different products, both views are correct. Yet it does not follow that the amount of money spent on advertising is socially justifiable or even that the advertising budget is economically justifiable to the sponsoring company. The "proofs" of advertising effectiveness are usually produced by advertising agencies, which cannot be regarded as patently disinterested investigators.

Defenders of advertising claim that it pays its way, even for the consumer, by expanding the market and thus making possible scale economies in production and reduced prices, while more people share the goodies. Opponents, not quite arguing to the same point, propound a "blackmail" theory of advertising. For established products (soap, cigarettes, toasters) they think advertising is used to change a company's *share* of the market, but this advantage is quickly countered by other producers. The net result may be no essential change except greatly increased advertising budgets (and employment of ad agencies) and a higher "useless" surcharge paid by the consumer.

I am convinced, but cannot prove, that there is a substantial irrationality in advertising expenditures, which the economy may be able to afford, but which, given the choice, it would prefer not to in view of other desirable ways of using money.

The use of covert manipulation of consumers, the angry thesis of Packard's *The Hidden Persuaders*, raises questions of tactics as well as morals. In an open society, with relatively free communication and criticism, any manipulative technique may be damaged by discovery. Monoply of knowledge, including the techniques of "motivation research," is difficult to maintain. The customer hates to be had. Open contempt for his intelligence (commercials pitched for the 11-year-old "adult" mind) or covert contempt for his rationality (firm, uncooked spaghetti, as a phallic symbol is better than limp, cooked *pasta*) may produce hostility rather than sales. Whatever the state of his subconscious, the customer is still capable of conscious memory of past foolishness.

X X I

PUBLIC: POLITICAL AND PROFANE

*WHEREIN the public in a democratically
governed nation is shown to have reserve powers
to control corporate conduct, and the moral questions
raised at the beginning remain unanswered
at the end.*

IN ANY society, whether democratic or totalitarian, it is a function of government to be the final authority on rules and their enforcement, the final arbiter among discordant interests. A crucial difference in political systems is how quickly that final authority is exercised—virtually at once in a totalitarian system and much later, reluctantly and perhaps tardily, in a democratic order. The idea of a self-regulating system with no need for political intervention is a myth in terms of social fact and contains basic errors in terms of social theory. Yet a democratic political order is to a remarkable degree "pluralistic," permitting wide diffusion of quasi-autonomy, of semi-final authority, of "privacy" in the ordering of social life and individual conduct.

The contemporary American business corporation, though legally a creature of the state from which it derives its charter, has a substantial but somewhat indefinite sphere of autonomy and privacy. Like the individual citizen, the corporation is taxed and regulated and may be rewarded with public employment (government contracts), punished for mischief by judicial action, and possibly called on for sacrifice in the national interest. How extensive and consistent the actions of government are and should be—the question of the boundaries between public and private interests—are matters of dispute and political difference, of negotiation and political action.

The plea for corporate self-regulation, for private responsibility without political interference, is made on grounds ranging from the grandly ideological to the meanly practical. The ideological arguments evoke both the doctrines of Nineteenth Century "liberalism" in economics, which did assume a virtually self-regulating economy, and even older political sentiments in favor of democratic pluralism, of liberty and choice, of avoiding regimentation by the omnipresent and stultifying agents of the state. The practical arguments, though never quite free of ideological overtones, rest upon the claims of private efficiency and public obfuscation, of freedom as a necessary condition for rational economic action.

As long as the discussions of corporate policies and of public policies toward corporations remain at such levels of generality, it is impossible for the inquisitive nonpartisan or the sensible citizen to come down on one side or the other. There are persuasive arguments on both sides, but they go past each other at high but undamaging speed more often than they meet in frontal clash.

Very few members of the American "business class" were ever truly anarchistic, desirous of an outright abolition of the state or its total separation from business matters. At the very least, there was general recognition that the state must keep order, defend private property against radical elements, and set up rules (the fewer the better, but not to the point of none).

When businessmen did, and do, make extreme, ideologically oriented pronouncements on freedom from political interference, it is surely fair to say that they do not mean to be taken with total seriousness, and in any event their actions belie their words. Often, in fact, the sayers and the doers are not the same people. The late Sam Lewisohn, for many years president of Miami Copper, commented in a small book, *Human Leadership in Industry,* that the extreme spokesmen of business ideology are more often lawyers and public relations men than they are practicing executives. A considerable part of the ideological output does not come from within corporate circles at all but from the staffs of trade associations and especially from the National Association of Manufacturers. These are generally men who, like professors and Congressmen, "have never met a payroll."

Business interests have generally sought governmental intervention of some kinds while generally opposing intervention of other kinds. The examples are so well known as to need no more than bare mention.

From the beginning of American industrialization, "protective" tariffs have been eagerly sponsored, and some "infant" industries doing over 5 billion dollars in annual sales still seek to be sheltered from the harshness of a competitive world market. The current arguments are likely to espouse the cause of American wage-earners and national defense, but the pleas for governmental help have an unbroken lineage with the more crudely profit-oriented claims of the past.

Business concerns have sought and received gifts of land from the public domain, tax abatements, direct subsidies from the public treasury, and governmental contracts at non-competitive prices. They have sponsored laws to restrain price competition in consumer goods (the so-called "fair-trade" laws) as well as all sorts of measures to restrain organized workers or other "hostile" interests.

Not all businessmen have sought all forms of governmental intervention. Many issues of public policy divide business opinion. Though non-rational sentiment cannot be dismissed as a factor in opinion, as when bankers have opposed regulations that would protect them from their own follies, one would be generally safe in assuming that the reaction will depend on "whose ox is gored." Again, it is primarily professional ideologies including politicians who give a spurious air of uniformity on issues that actually divide business opinion.

The Political Environment

The safest comment about the political environment of big business in the United States is that it is "mixed." Public hostility to size as such seems to have abated, although it has not disappeared and is capable of being fanned by such cases as the bidding conspiracy among electrical equipment manufacturers. (A periodic sampling of public opinion about the "monopoly power" of corporations revealed that large companies in industries far removed from that of the culprits received a marked upsurge of unwanted identification as companies having excessive power. Thus a particular situation of collusive pricing led to a resurgent opposition to size as such.)

It seems probable that the crucial role of large corporations (as well as many small ones, of course) in World War II and the subsequent Cold War has aided their public "image." Certainly the gain in public acceptance owes very little to the institutional advertising copy that attempts to depict the giant corporation as simply a larger and successful version of small business. By now nearly everyone but the courts has received the message that the stockholder is no longer in control, and many have understood the implications of size for the life of the corporate employee and the characteristics of markets. Even the courts are beginning to use concepts like "corporate citizenship" in rejecting stockholder complaints about corporate donations, for example. The idea that the large corporation is a distinctive institutional phenomenon has gained ground steadily, but the exact character of that institution is still largely in limbo. What I called in Chapter I the "moral crisis" of management, the uncertain justification of business power and responsibility and of the manager's own privileged position, is by no means solved. I do not even think that it is well on the road to a clear solution.

The attempt to develop a rationale for corporate power is halting at best. John Kenneth Galbraith can certainly not be called an "old fashioned" economist, but his diagnosis of *American Capitalism* strikes me as simply a modernized version of the self-regulating system. The American institutional system, Galbraith argues, does not tolerate persistent power imbalances. When power becomes extreme and irresponsible, as with the growth of Big Business in the early Twentieth Century, responsibility is enforced by countervailing power, including Big Labor.

Now countervailing power may result in stalemate rather than responsible action. Occasionally industrial disputes verge on precisely such stalemates. And the settlement of such disputes illustrates a point that I think Galbraith has not given sufficient weight. When a strike threatens to become crippling, when large populations of "third parties" or large sectors of the economy are seriously threatened, the government intervenes in one way or another. If the forms of intervention are haphazard and the powers of government unclear, these simply constitute further evidence of the "incomplete institutionalization," the uncertainty of public and private rights and responsibilities in the economy.

In a very real sense the labor union is as much a creature of the state as is the corporation. Both owe their existence to "enabling" legislation, and both play out their "private" interests within a changing but crucially important legal and political environment.

A variant on the notion that labor unions once served an important function but have outlived their usefulness is the current criticism of labor "monopoly power," or the view that unions have become "too strong." There are people who think that unions moved from the nursery (or perhaps the prison) to the throne rather quickly, without developing proper characteristics of mature restraint in the process. If political opinion supports that view, the curtailing of union power will not take place automatically by the appearance of some new "countervailing power," but it will be the result of deliberate governmental action. The countervailing power that circumscribes corporate or union action is likely to be the state either acting directly or as instigator and rule-maker for new non-governmental solutions.

The resolution of industrial disputes, I am suggesting, is not simply political in the sense that it tests the power of the contending parties but in the fuller sense that both their power and often the specific solutions are the consequence of state intervention. As the economy becomes increasingly interdependent and the power of the few to affect the lives of the many becomes more and more evident, I expect new forms of adjudication, perhaps compulsory arbitration or labor courts, to be instituted as mechanisms for reaching settlements. Autonomous action and private conflict may be too costly to be tolerated.

The Public Be Cultivated

In the United States there are more workers than managers and more members of the uncommitted voting public than either. There is perhaps more nearly a "managerial vote" than a "labor vote," but on many issues and in many elections there is neither. In any event, it would be a mistake to regard "labor policy" as the sole significant area in which the political opinion of the public is significant. It is difficult to find legislation without economic significance, for the economy like the polity includes everyone.

The great interest of corporations in "public opinion" clearly has faddish components but also has realistic foundations. The opinion of the public as such, as distinct from direct and indirect stockholders, union members, small businessmen, or customers, is pointless except in a political context. Although the government of a representative democracy is not always totally and immediately responsive to shades and shifts in opinion, a widespread and persistent hostility to big business would certainly have a pronounced influence on the course of legislation, and perhaps even on the course of judicial decision.

Ideology and realism in public relations occasionally come into conflict. The overt and insistent support by large corporations of state "right to work" laws, which would outlaw labor agreements that make union memberships a condition of continuing employment, probably succeed in creating a "labor vote" that would not otherwise exist. The aggressive, "fire-eating" spokesman for corporate interests commonly appears incapable of counting. One corporate spokesman, Lemuel Boulware of General Electric, sought to identify all the usual "thought leaders"—editors and politicans, union and P.T.A. officers, educators and clergymen—as either knaves or fools or both. The sole remaining sources of right-thinking virtue were, by default, the businessmen. Whatever the objective merits of that view, it represents political madness.

The cultivation of the public by corporations is likely to be defensive rather than positive as long as a clear rationale for corporate life is not at hand. It is perhaps more accurate to say that corporations can portray positive values piecemeal but do so by avoiding the Big Issues. Companies may point out contributions to national defense (in advertisements paid for largely or entirely by the taxpayer), to education and local welfare activities, to the well-being of their employees or to small businesses. They may link their activities to Patriotism, Science, and even Motherhood. They are understandably skittish about Democracy and tend to define Justice in a patently partial way. Nevertheless they seek a "favorable climate of opinion," chiefly so that vindictive and repressive legislation will not be forthcoming at some future time.

I do not claim that the cultivation of the public is necessarily deceitful or in other ways immoral. At times it is, but probably more often it is not. I only claim that in the nature of the case much of it is defensive and preventive, and that it tends to be loudest when the underlying uncertainty is greatest. Since corporate spokesmen must be assumed to be human until proved otherwise, this very human behavior is not very surprising.

The Uses and Abuses of Corporate Power

The castigating phrase, "the concentration of economic power," has now had currency for a half century, but it is now heard with less frequency than in earlier days among those of the "liberal" political persuasion. It is always easier, for purposes of political sentiment and allegiance, to identify the devil and keep his evil inviolate than it is to see the mixture of devilish and angelic qualities in the concrete behavior before us. Corporations have been unfair to critics by failing to behave with unmitigated sinfulness. The very man who dislikes in principle the monopoly power of American Telephone and Telegraph and in fact wishes he could threaten to take his business elsewhere, will in other situations, such as trying to reach someone served by an independent company, become impatient with A.T.&T. for not making their monopoly complete.

Certainly the alternative proposed by many critics of economic concentration, that of public ownership, could only exaggerate the problem. The actual concentration is generally less than total, the power implicit in concentration is constrained and constricted by external influences and some self-restraint, and concentrated power is occasionally appropriate to massive and integrated performance. Within organizations, executive power has its ethically questionable elements, but it is not total. Outside, many an executive would like to feel the sense of power attributed to him, but feels harassed with pressures rather than able to command the universe.

Although on some ideological issues business executives and even lesser managers seem to make common cause, I find that divisions of interests and values within and between corporate managements appear whenever the ideological fog lifts. The notion that virtually all power holders in all social fields constitute a single elite has been urged with fine prose and no evidence by C. Wright Mills in *The Power Elite*. It is a figment of a fevered

imagination comparable to the corporate public relations director's discovering a conspiracy against big business. The power concentrated in large corporations is sporadic and largely undisci-
plined, not disciplined and conspiratorial.

In some respects, the guilt of big business is the abdication of
power rather than its abuse. Product innovation, I have noted earlier, represents a minuscule output relative to the inputs for
research and development. Corporations often capture creativity
and contain it rather than release it. Too many incompetents in
high places (and in the complex technical world, every man is incompetent outside his own field) find it easier to be safe than
sorry and find all sorts of reasons for avoiding novelty. Problems
like urban transportation have technical solutions, and the solutions are prevented in part by anachronistic political structures,
which will finally be forced to solve them, if all else fails, as it
almost certainly will. Essentially "private" solutions *can* be imag-
ined, given any kind of political flexibility. It is quite unlikely,
however, that any large corporation would now venture on such
an enterprise as high-speed conveyors for urban commuters.

The concentration of economic power is a critical necessity for
modern productive technology and forms of mass organization.
Making that power responsible in a positive sense as well as accountable in a negative sense remains a large item of unfinished
business for the American public. The meaning of executive trusteeship, the qualities and ethical standards of managers, have yet to
be defined by law or established by custom. The idea of abolish-
ing big business is simply reactionary, a silly attempt to recreate a
simpler life, which was after all not very gracious. The national
economic welfare and indeed the national survival are deeply
dependent on the well-being of what Gardiner C. Means has
called "collective capitalism." I think the realization of our economic potential, the achievement of a balance between organized
effort and freedom, depends on finding a positive sense of mission
for the corporation and not simply on building stronger cages and
placing more bars in them. We know approximately what the
public is against, but what is the corporation for?

REFERENCES

F o r the reader who wants to explore further in the domains
of corporate life here are some of the most significant books. Many
of these contain extensive references to other publications, ranging
from the popular to the highly technical.

Chris Argyris, *Understanding Organizational Behavior* (Homewood,
Ill.: Dorsey Press, 1960). Summarizes theories and data included
in earlier, more specialized studies: *Executive Leadership* (New
York: Harper, 1953) and *Personality and Organization* (New
York: Harper, 1957).

Adolf A. Berle, Jr., and Gardiner C. Means, *The Modern Corporation
and Private Property* (New York: Macmillan, 1933). This "modern classic" explores the significance of the "separation of ownership and management" in the contemporary large corporation.
Berle has made further analyses of the emergence of new institutional patterns, especially in the social power and responsibility
of corporations in *The Twentieth Century Capitalist Revolution*
(New York: Harcourt, 1954) and in *Power Without Property*
(New York: Harcourt, 1959).

Melville Dalton, *Men Who Manage* (New York: Wiley, 1959). The
author compares the formal theory of administration with the
observed motives, attitudes, and actions of managers in concrete
situations. The results do not "discredit" theory but do serve to
humanize the managers.

Peter F. Drucker, *Concept of the Corporation* (New York: Day,
1946). An analysis of corporate behavior, based on a study of
General Motors. The author deals in this book primarily with
internal structures and policies, but in *The New Society* (New
York: Harper, 1950) he provides a friendly interpretation of the
external responsibilities of corporate managers.

Robert Dubin, *The World of Work* (Englewood Cliffs, N.J.: Prentice-
Hall, 1958). A wide-ranging discussion of the organization of
work in industrial societies, with special attention to the differences among various types of business and occupations.

John Kenneth Galbraith, *American Capitalism* (Boston: Houghton Mifflin, 1952). In this book a leading interpreter of economic structures and their implications for policy introduces the concept of "countervailing power" as the way in which large-scale interests and organizations—such as corporations and labor unions—are kept in appropriate balance.

Alvin W. Gouldner, *Patterns of Industrial Bureaucracy* (Glencoe, Ill.: Free Press, 1954). On the basis of an intensive case study the author attempts to integrate the theory of administration with the observational studies on "informal organization."

Edward S. Mason, ed., *The Corporation in Modern Society* (Cambridge: Harvard University Press, 1959). The authors of this book explore the significance of the large corporation in the operation of markets and also in public affairs. An especially valuable chapter by Eugene V. Rostow explores the question, "To Whom and for What Ends Are Corporate Managers Responsible?" The author's view that ways must be found to restore accountability to stockholders differs from the one presented in the volume in hand, but his position is well reasoned and the review of the controversy is excellent.

Wilbert E. Moore, *Industrial Relations and the Social Order*, rev. ed. (New York: Macmillan, 1951). The first edition of this book, in 1946, was the first general college-level textbook on "industrial sociology"—that is, the social organization of the industrial enterprise and its relations with society as a whole. The book includes extensive references to research studies and will again be revised in early 1963.

Clarence B. Randall, *The Folklore of Management* (Boston: Little, Brown, 1961). The retired president of Inland Steel takes a hard look at the myths and untested beliefs that underlie many managerial policies.

Francis X. Sutton and Others, *The American Business Creed* (Cambridge: Harvard University Press, 1956). The authors examine in critical detail the ideological pronouncements of spokesmen for business enterprise, and find that the ideological output grows with the increasing uncertainty concerning corporate functions and responsibilities.

William H. Whyte, Jr., *The Organization Man* (New York: Simon and Schuster, 1956). This widely read book has contributed its title to the American language, and its provocative thesis on corporate conformity has set off discussions throughout the business world and beyond.

INDEX

Accountants, 56, 121
Advertising, 254, 258, 274-276
Allis-Chalmers Company, 252
American Motors Company, 252
American Telephone and Telegraph Company, 138, 284
Antitrust Division, 232, 253
Argyris, Chris, 287
Aristotle, 202
Auditors, 56
Authority, in administrative organizations, 27-28, 48-52, 57-58, 88-90, 96-97, 133-134

Bakke, E. Wight, 241
Berle, Adolf A. Jr., 5-6, 8, 287
Bethlehem Steel Company, 252
Boulding, Kenneth, 80
Boulware, Lemuel, 283
Budgets, 118-121, 142-144
Bureaucracy, as administrative organization, 21-22, 28

Capital, supply to corporation, 226-230
Careers, 141, 142, 167-179; education, 169-170
Carnegie, Dale, 108
Change: cyclical, 198-201; deliberate, 193-196, 202-208; imitative, 196-197; related to tensions, 191-192; as result of competition, 111-112, 116-117; as result of solving problems, 38, 193. See also Technology

Chrysler Corporation, 252-253
Clerical workers, 45, 211-212
Cliques, 104-106
Collective bargaining: within management, 117-118; with unions, 236-242, 281-282
Collectivism, within the corporation, 144-147
Commitment, of workers, 156-157, 215-216
Communication: between specialists 65-66; formal, 60-64; general character, 59-60, 66-68; informal, 97-98; lateral, 63-64
Competence, as criterion of selection, 83-86, 107-108, 113
Competition, 110-123, 251-259; collective, within corporations, 116-121; in corporate markets, 251-260; and labor market, 26, 114; personal, within corporations, 113-116, 171, 174
Conflict, 124-136, 144-145; between line and staff, 133-136, 214; between management and labor, 129-133, 236-242; related to specialization, 126-127; between units in corporations, 126-129
Conformity, 158-166, 272-273
Consultants, 243-250; reasons for use, 245-246; types, 246-250
Cooperation, by-product of organization, 35-37, 152-155
Corporations: ideologies, 277-279,

ABOUT THE AUTHOR

WILBERT E. MOORE is Professor of Sociology at
Princeton University. He was born in Elma, Washington,
and holds degrees from Linfield College (Oregon), the
University of Oregon, and Harvard University. Mr. Moore
taught at the University of Oregon, Penn State, and Harvard before joining the faculty at Princeton in 1943. He
has been a research consultant for General Electric, an
editorial consultant for the *Encyclopedia Americana,* and is
a member of the U. S. National Commission for UNESCO
and of the Board of Directors of the Social Science Research Council. Mr. Moore is also the author of many
books in sociology, among them: *Economy and Society,
Industrial Relations and the Social Order,* and *Twentieth
Century Sociology.* His years of research in his field have
produced countless articles in magazines and professional
journals which, together with his books, have established
him as one of the leading authorities in the field of industrial sociology.

A NOTE ON THE TYPE

This book is set in Electra, a Linotype face designed by W. A. Dwiggins. This face cannot be classified as either modern or oldstyle. It is not based on any historical model, nor does it echo any particular period or style. It avoids the extreme contrasts between thick and thin elements that mark most modern faces, and attempts to give a feeling of fluidity, power, and speed.